INTEGRATING HUMAN RIGHTS INTO DEVELOPMENT

INTEGRATING HUMAN RIGHTS INTO DEVELOPMENT

DONOR APPROACHES, EXPERIENCES, AND CHALLENGES

Second Edition

THE WORLD BANK
Washington, D.C.

ORGANISATION FOR ECONOMIC
CO-OPERATION AND DEVELOPMENT

Contents

Boxes

Tables

Foreword

I welcome this second edition of *Integrating Human Rights into Development* as an invaluable resource for those committed to advancing engagement between human rights and development professionals and organizations.

During my term as United Nations High Commissioner for Human Rights, and over the course of my work with both Realizing Rights: The Ethical Globalization Initiative and the Mary Robinson Foundation–Climate Justice, I have highlighted the urgent need for human rights and development agendas to be mobilized together to eliminate poverty and promote equitable and sustainable development. Efforts to build bridges between the worlds of human rights and development continue to grow, and initiatives to advance these can be identified in a range of areas from climate justice to gender equity. Considerable progress has been made in forging the strategic and policy connections between human rights and development, particularly at the level of broad political commitment. The past seven years, since I wrote the preface to the first edition of this study, have witnessed particularly important milestones.

These support the view of an emerging convergence between human rights and development at the level of principles, values, and goals. Of particular relevance to the present publication was the DAC's 2007 Action-Oriented Policy Paper on Human Rights and Development, which included ten principles designed to serve as a basic orientation on human rights in key development areas, where donor harmonization is of particular relevance. At the international political level a number of milestones stand out: the 2008 Accra Agenda for Action recognizes respect for human rights as one of the cornerstones of sustainable development and signals the need for greater policy coherence. At the Fourth High-Level Forum on Aid Effectiveness, held in Busan in 2011, donors and partners again reaffirmed the importance of shared principles, which are consistent with their international commitments and form the foundation for cooperation for effective development. In the MDGs context, human rights have also enjoyed renewed recognition. The outcome document of the 2010 Millennium Summit, entitled *Keeping the Promises: United to Achieve the Millennium Development Goals,* is unequivocal in recognizing that respect for human rights is essential for achieving the MDGs. Finally, in the context of sustainable development, the Outcome Document from the 2012 UN Conference on Sustainable Development (Rio + 20) reaffirmed the importance of all human rights for sustainable development and the need for green economy policies in the context of sustainable development and poverty eradication to respect all human rights

   At the operational level, development priorities in areas such as education, social protection, adequate housing, and health care are increasingly framed in terms of human rights. This is apparent in the rise of economic and social rights litigation. As this second edition illustrates, the past six years have seen the continued growth of donor and partner experiences implementing human rights principles, tools, and programming approaches in a variety of sectors and projects. The range of these experiences speaks to both the depth of global commitment to human rights and the breadth of possibilities that exist in development cooperation. It reveals the importance of context and of tailoring approaches to institutional and policy frameworks to maximize actors' comparative advantage and respect the specificity of their roles internationally. Finally, the range of approaches supports a theory of complementary and mutually reinforcing approaches to integrating human rights in development.

   A great deal has been achieved in recent years, even if considerable work remains to be done to operationalize human rights in development policy and practice and ensure that human rights principles and obligations are integrated consistently. There are practical challenges to meet as well, in terms of developing effective tools and robust methodologies, including human rights impact assessments and human rights indicators. More emphasis is warranted in the areas of monitoring and evaluation frameworks to ensure that human rights are fully integrated into mainstream development policies, strategies, dialogues, and processes.

Finally, there is still some way to go to make the empirical case for the "value added" of human rights in instrumental terms, even as we hold fast to the primacy of intrinsic rationales for their place in development. Like the first, this edition remains the most comprehensive and up-to-date resource of its kind, by capturing key developments of the past seven years and including additional policy and legal dimensions, which are essential elements of the overall interface of human rights and development. It effectively summarizes recent progress by charting donor approaches and experiences without concealing the challenges attendant on these efforts. In this way, it contributes objectively to making the case that human rights are now part of development, and it goes some way to showing why they should be. I commend Siobhán McInerney-Lankford and her colleagues for their valuable work.

Mary Robinson
Former President of Ireland
Former United Nations High Commissioner for Human Rights
President, The Mary Robinson Foundation–Climate Justice

Preface

The past two decades have witnessed a convergence between human rights and development that is most evident at the level of international political statements and policy commitments, and the past seven years have been marked by particularly important milestones. Of direct relevance to this publication was the OECD Development Assistance Committee's 2007 Action Oriented Policy Paper (AOPP) which affirmed unequivocally that human rights are an essential part of development cooperation, noting the increasing convergence of the two areas. In the context of the Millennium Development Goals (MDGs), the 2010 UN World Summit Outcome Document confirmed the centrality of human rights to sustainable development. In the area of aid effectiveness, the 2005 Accra Agenda for Action and 2011 Busan Outcome Document both acknowledged the importance of human rights standards and principles. Finally, the Outcome Document from the 2012 UN Conference on Sustainable Development (Rio + 20) reaffirmed the importance of all human rights for sustainable development and the need for green economic policies, in the context of sustainable development, and poverty eradication to respect all human rights. In more applied terms, too, the links among rights violations, poverty, exclusion, environmental degradation, vulnerability, and conflict have continued to be explored. More positively, recognition of the intrinsic importance of human rights in a range of contexts is growing, as is recognition of their potential instrumental relevance for improved development processes and outcomes.

This second edition of *Integrating Human Rights into Development: Donor Approaches, Experiences, and Challenges* consolidates the findings and research compiled in 2006 with key developments and activities that have occurred in the intervening seven years. This edition is intended to build upon the review and findings of the first edition, rather than supplant them, so that much of that material in that first edition is preserved in this publication. Like the first edition, this study seeks to advance understanding of the nexus between development and human rights through a systematic consideration of donor approaches. It also seeks to enhance understanding among donors of how to work collectively to advance the strategic and coherent integration of human rights in development in light of agencies' roles and areas of comparative advantage.

This publication brings together the key political and policy statements of recent years with a discussion of the approaches and experiences of bilateral and multilateral agencies engaged in integrating human rights into their development cooperation activities. While it is acknowledged that the landscape of development cooperation has continued to evolve rapidly, marked by the emergence of new providers of development cooperation, this study retains a focus on providers reviewed in 2006 that have established positions on human rights, even where those are more implicit than strongly articulated. The 2008 financial crisis has also defined the context of aid, placing additional pressure on donors to demonstrate impact and results: this can be argued to underscore the need to establish the instrumental relevance and "value-added" of human rights. Nevertheless, the experience of the past seven years also attests to the sustained commitment of OECD member countries and multilateral donors to engage with human rights strategically, as a means for improving the delivery of aid and promoting sustainable and equitable development results.

Like the first edition, this study is based on a thorough examination of policy, guidance, and operational documents, evaluations, and other analyses of practical experience, as well as interviews with donor agencies. In a way similar to that of the 2006 edition, it reviews the approaches of different donor agencies and their rationales for working on human rights. It confirms the range of donor approaches to human rights: some donors adopt human rights–based approaches, others opt for more incremental but explicit approaches, and still others integrate human rights more implicitly into various dimensions of their development work. The study identifies the current practices in this field and looks at the common elements of those practices. It illustrates how aid agencies are working on human rights issues at the programming level and what donors have done over the past six years, charting significant changes and advances. Like the first edition, this study draws together lessons that form the core of the current evidence on the added value of human rights for development. It addresses both opportunities and challenges attendant to human rights in evolving development partnerships between donors and partner countries, as well as in the workings of the international aid system more broadly.

In aggregate terms, this second edition confirms the global trend toward recognizing the links between human rights and development at the level of international political statements and commitments, but it also confirms the diversity of approaches that exist between donors at the level of individual agency policies and operations. Donors maintain distinct rationales for engaging in human rights activities, based on their legal and policy mandates and their institutional roles and priorities. Nevertheless, in substantive and operational terms, the areas of engagement are often the same, with activities of different agencies sometimes overlapping substantially. Moreover, the past seven years evidence a shared emphasis on implementation, monitoring, and evaluation, as well as on results and impact.

It is hoped that this second edition can, like the first, serve as a reference for practitioners and those interested in exploring the connections between human rights and development. It is also hoped that this work can be of use to those pursuing the ways in which development cooperation can advance the realization of human rights, as well as the ways in which human rights approaches can make development interventions more effective, equitable, and sustainable. This update has therefore been undertaken with the aim of sustaining knowledge-sharing efforts among donors to improve donor coordination and support the realization of human rights in development.

Acknowledgments

The original publication of this work was the result of a collaborative effort by members of the DAC Network on Governance (GOVNET). It was based on a commissioned study written by Laure-Hélène Piron and Tammie O'Neil, of the UK Overseas Development Institute. We express our great appreciation to both authors for their excellent work. This second edition of the publication was commissioned by the World Bank Nordic Trust Fund Secretariat (NTF) under the guidance of Anders Zeijlon (NTF Coordinator) and Siobhán McInerney-Lankford (TTL and former Chair of the OECD DAC Human Rights Task Team). The NTF acknowledges the work of Royce Bernstein Murray, an independent human rights law consultant who undertook the bulk of the research work of this update in 2011–12. We thank the following people for their inputs and contributions to this second edition: Lisa Williams and Deborah Alimi, OECD Directorate for Development Cooperation; Dilani Edirisuriya and Michael Bergmann, Australian Agency for International Development (AusAID); Georg Huber-Grabenwarter, Austrian Development Agency (ADA); Anton Mair, Austrian Federal Ministry for European and International Affairs, Department of Development Cooperation; Petra Schirnhofer, Austrian Development Agency; Robyn Chomyshyn, Canadian International Development Agency; Nina Berg, Thea Lund Christiansen, Anne Birgitte Hansen, and Frode Neergaard, Royal Danish Ministry of Foreign Affairs; Aurelia Willie, European Commission; Serena Pepino, Food and Agriculture Organization of the United Nations (FAO); Merja Lahtinen and Rauno Merisaari, Ministry of Foreign Affairs of Finland; Marita Steinke and Ute Möhring, German Federal Ministry for Economic Cooperation and Development (BMZ); Juliane Osterhaus, German Agency for International Development (GIZ); Dónal Cronin, Irish Department of Foreign

Affairs; Corina Van der Laan, Netherlands Ministry of Foreign Affairs; Sally Jackman and Michelle Mcgillivray, New Zealand Aid Programme (NZAID); Alfonso Barragues (UNFPA); Saranbaatar Bayarmagnai and Mac Darrow, Office of the High Commissioner for Human Rights (OHCHR); Snjezana Bokulic, Organization for Security and Cooperation in Europe (OSCE); Sonia Franco Alonso and Miguel Soler Gomis, Spanish Planning and Evaluation Development Policies Directorate General (DGPOLDE); Lisa Fredriksson and Helena Lagerlof, Swedish International Development Cooperation Agency (Sida); Corinne Huser, Swiss Agency for Development and Cooperation (SDC); Adriana Jacinto and Patrick van Weerelt, United Nations System Staff College; Daniel Seymour and Wendy Isaack, UN Women; Sarah Rattray, UNDG HuriTalk; Irina Zoubenko-Laplante, UNESCO; Simone Schwartz-Delgado, UNHCR; Cormac O'Reilly and Hedda Oehlberger-Femundsenden, UNIDO; Sylvia Bluck and Lu Eccelstone, UK Department for International Development (DFID); Fina Pattugalan, World Food Program; Helena Nygren-Krug and Yehenew Walilegne, World Health Organization (WHO); Behnaz Bonyadian, Charles Di Leva, Varun Gauri, Sara Gustafsson, Bernard Harborne, Stephen Lintner, Alexandre Marc, Andre Medici, Hans-Otto Sano, Dena Ringold, and Ethan Yeh, World Bank; and Felicia Kolp, International Finance Corporation (World Bank/IFC). Additional thanks are due to Emilie Filmer-Wilson for sharing data from the 2010 UNDG-HRM Mapping of UN Agency Human Rights Mainstreaming Policies and Tools, and to Tom Gilliams, Senior Counsel at the European Investment Bank for sharing the summary by Alfonso Querejeta of the 2011 survey of human rights and the activities of the international financial institutions.

We acknowledge the key contributions of the following to the original publication in 2006: Rahel Boesch (former Chair of the GOVNET Task Team on Human Rights and Development); Lisa Fredriksson (former Co-Chair); and Sebastian Bartsch (former OECD Directorate for Development Cooperation), who together managed and provided guidance for the entire process, as well as the members of the Task Team's core group in 2006, Jane Alexander, Sarita Bhatla, Mac Darrow, Christiane Hieronymus, Siobhán McInerney-Lankford, Juliane Osterhaus, Garett Pratt, Maria-Luisa Silva, Birgitta Tazelaar, Patrick van Weerelt, Lee Waldorf, and Franziska Walter, whose commitment to this project was exceptional. We would also like to thank many other representatives of donor agencies and NGOs and DAC Secretariat staff who made themselves available for interviews, shared documentation, and submitted written or oral comments on the manuscript. A team of OECD staff prepared the original publication: Sebastian Bartsch acted as the main editor, and Carola Miras and Misha Pinkhasov provided advice and practical assistance on all stages of the publication process. Invaluable external editorial assistance was contributed by Laura Boutin. From World Bank EXTOP we acknowledge the assistance of Stephen McGroarty, Mayya Revzina, Deborah Appel-Barker, and Rick Ludwick. We thank them all.

Abbreviations

AAA	Accra Agenda for Action
ADA	Austrian Development Agency
ADB	Asian Development Bank
ADC	Austrian Development Cooperation
ADG/FWC	Assistant Director General, Family, Women's and Children's Health Cluster
AECID	Spanish Agency for International Development Cooperation
AfDB	African Development Bank
AIBEP	Australia-Indonesia Basic Education Program
AOPP	Action-oriented Policy Paper
ASEAN	Association of Southeast Asian Nations
AusAID	Australian Agency for International Development
BCLR	Butterworths Constitutional Law Reports (South Africa)
BMZ	German Federal Ministry for Economic Cooperation and Development
BSTDB	Black Sea Trade and Development Bank
CCA	Common Country Assessment (UN)
CEB	Council of Europe Bank
CEDAW	Convention on the Elimination of All Forms of Discrimination against Women
CESR	Center for Economic and Social Rights
CFSP	Common Foreign and Security Policy
CIDA	Canadian International Development Agency
CRC	Convention on the Rights of the Child
CSO	Civil society organization

DAC	Development Assistance Committee (OECD)
DED	German Development Service
DFID	Department for International Development (UK)
EBRD	European Bank for Reconstruction and Development
EC	European Commission
EIB	European Investment Bank
EIDHR	European Instrument for Democracy and Human Rights
EU	European Union
FAO	Food and Agricultural Organization of the United Nations
FTP	Fellowship Training Programme (Ireland)
GIZ	Deutsche Gesellschaft für Internationale Zusammenarbeit (Germany)
GHRSP	Global Human Rights Strengthening Programme, 2008–11 (UNDP)
GJLOS	Governance and Justice Sector Programme
GOVNET	Network on Governance (DAC)
GPDD	Global Partnership on Disability and Development
GTZ	German Technical Agency for Cooperation
HIV/AIDS	Human immunodeficiency virus infection/acquired immunodeficiency syndrome
HR	Human rights
HRBA	Human rights–based approach
HRIAM	Human Rights Impact Assessment and Management
HRTT	Human Rights Task Team (DAC-GOVNET)
HURIST	Global Human Rights Strengthening Programme, 1999–2005 (OHCHR/UNDP)
ICESCR	International Covenant on Economic, Social, and Cultural Rights
ICHRP	International Council on Human Rights Policy
IDA	International Development Agency
IDB	Inter-American Development Bank
IFC	International Finance Corporation
ILO	International Labour Organization
INSTRAW	International Research and Training Institute for the Advancement of Women
Inwent	Capacity Building International (Germany)
J4P	Justice for the Poor

KfW	German Development Bank
KP	Knowledge product
LGBT	Lesbian, Gay, Bisexual, and Transgender
MAF	MDG Acceleration Framework
MAINIAC	Mainstreaming in Action
MCC	Millennium Challenge Corporation
MDAs	Ministries, Departments and Agencies
MDG	Millennium development goal
MOU	Memorandum of Understanding
MRG	Minority Rights Group International
NGO	Nongovernmental organization
NHRI	National Human Rights Institution
Norad	Norwegian Agency for Development Cooperation
NTF	World Bank Nordic Trust Fund Secretariat
NZAID	New Zealand Agency for International Development
ODAAA	Official Development Assistance Accountability Act (Canada)
OECD	Organisation for Economic Co-operation and Development
OHCHR	Office of the UN High Commissioner for Human Rights
PRSP	Poverty Reduction Strategy Paper
SADEV	Swedish Agency for Development Evaluation
SCRPD	Secretariat for the Convention on the Rights of Persons with Disabilities
SDC	Swiss Agency for Development and Cooperation
SLA	Sustainable Livelihoods Approach
Sida	Swedish International Development Cooperation Agency
UN	United Nations
UNAIDS	Joint United Nations Programme on HIV/AIDS
UNCAC	United Nations Convention Against Corruption
UNCT	United Nations Country Team
UNDAF	United Nations Development Assistance Framework
UNDESA	United Nations Department of Economic and Social Affairs
UN-DOCO	United Nations Development Operations Coordination Office
UNDG	United Nations Development Group

UNDP	United Nations Development Programme
UNDG-HRM	United Nations Development Group-Human Rights Main-streaming Mechanism
UNEP	United Nations Environment Programme
UNESCO	United Nations Educational, Scientific, and Cultural Organization
UNFPA	United Nations Population Fund
UNHCR	United Nations High Commissioner for Refugees
UNICEF	United Nations Children's Fund
UNIDO	United Nations Industrial Development Organization
UNIFEM	United Nations Development Fund for Women (replaced by UNWomen in 2010)
UNOPS	United Nations Office for Project Services
UNSSC	United Nations System Staff College
UN Women	United Nations Entity for Gender Equality and the Empowerment of Women
UPR	Universal periodic review
USAID	United States Agency for International Development
WFP	World Food Programme
WHO	World Health Organization

Overview

Human rights are an important aspect of development policy and programming. The 1993 Vienna World Conference on Human Rights, the 2000 Millennium Summit, and the 2005 and 2010 World Summits all recognized that development and human rights are interdependent and mutually reinforcing. In the 2010 World Summit Outcome document, UN member states affirmed:

> that peace and security, development and human rights are the pillars of the United Nations system and the foundations for collective security and well-being. We recognise that development, peace and security and human rights are interlinked and mutually reinforcing. We reaffirm that our common fundamental values, including freedom, equality, solidarity, tolerance, respect for all human rights, respect for nature and shared responsibility, are essential for achieving the Millennium Development Goals.

The UN system has been actively engaged in the process of human rights mainstreaming since 1997 and, in 2003, agreed on an interagency Common Understanding of a Human Rights–Based Approach to Development Programming ("UN Common Understanding"). This definition highlights:

- The relationship between development cooperation, the Universal Declaration of Human Rights. and international human rights instruments
- The relevance for development programming of human rights standards and principles derived from those instruments (e.g., equality and nondiscrimination, participation and inclusion, accountability and the rule of law)
- The contribution that development cooperation can make to building the capacities of "duty-bearers" and "rights-holders" to realize and claim rights.

This study, first commissioned and published in 2006 by the DAC Network on Governance (GOVNET), reviews the approaches of different donor agencies and their rationales for working on human rights. It identifies the current practice in this field and draws together lessons that form the core of the current evidence on the contribution of human rights to development. It discusses both new opportunities and conceptual and practical challenges to integrating human rights. Those challenges arise in the development partnerships between donors and partner countries, as well as in the institutions and processes of the international aid system more broadly. This second edition, commissioned by the Nordic Trust Fund of the World Bank, identifies developments and trends from the past seven years.

Donor Policies and Rationales

There is no single approach to integrating human rights into development. Over the past 15 years, most bilateral and multilateral donors have established human rights policies or policies based on a human rights–based approach (HRBA) or that integrate human rights principles. Some of these policies promulgate binding requirements, which must be complied with, while others may be more aspirational, embodying general principles that serve as guidance; some policy examples combine both. The policies of some donors have evolved over time, with a number adopting "second-generation" policies based on their experiences incorporating human rights into development. An important distinction to note is that some agencies have an explicit mandate to promote human rights in the course of their work, while others do not. Such a mandate may derive from an agency's constituent instrument or from its policy framework. However, even agencies without an explicit human rights mandate or policy engage in work related to human rights in implicit ways, such as through projects and programs that promote good governance and access to justice. It is worth noting also that the aid context is a fast-changing one, in which new actors and donors are emerging in ways that makes the donor landscape more varied and more complex. Many of these new donors are playing an increasingly important role in providing development assistance (and sometimes humanitarian assistance) to countries in the global South. For the purpose of the present study, the complexity of the picture is compounded by the fact that many of the new emerging donors have not developed explicit positions on human rights. Nevertheless, a number of landmark political and policy statements of recent years signal some coalescence around certain core commitments and principles. Thus, following the 2006 Study on Integrating Human Rights into Development, the 2007 DAC Action-Oriented Policy Paper on Human Rights elaborated 10 principles to help guide donors to effectively engage on human rights.

Human rights work may be seen as both an objective in its own right and as contributing to improving the quality and effectiveness of development assistance. The intrinsic reasons for integrating human rights in development relate to moral and ethical imperatives connected with human dignity and freedom and may also draw on the legal obligations emanating from the international human rights framework. States party to human rights instruments have obligations to respect, protect, and fulfill human rights. Donors also focus on human rights for instrumental purposes—as a means to an end—to improve development outcomes in relation to governance, poverty reduction, and aid effectiveness.

Human rights frameworks may help advance accountability by holding duty-bearers to account for their actions, as marginalized communities are empowered to demand that the state respect, protect, and fulfill their rights. Some donors are constrained by mandates that limit explicit engagement in human rights work. Political challenges can also arise: some partner countries may be less receptive to development cooperation linked to human rights considerations. Practical challenges of operationalizing human rights in development programming or enforcing human rights policy requirements are important considerations as well. Moreover, some donors continue to question the added value of human rights to their development work and the link between human rights and development effectiveness.

Donor Approaches to Programming Experiences

The integration of human rights into development can occur in a variety of ways. A number of agencies have adopted **human rights–based approaches (HRBAs),** which are the strongest articulation of donor and partner commitment to human rights in development. HRBAs recognize human rights as a primary goal of development cooperation and require that they inform all stages of the development process. They require institutional policy commitments, changes in the provision of aid, and an articulation of human rights an explicit goal of development programming.

Many bilateral and multilateral agencies have adopted human rights **mainstreaming** policies, which direct the integration of human rights into country programs or existing aid interventions in different sectors or toward particular groups, such as children's rights, women's rights, the rights of minorities and indigenous peoples, health, education, and livelihoods. Infrastructure programs can likewise benefit from human rights frameworks, as the risk of causing human rights violations can be mitigated by "do no harm" policies based implicitly or explicitly on human rights. Increased emphasis has been placed in recent years on mainstreaming human rights into programs that promote the rights of persons with disabilities. More generally, the principle of "do no harm" can be seen to support an emphasis on policy coherence, such that policies underpinning development and related areas should not undermine the standards of protection afforded by human rights treaties to which donors and partners have committed themselves.

As a complement to these efforts, donors may engage in human rights **dialogue**, often undertaken within the context of foreign policy discussions. Donors may seek out entry points for dialogue on sensitive subjects or review compliance with human rights clauses and other provisions that condition development cooperation agreements.

The most common forms of assistance are **projects**, often targeted at the realization of specific rights, the protection of particular groups, or in support of human rights organizations. Considerable support continues to be provided to human rights projects at the country and local levels, often through civil society organizations, to build the capacity of rights-holders to claim and enforce their rights. Some of these projects receive funding, training, or advice from institutional entities with human rights expertise, such as the World Bank Nordic Trust Fund or UN System Staff College.

In agencies that do not explicitly use a human rights framework, an **implicit integration** of human rights can sometimes be identified. This may be visible in governance interventions that indirectly address civil and political rights or increasingly in activities that promote access to justice and combat corruption. Finally, some agencies employ several approaches at once, or a combination of approaches depending on sector, country, and context. Many of the approaches identified are complementary and overlapping.

Preliminary Lessons: Integrating Human Rights Dimensions, Principles, and Obligations

Based on donor experiences, it has been possible to identify a set of preliminary lessons concerning the contribution of human rights for development.

The intrinsic value of human rights offers development actors an explicit normative and analytical framework, grounded in a consensual global legal regime of international human rights treaties. States' legal obligations under the international human rights treaty framework anchor the normative agenda being pursued under HRBAs and potentially bridge the accountability gaps that can arise. That framework can be adapted to different political and cultural environments. In some countries, it has proved more fruitful to take a more gradual and implicit approach. Operational human rights principles drawn from international human rights treaties, such as inclusion, nondiscrimination, participation, and accountability have made it easier to integrate human rights into development programming. In fact, it has been possible to integrate human rights (using principles derived from the human rights framework) without an explicit approach, as can be seen in the work of some of the international financial institutions. A potential shortcoming of such an approach is the risk of "rhetorical repackaging," which involves a superficial use of human rights terms in development without a full incorporation of human rights obligations or principles.

Human rights also have instrumental value for the governance agenda, as they highlight the need to build both the capacity of states to deliver on human rights commitments and the capacity of citizens to claim their entitlements. Human rights can enhance the design and impact of aid in terms of poverty reduction goals, building on the commitments of the 2010 UN World Summit. They can provide a lens through which to examine the structural determinants of poverty, including inequality and exclusion as barriers to poverty reduction, and thereby advance poverty reduction goals. Human rights demand a better understanding of the context and power relations within which aid operates, potentially elucidating the context and causes of poverty and the factors that contribute to cycles of conflict, powerlessness, and lack of voice. The principles of equality and nondiscrimination focus attention squarely on excluded and marginalized individuals and groups (and emphasize the importance of disaggregated data), again potentially advancing development goals aimed at reducing inequalities and inequity. Human rights principles may also demonstrate instrumental value in complementing aid effectiveness principles articulated in the Paris Declaration: alignment, harmonization, results-based management, mutual accountability, and ownership.

Challenges and Opportunities

Donors confront several challenges and opportunities as they pursue the integration of human rights into development.

First, the success of those efforts depends on a deepened institutionalization of human rights considerations, with attention to systems, procedures, and staff incentives and allocating adequate resources to better translate their policies into practice. A number of factors could contribute to success in this area: a supportive international and domestic political context; domestic legal environments amenable to development and fostering human rights; senior-level commitment, accountability, and communication; a strengthening of staff capacities and incentives; provision of new tools and procedures; and adaptation to a decentralized context. However, many agencies acknowledge that they need to invest more in knowledge management to advance their policy development and improve the basis for harmonized policies and approaches. Agencies and institutions that use an implicit human rights–based approach may face additional challenges in measuring progress in human rights realization, particularly where programs do not lend themselves to measurement according to human rights based indicators.

Second, aid agencies have found engagement with partner countries (and fragile states, in particular) difficult because of weaknesses in the capacity to implement human rights. Agencies also face political barriers, in particular when their partner's commitment is weak, or when there is overt resistance to human rights in general, or to sensitivities surrounding particular human rights issues. Practitioners working on fragile states and human rights share a common interest in the prioritization of key features of the partner state: the legitimacy and accountability of state structures and the state's ability to create an enabling environment. Human rights can also offer analytical and operational approaches for donor engagement in these difficult environments. Member states have made several commitments, most recently at the UN 2010 World Summit, to integrate the promotion and protection of human rights into national policies. These provide entry points to strengthen the national ownership of human rights in the context of development partnerships, in particular around poverty reduction strategies.

Third, aid agencies need to continue to explore the place of human rights into thinking and practice around new aid effectiveness processes, instruments, and modalities. Examples in the context of the Millennium Development Goals (MDGs) include linking the goals to specific human rights standards; drawing on the Millennium Declaration, which makes explicit reference to human rights; and adopting human rights–based approaches toward meeting the MDGs. The Outcome Document of the 2010 World Summit reaffirmed that respect for human rights is critical for reaching the MDGs. The GOVNET has also explored the relevance of human rights for aid effectiveness, including in its 2007 DAC Action-Oriented Policy Paper on Human Rights, which recommends that donors "consider human rights in decisions on alignment and aid instruments" (Principle 6) and "consider mutual reinforcement between human rights and aid effectiveness principles" (Principle 7). Likewise, the Accra Agenda for Action explicitly recognizes the connection between human rights and aid effectiveness:

We need to achieve much more if all countries are to meet the Millennium Development Goals (MDGs). Aid is only one part of the development picture. Democracy, economic growth, social progress, and care for the environment are the prime engines of development in all countries. Addressing inequalities of income and opportunity within countries and between states is essential to global progress. Gender equality, respect for human rights, and environmental sustainability are cornerstones for achieving enduring impact on the lives and potential of poor women, men, and children. It is vital that all our policies address these issues in a more systematic and coherent way.

In paragraph 13(c) it goes on to say, "Developing countries and donors will ensure that their respective development policies and programs are designed and implemented in ways consistent with their agreed international commitments on gender equality, human rights, disability and environmental sustainability." Other research points to the congruence between human rights and a number of aid effectiveness principles related to strengthening partner countries' capacities, greater transparency, managing for results, and policy coherence (see DAC HRTT 2007 update "Human Rights and Aid Effectiveness," an information sheet entitled "Human Rights and Aid Effectiveness: Key Actions to Improve Inter-Linkages," and a report from the DAC Network on Governance (GOVNET), "Linking Human Rights and Aid Effectiveness for Better Development Results: Practical Experience from the Health Sector").

Finally, the 2011 outcome document from the Fourth High-Level Forum on Aid Effectiveness, in Busan, explicitly preserves the commitments of the Accra Agenda for Action, which include provisions on human rights. In addition, it provides for the right to development and confirms the "common principles which consistent with our agreed international commitments on human rights, decent work, gender equality, environmental sustainability and disability, form the foundation of our cooperation for effective development" (paragraph 11).

Trends and Conclusions

The past decade, and the last six years in particular, have witnessed a steady trajectory of integration of human rights principles into development cooperation. There have been significant developments on the international stage, such as high-level political statements like the 2008 Accra Agenda for Action, the 2010 Millennium Outcome Document, and the outcome document of the Fourth High-Level Forum on Aid Effectiveness, in Busan, Korea, as well as events surrounding the 25th anniversary of the Declaration on the Right to Development at the end of 2011. At the national level, some donors have followed through with more explicit commitments to incorporating human rights into their development work, but significant challenges persist in the implementation and operationalizing of a human rights–based approach. There has been considerable activity at the level of projects, though it remains unclear whether that reflects a greater difficulty integrating human rights at a policy or programmatic level. Other actors, particularly the multilateral development banks, have shown greater interest in engaging on these issues, particularly in terms of improving risk mitigation and promulgating or updating environmental and social safeguard policies, and adhering to a "do no harm" principle. Overall, these activities do not represent a seismic shift in donor approaches. Rather they confirm that in substantive terms, and at the operational level, wide areas of convergence exist among donor approaches. They also reveal common areas of emphasis in relation to implementation, monitoring, and evaluation, as well as on results and impact. To sustain progress, all development actors should leverage their expertise and comparative advantage to better understand the synergies between human rights and development so as to contribute in complementary ways to both.

Part I

Analytical Perspectives

Donor Policies and Rationales

There is no single approach to integrating human rights into development. Some donors have developed human rights policies that inform and guide their development assistance, whereas others incorporate human rights principles in less explicit ways. Some human rights policies promulgate binding requirements; others may be more aspirational, embodying general principles that serve as guides; a number of policies can be seen to contain a combination of both. Such policy efforts may be grounded in legal and ethical obligations, but they can also be viewed in a more functional light, under which a focus on human rights is viewed as improving development and helping to avoid and mitigate risk in aid interventions. The implementation of human rights approaches remains challenging, even for donors and agencies with an explicit legal and political mandate to do so.

Policies

The trend is clear and sustained among "traditional donors": both bilateral and multilateral agencies have adopted or are in the process of adopting or refining policies on human rights and development. Among bilaterals, a first wave of foreign policy statements in the 1990s was later complemented by aid agency–specific documents on human rights and development. They often emphasize the positive measures that donors can support through financial or technical assistance and dialogue to promote human rights in partner countries. Multilaterals, such as the UN system, the OECD Development Assistance Committee (DAC), or the European Commission, have also developed human rights explicit policy frameworks, but not all of the international financial institutions have done so.

As table 1.1 illustrates, the majority of agencies surveyed have either adopted human rights policies or are in the process of developing or updating them in light of experience gained over the past 15 years. By comparison, fewer agencies and institutions have no human rights policies at all. Agencies without explicit policies may still refer to human rights in other documents or work on human rights in indirect ways, as described in table 1.1 (the table is not intended to be comprehensive).

The 2007 DAC Action-Oriented Policy Paper on Human Rights elaborated 10 principles to serve as basic orientations in areas where harmonized donor action is of particular importance (OECD 2007a; see box 1.1). Given their place in many states' domestic legal and policy frameworks, human rights may play a part in setting national development priorities whose implementation the donors can support. In addition, a strong congruence exists between, on the one hand, building partners' capacity and ensuring that aid does not undermine national capacities and, on the other, the principle that states are the primary duty-bearers and that aid can be used to assist them in meeting their human rights obligations.

Rationales

Why have agencies adopted such policies? The principle reason lies in the changing international context. Human rights remained a highly politicized issue during the Cold War,[3] with a division between states that prioritized civil and political rights and those that promoted economic, social, and cultural rights. At the 1993 Vienna World Conference on Human Rights, a consensus was reached that recognized that "All human rights are universal, indivisible and interdependent and

Table 1.1 Policy Statements on Human Rights and Development

Type	Illustrations
No overall human rights policies but occasional references to human rights limited to sector policies; human rights may be captured in more general, aspirational terms rather than as a strict policy requirement to be complied with.	African Development Bank (AfDB) Asian Development Bank (ADB) (indigenous peoples, gender and development, involuntary resettlement) Black Sea Trade and Development Bank (BSTDB) IFC (sustainability policy; performance standards on social and environmental assessment and management systems; community health, safety, and security; land acquisition and involuntary resettlement; indigenous peoples; cultural heritage) Inter-American Development Bank (IADB) (indigenous peoples, gender equality in development, involuntary resettlement, environmental and social sustainability) International Finance Corporation (IFC) Islamic Development Bank (IDB) Nordic Investment Bank (NIB) (indigenous people and other vulnerable groups) UN Environment Programme (UNEP) UN-HABITAT UN Industrial Development Organization (UNIDO) UNOPS World Food Programme (WFP) World Health Organization (WHO) Australian Agency for International Development (AusAID) U.S. Agency for International Development (USAID) (internally displaced people, trafficking, civilian protection) World Bank IBRD/IDA—one reference in indigenous peoples policy;
Established human rights policies and policies based on a human rights–based approach (HRBA).	Canadian International Development Agency (CIDA 1996; 2005a; Canada 2008) Swiss Agency for Development and Cooperation (SDC 1997; 2006a) Swedish International Development Cooperation Agency (Sida 1997; Government of Sweden 2003b) United Nations High Commissioner for Refugees (UNHCR 1997) United Nations Development Program (UNDP 1998a) and Various Practice Notes (such as UNDP 2003a; 2004a; 2005) UNICEF (1998; 2001) Ministry for Foreign Affairs of Finland (2000; 2004) U.K. Department for International Development (DFID 2000a) European Commission (2001) Netherlands Ministry of Foreign Affairs (2001) New Zealand Agency for International Development Cooperation (NZAID 2002) UNESCO (2003) German Federal Ministry for Economic Cooperation and Development (BMZ 2004) United Nations Population Fund (UNFPA 2004a) United Nations Development Fund for Women (UNIFEM 2004a)[a]

(cotinued next page)

Table 1.1 (Continued)

Type	Illustrations
	Austria Development Cooperation (ADC 2006a) Government of Spain (2008) Office of the High Commissioner for Human Rights (OHCHR 2009) Ministry of Foreign Affairs of Denmark (2010b)
"Second-generation" policies.	German Federal Ministry for Economic Cooperation and Development (2011) Netherlands Ministry of Foreign Affairs (2007; 2011) Ministry for Foreign Affairs of Sweden (2010a) Ministry of Foreign Affairs of Denmark (2012) UNICEF (2010a; 2010b) UNFPA (2010) OHCHR
Human rights as part of the overall agency/institutional mandate.[b]	International Labour Organization (ILO) UN Department of Economic and Social Affairs (DESA) UNAIDS UN-HABITAT UNHCR UN Women[a] World Food Program (WFP) World Health Organization (WHO) Council of Europe Bank (CEB) European Bank for Reconstruction and Development (EBRD) European Instrument for Democracy and Human Rights (EIDHR) European Investment Bank (EIB)
Interagency or multilateral agreements on or referencing human rights and development.	UN Vienna Human Rights Declaration and Program of Action (UN 1993) UN Millennium Declaration (2000) DAC Guidelines on Poverty Reduction (OECD 2001) UN Interagency Common Understanding of an HRBA (2003) UN World Summit Outcome Document (2005a) DAC Action-Oriented Paper on Human Rights and Development (OECD 2007a) Accra Agenda for Action (2008) UN MDG 2010 Summit Outcome Document (UN 2010d) Busan Outcome Document (2011) The 25th Anniversary of the Declaration on the Right to Development, Joint Statement of Chairpersons of the UN Treaty Bodies (UN 2011a) Joint Statement on the Occasion of the 25th Anniversary of the UN Declaration on the Right to Development (UN 2011b) UN Conference on Sustainable Development (Rio + 20) Outcome Document (UN 2012)

Note: The term "policy" admits of a wide set of definitions. It is employed broadly here to include a range of types of policies, from those establishing binding requirements to those embodying general principles that serve as guidance, as well as policies containing both.

a. UN Women was created in July 2010 (UN 2010a) to replace UNIFEM and has been in the process of developing its own human rights policy. The FAO has also been developing its own Right to Food Mainstreaming Strategy (UNDG-HRM 2011).

b. For more information about the status of UN agency human rights mainstreaming policies, see UNDG-HRM 2011.

Box 1.1 DAC Action-Oriented Policy Paper on Human Rights (AOPP)

In 2007, the DAC elaborated 10 principles for promoting and integrating human rights in development:

1. Build a shared understanding of the links between human rights obligations and development priorities through dialogue.
2. Identify areas of support to partner governments on human rights.
3. Safeguard human rights in processes of state-building.
4. Support the demand side of human rights.
5. Promote nondiscrimination as a basis for more inclusive and stable societies.
6. Consider human rights in decisions on alignment and aid instruments.
7. Consider mutual reinforcement between human rights and aid effectiveness principles.
8. Do no harm.
9. Take a harmonized and graduated approach to deteriorating human rights situations.
10. Ensure that the scaling-up of aid is conducive to human rights.

Source: OECD 2007a

---

interrelated" (UN 1993), implying that states and their aid agencies should not prioritize one set of rights over the other. The Vienna Consensus also affirmed that:

> Democracy, development and respect for human rights and fundamental freedoms are interdependent and mutually reinforcing … The international community should support the strengthening and promoting of democracy, development and respect for human rights and fundamental freedoms in the entire world. (UN 1993)

More recently, as UN member states took stock of the progress made toward achievement of the Millennium Development Goals (MDGs), the 2010 World Summit Outcome document on human rights acknowledged:

> that peace and security, development and human rights are the pillars of the United Nations system and the foundations for collective security and well-being. We recognise that development, peace and security and human rights are interlinked and mutually reinforcing. We reaffirm that our common fundamental values, including freedom, equality, solidarity, tolerance, respect for all human rights, respect for nature and shared responsibility, are essential for achieving the Millennium Development Goals. (UN 2010d)

As illustrated by the 1997 DAC statement that "respect for human rights is seen as an objective in its own right but also as a critical factor for the longer-term sustainability of development activities" (OECD 1997a), there are two main rationales for agencies' work on human rights as part of development cooperation: intrinsic and instrumental. Although they are discussed separately here, they are not mutually exclusive and can be linked in policy and practice.

Intrinsic Rationale

Intrinsic reasons start from moral or ethical norms, which are reflected in legal obligations that form part of the international human rights framework for the protection of the equal dignity of all human beings. This universal framework of common values was reaffirmed at the 2010 and 2005 UN World Summits, including freedom, equality, solidarity, and tolerance.

All states that are party to the relevant international human rights instruments have a duty to respect, protect, and fulfill human rights, including doing so through international cooperation. The UN, which is the guarantor of the international human rights system, has since 1997 worked to mainstream human rights in all its activities. The 2005 UN World Summit called for further mainstreaming of human rights throughout the UN system, strengthening of the Office of the High Commissioner for Human Rights (OHCHR) and closer cooperation between OHCHR and all relevant United Nations bodies (UN 2005a). The 2010 UN World Summit reaffirmed that respect for all human rights is essential for achieving the Millennium Development Goals (UN 2010d). The 2003 UN interagency definition of a human rights–based approach (HRBA) explicitly states that development cooperation should further the realization of human rights as laid out in international human rights instruments (box 1.2). A number of bilateral agencies have also adopted the view that development and human rights are interlinked and that aid should be used to foster human rights objectives. Nevertheless, the fact that a normative agenda is increasingly pursued under HRBAs does not necessarily result in an emphasis on human rights as legal obligations or as the subject of binding international treaty obligations in the context of development cooperation for either donors or partners (McInerney-Lankford 2009).

> **Box 1.2 UN Interagency Common Understanding of a Human Rights–Based Approach**
>
> 1. All programs of development cooperation, policies and technical assistance should further the realization of human rights as laid down in the Universal Declaration of Human Rights and other international human rights instruments.
> 2. Human rights standards contained in, and principles[a] derived from, the Universal Declaration of Human Rights and other international human rights instruments guide all development cooperation and programming in all sectors and in all phases of the programming process.
> 3. Development cooperation contributes to the development of the capacities of "duty-bearers" to meet their obligations and/or of "rights-holders" to claim their rights.
>
> *Source:* UN 2003a.
> a. The human rights principles identified in this agreement are universality and inalienability; indivisibility; interdependence and interrelatedness; equality and nondiscrimination; participation and inclusion; accountability and rule of law.

Not all aid agencies accept that they are under a legal obligation to promote and respect human rights through their assistance, and intrinsic arguments are not limited to legal ones: the concepts of humanity and human dignity underlying the human rights framework are strong factors behind most policies. Ethical arguments thus drive a positive association between human rights and aid, centered on human dignity and the need to combat poverty. Political factors can also drive agencies to integrate human rights, for example, when there is public outcry over substantial amounts of aid given to governments that use excessive force against their own citizens or that practice ethnic discrimination.

Intrinsic reasons also include arguments in which the realization of human rights is seen as constitutive of development:

- Drawing on Sen's capabilities framework (1999), the Human Development Report 2000 highlights the common vision and common purpose of human development and human rights "to secure the freedom, well-being and dignity of all people everywhere" (UNDP 2000).
- The multidimensional definition of poverty in the DAC Guidelines on Poverty Reduction maps on to the various human rights codified under the international framework (OECD 2001). These guidelines and other DAC documents describe human rights, alongside

governance, democracy and the rule of law, as part of the qualitative elements of development.

- The World Bank's *Voices of the Poor* reports confirmed that poor people care about civil and political rights, such as safety and security, as much as food and water, and that they are legitimate poverty reduction goals (Narayan et al. 2000a; 2000b; Narayan and Petesch 2002).

As aid agencies have become more familiar with the human rights framework, human rights organizations too have started to address poverty and development more directly. The Office of the United Nations High Commissioner for Human Rights has taken a particular interest in poverty reduction, and international human rights NGOs are increasingly addressing economic, social, and cultural rights.

Instrumental Rationale

Instrumental reasons recognize the place of the international human rights framework but in addition argue that a focus on human rights can improve processes and outcomes in relation to development assistance, security, and other international priorities. They can thus be seen as a means to an end, such as sustainable development, or as part of upholding a principle of "do no harm." Starting from a traditional focus on civil and political rights, the integration of human rights in development can contribute to good governance. Human rights frameworks help people hold duty-bearers accountable, inasmuch as they empower individuals and communities to demand that the state respect, protect, and fulfill their rights.

For some agencies, such as the Swiss Agency for Development and Cooperation (SDC), the Austrian Development Cooperation, and the Canadian International Development Agency (CIDA), human rights are defined as a subcategory of governance. For other agencies, human rights, democracy, and the rule of law are seen as additional dimensions to a more technical core definition of governance around the management of public resources (European Commission 2001). The human rights principles of accountability, rule of law, and participation are seen as contributing to more effective, legitimate, and accountable governance (World Bank 2010a). The Swedish International Development Cooperation Agency (Sida) closely links democracy and human rights objectives. It considers that poverty, understood in its broadest sense, is a state wherein almost all human rights are violated, and that a lack of democracy leads to greater poverty in the long term. Under the umbrella of "democratic governance," Sida supports initiatives on human rights, democratization, rule of law, people's participation, and good governance, all of which are seen to contribute to poverty reduction and to highlight the political dimensions of development.

Integrating human rights into development cooperation can also help to achieve more effective poverty reduction and better social outcomes. A commitment to human rights calls for urgent steps to tackle extreme poverty and social exclusion, which violate human dignity and the human rights of the poorest. The Outcome Document from the 2010 UN Summit on the Millennium Development Goals (UN 2010d), as well as the 1995 Copenhagen World Summit on Social Development, set out international commitments in this area. A focus on vulnerable and excluded groups and the principles of universality, equality and nondiscrimination, participation and inclusion are particularly relevant here. The UK Department for International Development (DFID) has emphasized an empowerment approach aimed at participation, inclusion, and realizing the rights of the very poorest (DFID 2000a). SDC's policy strengthens its commitment to empowerment and participation by explicit reference to human rights (SDC 2006a). The World Bank's social development policy (2005a) is based on its experience that inclusion, cohesion, and accountability make development interventions more effective and sustainable.

Finally, agency statements often argue that a focus on human rights can improve the coherence, quality, and effectiveness of aid. For example, Dutch policy highlights the links between human rights, foreign policy, and development, and the use of political instruments to achieve both human rights and development objectives.

Legal and Policy Considerations

Donor agencies do not endorse the different rationales for working on human rights and development to the same degree. Some agencies point to legal constraints. For example, some are concerned that there may be conflicts with their mandate if they work explicitly on human rights because of the political prohibitions in their constituent instruments. This is the case for the World Bank, where human rights have traditionally been seen as political, and therefore outside of the Bank's mandate because of the political prohibitions of its Articles of Agreement. For the World Bank, human rights are "relevant only when there are economic consequences" (Dañino 2004). Such legal considerations are compounded by the practical challenges of defining the parameters of human rights considerations or ensuring compliance with human rights obligations. In addition, it is argued that existing human development initiatives already contribute to economic and social rights. Several of the Bank's *World Development Reports* address human rights themes: the WDR 2006 on Equity (World Bank 2005c) makes explicit reference to human rights, and both the WDR 2012, on gender, and WDR 2013, on jobs, address the relevance of human rights to their themes. In addition, some of the World Bank conceptual frameworks (for example, empowerment, accountability) or interventions toward particular social groups, such as indigenous peoples (World Bank 2005d) or persons with disabilities (World Bank and WHO 2011) or HIV/AIDS (World Bank 2011k; 2012a), have strong human rights content. Another important World Bank initiative is the Nordic Trust Fund, created in 2008 as an internal "knowledge and learning initiative" to help develop an informed view among Bank staff on how human rights relate to the Bank's core work (for further discussion of the Nordic Trust Fund, see box 2.14 and chapter 8). European financial institutions address these issues in their own distinct ways (box 1.3).

Legal constraints are often related to political ones. Not all partner countries may be receptive to having development cooperation linked to human rights considerations. Moreover, domestic political environments in donor countries may be more or less conducive to grounding aid in an international human rights framework. For example, Sweden's global policy, which requires that a "rights perspective" (a type of human rights–based approach) be integrated into all aspects of foreign policy (including aid), contrasts with that of the United States, where there is a more selective endorsement of the international human rights framework, illustrated by the nonratification of the International Covenant on Economic, Social and Cultural Rights, the Convention on the Rights

Box 1.3 Human Rights Policy Frameworks at European Financial Institutions

Financial institutions of the European Union, such as the European Investment Bank (EIB), are bound by the Charter of Fundamental Rights of the European Union to respect and promote the charter's rights and principles. The EIB's Statement of Environmental and Social Principles and Standards (EIB 2009) sets forth the Bank's human rights approach generally, which is implemented in part by five "Social Assessment Guidance Notes" (attached to the EIB's Environmental and Social Practices Handbook) on issues that may cover human rights concerns: involuntary resettlement; rights and interests of vulnerable groups; labor standards; occupational and community health and safety; and public consultation and participation (EIB 2006).

Preambular language in the foundational legal instrument of the European Bank for Reconstruction and Development (EBRD) notes that contracting parties are "[c]ommitted to the fundamental principles of multiparty democracy, the rule of law, respect for human rights and market economies" (EBRD 1990). It further describes the EBRD's mission as facilitating the transition toward market economies and in member countries committed to democracy and pluralism. This enables the EBRD to emphasize human rights in the course of its work. Although the EBRD does not have an explicit human rights policy, its emphasis on political and civil rights is reflected in the EBRD's "Procedures to Implement the Political Aspects of the Mandate of the European Bank for Reconstruction and Development" (EBRD 1991) and the "Political Aspects of the [EBRD's] Mandate in Relation to Ethnic Minorities" (EBRD 1993). Additional attention is paid to specific human rights in the EBRD's "Environmental and Social Policy" (EBRD 2008) as well as its "Gender Action Plan" (EBRD 2010).

Although the Council of Europe Bank (CEB) does not have a foundational document explicitly establishing human rights responsibilities for the bank, it is institutionally grounded in human rights as well. The CEB is administered under the authority of the Council of Europe, the main purpose of which is to promote human rights, democracy, and rule of law. The Secretary General of the Council of Europe is required to review every project application to assess whether it conforms to the political and social aims of the Council of Europe (CEB 2010a). The CEB's human rights framework includes loan regulations that require projects to conform to the provisions of the Convention for the Protection of Human Rights and Fundamental Freedoms and the European Social Charter (CEB 2010a). These CEB contractual covenants are a unique feature, as CEB can suspend, cancel, or demand early reimbursement of a loan if a project's implementation leads to a human rights violation (see, for example, Article 3.3(g)(iii) of the CEB Loan Regulations). Its Environmental Policy also mandates that "the CEB will not knowingly finance projects which are identified as undermining human rights" (CEB 2010).

of the Child, and other international instruments. This means that the poverty reduction efforts of the U.S. Agency for International Development (USAID) cannot be conceptualized from the perspective of economic and social rights and state obligations.

Even in such circumstances, aid agencies have been working on aspects of the human rights agenda (either narrowly on civil or political rights, or without using explicit human rights language) or are currently considering how to adapt their policy frameworks. Processes of stock-taking or mainstreaming of human rights work (without an overarching policy) are among the entry points (box 1.4).

For some agencies that have not adopted human rights policies the reasons are pragmatic ones. For example, Australia engages in international dialogue on human rights and provides grant funding to nongovernment organizations and human rights institutions based or operating in developing countries to promote and protect human rights. In 2011–12, Australia provided $3.7 million through its Human Rights Grants Scheme to fund 41 projects across the Asia-Pacific,

---

Box 1.4 Entry Points for Human Rights in the Absence of Policy Statements

"Protection from abuse"—whether in international conflicts, human trafficking, internally displaced people, or the rule of law—is an entry point for USAID, which had compiled a list of human rights interventions and had appointed human rights advisers in its Office of Transition Initiatives.

The World Food Program (WFP) does not have an explicit human rights policy but does have policy frameworks that relate directly or indirectly to human rights, such as the 2008–13 WFP Strategic Plan, stating that food security shall be delivered "in ways that contribute to the safety and dignity of affected populations." Its protection approach is consistent with human rights–based programming, including a right-to-food approach (WFP 2010). WFP also commenced the "Protection Project," funded through external sources, which engages in the training of WFP staff and partners on protection (including trainings of trainers), a study on gender-based violence in the context of food assistance in displacement settings, and continuous program support to country offices, such as assessment, implementation, and monitoring tools. Thus far, the project guidance and tools have been mainstreamed at the field level with country offices; the next step would be to have them incorporated at headquarters (particularly as part of the monitoring process) (UNDG-HRM 2011). Similarly, the UN Food and Agricultural Organization (FAO) does not yet have a human rights mainstreaming policy but has other strategic tools, such as the Voluntary Guidelines on the Right to Food (FAO 2005), which represent a consensus on how to achieve the right to adequate food and how to promote it in the context of food security (UNDG-HRM 2011).

Although the World Health Organization (WHO) has not adopted an explicit and overarching human rights mainstreaming policy, it has launched a mainstreaming process in the context of its current reform process, which brings together gender, equity, and human rights. A new team, responsible for institutional mainstreaming and located within the Office of the Assistant Director-General, Family, Women's and Children's Health Cluster (ADG/FWC), has been established to play a central role in fostering greater cooperation across the organization. It will stimulate action with headquarters departments, regional offices, and through the regional offices, with WHO country offices and their national counterparts (WHO 2012).

Middle East, and Africa. Although Australia does not have a stand-alone human rights policy, enhancing human rights is included within "Effective Governance"—one of five core strategic goals of the Australian aid program (AusAID 2012).

Human rights principles are also applied in AusAID's Gender Thematic Strategy (AusAID 2011a), as well as in AusAID's Development for All strategy, which reflects the rights-based approach of the United Nations Convention on the Rights of Persons with Disabilities (AusAID 2008). Australia's Humanitarian Action Policy highlights protecting the safety, dignity, and rights of affected populations as core to its humanitarian action, and it includes as a guiding principle a commitment to working with governments and humanitarian partners to advocate for the rights and protection of affected populations (AusAID 2011b).

The further development or implementation of agencies' human rights policies presents a number of empirical challenges. Some aid agency staff consider that aid or national policies based on human rights standards may constrain, rather than facilitate, poverty reduction, conflict resolution, or other objectives. Peace or health outcomes may be hindered by paying attention to the processes to reach those outcomes, social spending on economic and social rights goals can slow economic growth, and labor standards can result in incentives that have a negative impact on growth (for example, if the minimum wage is set too high, or if implementing health and safety standards is prohibitively expensive for employers).

Practical and empirical challenges tend to be more amenable to evidence-based discussions than legal and political ones. Research and multidisciplinary exchanges can contribute to the development and application of policies so as to reach a wider set of agency staff and partners (box 1.5).

As part of its Human Rights Mainstreaming Case Study initiative, the United Nations Development Group Human Rights Mainstreaming Mechanism (UNDG-HRM; See box 2.13, chapter 2) launched a call for examples of successful human rights mainstreaming at country level in April 2012. The case study project responds to one of the central findings from the UNDG-HRM's 2011 Survey to United Nations Country Teams (UNCTs) on their needs, challenges, and opportunities for human rights mainstreaming. A large number of UNCTs requested more practical examples and lessons learned on human rights mainstreaming.

Box 1.5 Building the Evidence Base for Human Rights Policies

The Asia-Pacific Regional Office of the High Commissioner for Human Rights developed the Lessons Learned Project (in collaboration with several other organizations) to help integrate human rights policy and practice in all UN activities. Project staff culled programs and projects of the UN system and its many partners for experiences in using a human rights–based approach to development. Project activities included writing up the lessons learned (both positive and negative) and provision of assistance to UN country teams (UNCTs) across the region (Banerjee 2005; UNESCO 2008b).

Research is ongoing in the World Bank's Development Research Group focusing on the role of judiciaries and legal institutions in promoting state accountability (World Bank 2011d), the impact of legal strategies to claim economic and social rights (World Bank 2011c), administrative law mechanisms for redressing complaints regarding the provision of basic services (World Bank 2011e), and the costs of compliance with human rights treaties (World Bank 2011f). Other recently published research addresses the impacts of human rights–based approaches (World Bank 2012b). The World Bank also recently published a study on the relevance of human rights indicators for development, which also provided an overview of methodological approaches on human rights measurement (World Bank 2010b). Earlier research undertaken in the World Bank Institute found that "there are consistent, statistically significant and empirically large effects of civil liberties on investment project rates of return," that state capture impairs socioeconomic development, and that "the extent of capture and crony bias is related to the degree of civil liberties in a country" (Kaufmann 2005).

From an initial review of UN country examples of human rights mainstreaming, the role of UNCTs in supporting governments' engagement with, and follow-up to, human rights mechanisms can be powerful. For example, advocacy efforts by the UNCT in Azerbaijan were instrumental in that country's ratification of the Convention on the Rights of Persons with Disabilities. Subsequently, the UNCT developed joint programs to support major legal and policy changes in the country, as well as concrete activities to enable people with disabilities to better exercise their rights. In Uruguay, following the visit of the Special Rapporteur on torture and other cruel, inhuman, or degrading treatment or punishment, the UNCT developed joint programs on penal reform that mobilized and supported the government to carry out a sweeping penal reform program.

In Tanzania, the UNCT played an important role in supporting the engagement of government and civil society with the Universal Periodic Review (UPR) process (chapter 6). It also used that process to raise human rights issues on the public agenda. Following the intergovernmental dialogue in Geneva, the UN country team developed a UPR follow-up assistance strategy to ensure that the recommendations inform national development policies and programs, as well as the United Nations Development Assistance Plan (UNDAP 2011–2015).

A number of UNCTs, as illustrated by Ecuador, Kenya, and the Philippines, are moving beyond applying a human rights–based approach to UN programming only. At the request of the respective governments, these teams are supporting national partners in applying the approach to national development policies and processes as well.

From Policy to Practice

Agencies have adopted different approaches to implementing policies, reflecting their mandates, policy frameworks, and different modes of engagement. Most common have been human rights projects, usually linked to the promotion and protection of civil and political rights. Some agencies have committed to human rights mainstreaming, which usually leads to working on human rights issues in nongovernance sectors. Many bilateral aid agencies also undertake some form of human rights dialogue, often linked to their foreign policies. Where political or legal constraints to these approaches exist, donors engage in implicit human rights work without referring explicitly to human rights or adopting an HRBA. Chapter 2 offers a framework for further examination of these approaches.

References

Accra Agenda for Action. 2008. Third High-Level Forum on Aid Effectiveness, September 4, 2008, Accra.

ADC (Austrian Development Cooperation). 2006a. Human Rights Policy Document, Vienna.

AusAID (Australian Agency for International Development). 2001. "Putting Things to Rights: The Use of Foreign Aid to Advance Human Rights in Developing Nations." Submission from the Australian Agency for International Development to the Human Rights Sub-Committee of the Joint Standing Committee on Foreign Affairs, Defence and Trade on its Inquiry into the Link Between Aid and Human Rights, Canberra.

———. 2008. Development for All: Towards a Disability-Inclusive Australian Aid Program, 2009–2014. Canberra.

———. 2011a. "Promoting Opportunities for All: Gender Equality and Women's Empowerment, Thematic Strategy, November 2011." December, Canberra.

———. 2011b. "Humanitarian Action Policy." December, Canberra.

———. 2012. "An Effective Aid Program for Australia: Making a Real Difference—Delivering Real Results." June, Commonwealth of Australia, Canberra.

Banerjee, Upala Devi, ed. 2005. *Lessons Learned from Rights-Based Approaches in the Asia Pacific Region: Documentation of Case Studies.* Office of the United Nations High Commissioner for Human Rights, Regional Office for Asia-Pacific, Bangkok.

BMZ (German Federal Ministry for Economic Cooperation and Development). 2004. *Every Person Has a Right to Development: Development Policy Action Plan on Human Rights 2004–2007.* BMZ Concept no. 128, Bonn.

Buson Outcome Document. 2011. Busan Partnership for Effective Development Cooperation, Fourth High-Level Forum on Aid Effectiveness, November 29–December 1.

Canada. 2008. *Official Development Assistance Accountability Act,* June 28, 2008, S.C. 2008, c. 17, Minister of Justice, Québec.

CEB (Council of Europe Bank). 2010a. "Policy for Loan and Project Financing." Adopted in June 2006 under Administrative Council Resolution 1495, Paris.

———. 2010b. "Environmental Policy." September, Paris.

Centre for Democratic Institutions. 2001. "Human Rights and Corruption," prepared by Zoe Pearson. CDI, Canberra.

CIDA (Canadian International Development Agency). 1996. *Government of Canada Policy for CIDA on Human Rights, Democratization and Good Governance.* Québec: CIDA.

———. 2005a. *A Role of Pride and Influence in the World—Development.* Canada's International Policy Statement, Québec.

Dañino, Roberto. 2004. "The World Bank: A Lawyer's Perspective." Lecture at Harvard Law School, International Finance Seminar, November 1, Washington, DC.

DFID (U.K. Department for International Development). 2000a. "Realising Human Rights for Poor People." Policy paper, DFID, London.

EBRD (European Bank for Reconstruction and Development). 1990. *The Agreement Establishing the European Bank for Reconstruction and Development* [signed May 29, 1990; entered into force March 28, 1991], Paris.

———. 1991. "Procedures to Implement the Political Aspects of the Mandate of the European Bank for Reconstruction and Development." EBRD, London.

———. 1993. "Political Aspects of the Mandate of the EBRD." April; updated April 2010, EBRD, London.

———. 2010. "The EBRD's Gender Action Plan." January, EBRD, London.

EIB (European Investment Bank). 2006. "Social Assessment Guidance Notes." July, EIB, Luxembourg.

———. 2009. "EIB Statement of Environmental and Social Principles and Standards." February 3, EIB, Luxembourg.

European Commission. 2001. "The European Union's Role in Promoting Human Rights and Democratisation in Third Countries." Communication from the Commission to the Council and the European Parliament, May 8, Brussels.

FAO (Food and Agriculture Organization of the United Nations). 2005. "Voluntary Guidelines to Support the Progressive Realization of the Right to Adequate Food in the Context of National Food Security." Adopted in November 2004, Rome.

Government of Spain. 2008. *Human Rights Plan.* December 12, Madrid.

Government of Sweden. 2003b. "Human Rights in Swedish Foreign Policy." Government Communication no. 2003/04:20, Stockholm.

Kaufmann, Daniel. 2005. "Human Rights and Governance: The Empirical Challenge." In *Human Rights and Development: Towards Mutual Reinforcement,* ed. Philip Alston and Mary Robinson, 352–402. Oxford: Oxford University Press.

McInerney-Lankford, Siobhán. 2009. "Human Rights and Development: A Comment on Challenges and Opportunities from a Legal Perspective." *Journal of Human Rights Practice* 1 (1): 51–82.

Ministry for Foreign Affairs of Finland. 2000. *Democracy and Human Rights: A Pathway to Peace and Development*

———. 2004. *Development Policy: Government Resolution 2004.* February 5,

Ministry for Foreign Affairs of Sweden. 2010a. *Change for Freedom: Policy for Democratic Development and Human Rights in Swedish Development Cooperation, 2010–2014.* Stockholm.

Ministry of Foreign Affairs of Denmark. 2010b. *Freedom from Poverty, Freedom to Change.* July, Copenhagen.

———. 2012. *The Right to a Better Life. Strategy for Denmark's Development Cooperation.* June, Copenhagen.

Narayan, Deepa, with Raj Patel, Kai Schafft, Anne Rademacher, and Sarah Koch-Schultz. 2000a. *Voices of the Poor: Can Anyone Hear Us?* Published for the World Bank. New York: Oxford University Press.

Narayan, Deepa, Robert Chambers, Meera Shah, and Patti Petesch. 2000b. *Voices of the Poor: Crying Out for Change.* Published for the World Bank. New York: Oxford University Press.

Narayan, Deepa, and Patti Petesch. 2002. *Voices of the Poor: From Many Lands.* Published for the World Bank. New York: Oxford University Press.

Netherlands Ministry of Foreign Affairs. 2001. "2001 Memorandum on Human Rights Policy." Human Rights and Peace Building Department, The Hague.

———. 2007. *Human Dignity for All: A Human Rights Strategy for Foreign Policy.* The Hague: Netherlands Ministry of Foreign Affairs.

———. 2011. "Responsible for Freedom: Human Rights in Foreign Policy." Memorandum, April., Netherlands Ministry of Foreign Affairs, The Hague.

NZAID (New Zealand Agency for International Development). 2002. *Human Rights Policy Statement.* Wellington: NZAID.

OECD (Organisation for Economic Cooperation and Development). 1997a. "Final Report of the Ad Hoc Working Group on Participatory Development and Good Governance." OECD, Paris.

———. 2001. *Poverty Reduction.* DAC Guidelines, OECD, Paris.

———. 2007a. "DAC Action-Oriented Policy Paper on Human Rights and Development." February, OECD, Paris.

OHCHR (Office of the UN High Commissioner for Human Rights). 2009. *High Commissioner's Strategic Management Plan, 2010-2011.* Geneva: OHCHR.

SDC (Swiss Agency for Development and Cooperation). 1997. "Promoting Human Rights in Development Cooperation—Guidelines." Bern: SDC.

———. 2006a. *SDC's Human Rights Policy: Towards a Life in Dignity. Realising Rights for Poor People.* Bern: SDC.

Sen, Amartya. 1999. *Development as Freedom.* Oxford: Oxford University Press.

Sida (Swedish International Development Cooperation Agency). 1997. "Justice and Peace: Sida's Programme for Peace, Democracy and Human Rights." Sida, Stockholm.

UN (United Nations). 1993. "Vienna Declaration and Program of Action." Adopted by the World Conference on Human Rights, June 25, Vienna.

———. 2000. "United Nations Millennium Declaration," September 8, A/RES/55/2, UN, New York.

———. 2003a. "The Human Rights–Based Approach to Development Cooperation. Towards a Common Understanding among UN Agencies." Statement agreed at the Interagency Workshop on a Human Rights–Based Approach, May 3–5, Stamford, CT.

———. 2005a. "2005 World Summit Outcome." Resolution adopted by the UN General Assembly, A/RES/60/1, New York.

———. 2010d. "Keeping the Promise: United to Achieve the Millennium Development Goals." A/RES/65/L.1, October 19, UN, New York.

———. 2011a. "The 25th Anniversary of the Declaration on the Right to Development." Joint Statement of Chairpersons of the UN Treaty Bodies," July 1, UN, Geneva.

———. 2011b. "Joint Statement on the Occasion of the 25th Anniversary of the United Nations Declaration on the Right to Development," September 14, Geneva.

———. 2012. *The Future We Want.* UN Conference on Sustainable Development ("Rio + 20") Outcome Document, A/RES/66/288, September 11, New York.

UNDG-HRM (United Nations Development Group Human Rights Mainstreaming Mechanism). 2011. "Mapping of UN Agency Human Rights Mainstreaming Policies and Tools." April 18, UNDG, New York.

UNDP (United Nations Development Programme). 2000. *Human Development Report 2000: Human Rights and Human Development.* New York: UNDP.

———. 1998a. "Integrating Human Rights with Sustainable Human Development." UNDP Policy Document, UNDP, New York.

————. 2003a. "Poverty Reduction and Human Rights." Practice Note, New York.

————. 2004a. "Access to Justice." Practice Note, New York.

————. 2005. "Human Rights in UNDP." Practice Note, New York.

UNESCO (United Nations Educational, Scientific, and Cultural Organization). 2003. *Strategy on Human Rights*. Paris: UNESCO.

————. 2008b. "Undertaking a Human Rights–Based Approach: Lessons for Policy, Planning and Programming—Documenting Lessons Learned for the Human Rights–Based Approach to Programming: An Asia-Pacific Perspective—Implications for Policy, Planning and Programming." UNESCO, Bangkok.

UNFPA (United Nations Population Fund). 2004a. "Policy Note on Implementing a Human Rights–Based Approach to Programming in UNFPA." UNFPA, New York.

————. 2010. "Integrating Gender, Human Rights and Culture in UNFPA Programmes." Policy Guidance Note, UNFPA, New York.

UNHCR (UN High Commissioner for Refugees). 1997. "UNHCR and Human Rights." August 6, Geneva.

UNICEF (UN Children's Fund). 1998. "A Human Rights Approach to UNICEF Programming for Children and Women: What It Is, and Some Changes It Will Bring." Executive Directive, CF/EXD/1998-04, April 21, UNICEF, New York.

————. 2001. "Medium-Term Strategic Plan, 2002–2005." UNICEF, New York.

————. 2010a. "Narrowing the Gaps to Meet the Goals." September 7, New York.

————. 2010b. "The Approach of UNICEF to Capacity Development." E/ICEF/2010/CRP.20, August 3, New York.

UNIFEM (United Nations Development Fund for Women). 2004a. "Multi-Year Funding Framework, 2004-2007." UN, New York.

WFP (World Food Program). 2010. *Revolution: From Food Aid to Food Assistance, Innovations to Overcoming Hunger*. Ed. Steven Were Omamo, Ugo Gentilini, and Susanna Sanström. Rome: WFP

World Bank. 2005a. "Empowering People by Transforming Institutions: Social Development in World Bank Operations." January 12, World Bank, Washington, DC.

————. 2005c. *Equity and Development. World Development Report 2006*. Washington, DC: World Bank.

————. 2005d. "Indigenous Peoples." Operational Policy 4.10, July, World Bank, Washington, DC.

———— 2010a. *Demanding Good Governance: Lessons from Social Accountability Initiatives in Africa*, ed. Mary McNeil and Carmen Malena. Washington, DC: World Bank.

————. 2011d. *Courts and the Domestic Practice of Human Rights*, by Daniel M. Brinks and Varun Gauri. Preliminary draft dated April 15, 2011, Washington, DC. Cited with permission of the authors.

————. 2011e. "Redressing Grievances and Complaints Regarding Basic Service Delivery," by Varun Gauri. Policy Research Working Paper 5699, June, World Bank, Washington, DC.

————. 2011f. *The Costs of Complying with Human Rights Treaties: The Convention on the Rights of the Child and Basic Immunization,* by Varun Gauri. Washington, DC: World Bank.

————. 2011k. "The Global HIV Epidemics among Men Who Have Sex with Men." World Bank, Washington, DC.

————. 2012a. "Working for a World Free of AIDS." World Bank, Washington, DC.

————. 2012b. "Human Rights–Based Approaches to Development: Concepts, Evidence and Policy." January, World Bank, Washington, DC.

World Bank and WHO. 2011. *World Report on Disability*. Washington, DC: World Bank and WHO.

2

Donor Approaches to Development Programming

Agencies employ a range of approaches to incorporate human rights into their development work. Some approaches are driven by the donor's human rights policies, whereas others are constrained by the parameters of agency mandates, capacity, or comparative advantage in the field. At times, agencies adopt different approaches in different areas or use multiple approaches simultaneously; these delineations can also be blurred by overlapping nomenclatures. Nevertheless, five basic approaches to human rights in development programming can be identified: a human rights–based approach, or HRBA; human rights mainstreaming; dialogues and conditionality; projects and global initiatives; and implicit human rights work (table 2.1).

HRBAs indicate a stronger commitment to systematically taking human rights into account. Ultimately, this approach calls for a transformation of institutional practices. Projects, mainstreaming, and dialogue/conditionality are part of the implementation menu, but the overall rationale is usually different. In the UN definition, human rights are explicitly part of the goal of development assistance, leading to a different approach to the provision of aid. As one examination of human rights and development notes:

Table 2.1 Donor Approaches to Integrating Human Rights and Indicative Activities

Human rights–based approaches	Human rights mainstreaming	Human rights dialogue	Human rights projects	Implicit human rights work
Human rights considered constitutive of the goal of development, leading to a new approach to aid and requiring institutional change.	Efforts to ensure that human rights are integrated into all sectors of existing aid interventions (e.g., water, education). This may include "do no harm" aspects.	Foreign policy and aid dialogues include human rights issues, sometimes linked to conditionality. Aid modalities and volumes may be affected in cases of significant human rights violations.	Projects or programs directly targeted at the realization of specific rights (e.g., freedom of expression), specific groups (e.g., children), or in support of human rights organizations (e.g., in civil society).	Agencies may not explicitly work on human rights issues and prefer to use other descriptors ("protection," "empowerment," or general "good governance" label). The goal, content, and approach can be related to other explicit forms of human rights integration rather than "repackaging."

At the highest level of integration, agency mandates are redefined in human rights terms, seeking to create a more structural and holistic approach to development and social change. Here we face a fundamental rethinking of the entire development practice: its ideology, its partners, its aims, its processes, its systems and procedures. (Uvin 2004)

In addition to the UN system, in which nearly all agencies have explicit human rights mainstreaming policies (UNDG-HRM 2011), a significant number of bilateral agencies have adopted HRBAs. Some have not redefined their mandates in human rights terms: they see the human rights policy as one among many contributing to the achievement of poverty reduction and empowerment. The boundary between human rights mainstreaming and HRBAs is not watertight either, as genuine efforts to mainstream across sectors rapidly lead to taking human rights into account more systematically across the organization. The human rights mainstreaming action plan of the New Zealand Aid Program (NZAID), for example, is very close to the UN's definition of a human rights–based approach (chapter 5). However, agencies exist that are committed on paper to an HRBA that have not invested as much in institutional transformation.

Finally, some agencies do not explicitly use a human rights framework at a policy level, but aspects of their policies or programming are consistent with what an HRBA would call for, such as a focus on empowerment and inclusion; otherwise, there may be strong congruencies at a sector level, for example, with civilian protection or gender. It should be noted in this connection that distinguishing implicit human rights work from good development practice may not be that easy to do.

Human Rights–Based Approaches

On the spectrum of incorporating human rights in development, HRBAs are the strongest articulation of donor and partner commitment. As a conceptual framework, an HRBA explicitly positions human rights as a primary goal of development cooperation. Attention is placed on the political dimensions of poverty and power dynamics within a society that cause and reinforce exclusion and discrimination, with capacity building presented as a key feature of programming. HRBAs help articulate the role and obligations of the state as duty-bearer and the corresponding entitlements of the people as rights-holders. HRBAs can support governments to become better equipped to identify and meet needs within and across communities. People, including marginalized and vulnerable groups, are given a voice and become empowered to participate in decision making.

A human rights–based approach can be employed at different stages of the development process: planning, implementation, and evaluating results. These steps typically draw on an agency's human rights policy or institutional mandate, which provide guidance throughout the process. box 2.1 highlights the example of Germany's human rights policy.

Whereas many donors now have human rights policies, and the value of a human rights–based approach is increasingly understood, the challenges of implementing and evaluating the results of HRBAs remain. Outcomes of HRBAs can be hard to quantify, as they are focused on long-term, sustainable changes to power dynamics and

Box 2.1 Germany's Human Rights Policy Framework

Germany developed its first Development Policy Action Plan on Human Rights for 2004–07, and it was later updated for 2008–10 (BMZ 2008). The Federal Ministry for Economic Cooperation and Development (BMZ) also produced a guidance paper in 2009 (GTZ 2009a) and fact sheets in 2010 on applying an HRBA to different sectors (BMZ 2010). In May 2011, BMZ launched a new, overarching human rights policy that defines human rights as a guiding principle and a cross-sectoral issue in its development policy. The policy promotes a dual track approach, which combines support for specific human rights projects with mainstreaming an HRBA in all fields of intervention (BMZ 2011a). It is both retrospective, in its discussion of Germany's past experience with a human rights–based approach, and forward looking, in its description of approaches to future development activities. Moreover, the policy gives attention to the linkages between human rights and the Millennium Development Goals. The policy is a binding requirement for agencies implementing official development assistance (ODA), such as the German Development Bank (KfW) and GIZ, which was created by the merger in January 2011 of DED, the German Development Service; GTZ, or German Technical Cooperation; and Capacity Building International–Germany, known as Inwent. Civil society organizations funded by the BMZ can use it as a guide in their business activities. Guidelines to support implementation of the new policy have been produced since mid-2011. They include guidance on how to assess and mitigate risks and possible negative human rights impacts at program formulation and on how to integrate human rights standards (based on the treaties and the General Comments) into sector programming.

The 2011 document is the overarching human rights policy, but human rights have also been mainstreamed in earlier German strategies, for example, the ones on good governance (BMZ 2009a), water (BMZ 2006), and health (BMZ 2009b).

political participation. However, emerging work on human rights indicators has potential relevance for measuring the impacts of HRBAs, and development indicators that account for HRBAs are also being used to demonstrate the effects of such an approach (chapter 4).

Human Rights Mainstreaming

Efforts to mainstream human rights entail incorporating human rights into all projects and programs and screening activities for human rights implications. Mainstreaming efforts may involve "do no harm" policies, in which any adverse human rights impacts are identified and mitigated. NZAID has developed a useful set of screening questions for evaluating the implementation of its human rights mainstreaming policy, which can be considered at all stages of the program cycle and evaluation process. They include:

- Which rights are affected by this strategy or program?
- Is there a risk of acting in any way that is inconsistent with its human rights commitments? A risk of reducing the ability of the partner government to fulfill its human rights obligations? Or a risk of reducing participants' ability to exercise their rights?
- Has the strategy or program been developed and implemented using participatory methodologies?
- Does the strategy or program contain clear accountability mechanisms and measures that reinforce legal accountabilities within both the partner country and New Zealand?
- Is the strategy or program inclusive? Does it discriminate (directly or indirectly) against any group of people, or bar them from benefiting from the program's benefits, or does it support discriminatory laws and regulations?
- Does the monitoring and evaluation framework include the collection of disaggregated data? (NZAID 2009)

Mainstreaming also reflects the principle that responsibility for human rights does not lie with any one specialized office of a development agency, but rather should be incorporated into the work of all staff across all sectors. This type of organizational approach fosters an institutional culture that understands and applies human rights principles to development practice more comprehensively and systematically. In practice, it is not uncommon for human rights responsibilities to be housed within governance units, which may result in greater focus by agencies on civil and political rights interventions.

Country Programs

Another strategic form of support integrates human rights in the design of a country strategy. The United Nations Population Fund (UNFPA) has published a detailed manual on implementing an HRBA into country programming (UNFPA and the Harvard School of Public Health 2010). It explains how to integrate human rights principles into each of the four stages of the country program cycle: (1) situation assessment and analysis; (2) planning and design; (3) implementation; and (4) monitoring and evaluation. Throughout these stages, aid practitioners are encouraged to integrate core human rights principles (universality and inalienability; indivisibility; interdependence and interrelatedness; participation and inclusion; equality and nondiscrimination; and accountability and rule of law) into the agency's policy dialogue and support of programmatic work. Each programming stage should also systematically include a focus on cultural sensitivity (see box 4.11, in chapter 4) and gender equality.

Chapter 7 describes three country programs in detail: UNICEF in Vietnam, the Swedish International Development Cooperation Agency, or Sida, in Kenya (box 2.2), and the U.K. Department for International Development, or DFID, in Peru. Country-level approaches also create opportunities to mainstream human rights into other sectors, for example, encouraging a focus on human rights principles (for example, participation and accountability) in more technical areas (such as roads or water), or supporting the realization of economic and social rights (for example, labor standards or social protection). The relevance of human rights also comes to the fore in the criteria used for selection of partner countries, aid allocations, and modes of delivery, as well as in policy dialogue between donors and developing countries.

In addition to country programming, human rights are frequently mainstreamed across sectors. This allows for general human rights principles, such as participation, nondiscrimination, and empowerment, to be considered alongside more specific human rights obligations that are tailored to the particular thematic area. The foregoing also illustrates the fact that donors may employ different approaches to integrate human rights simultaneously or in an overlapping and interchangeable way.

Children's Rights

A significant number of agencies have invested in children's rights. In addition to UNICEF and NGOs, such as the International Save the Children Alliance, a range of bilateral agencies have developed approaches to children, based on the Convention on the Rights of the Child (CRC). For example, the Canadian International Development Agency's (CIDA)

Box 2.2 Sweden's Kenya Program

In Kenya, the Swedish embassy has worked on human rights and democracy at three levels. First, a range of direct interventions included work in the Governance and Justice Sector program, a government of Kenya–led reform initiative focused on improving access to justice, strengthening the rule of law, capacity building, and fighting corruption. It was the first sectorwide approach to reforms in Kenya, and it recognized the interdependence of 32 different ministries, departments, and agencies that make up the country's governance and justice institutions. Seven thematic groups, including one on democracy, human rights, and rule of law, were organized and became the main entry points for HRBA programming in the governance and justice sector (SADEV 2008).

Second, a Mainstreaming in Action approach (MAINIAC) was set up to integrate human rights and democracy principles into sector programs (such as roads, water, health, justice, and agriculture). The approach reflected the understanding that the nonfulfillment of democracy and human rights was the root cause of poverty in Kenya. MAINIAC aimed to build the capacity of key actors, including embassy staff and Kenyan duty-bearers, so that they could identify and use human rights mainstreaming indicators, implement activities in a manner that promotes mainstreaming, participate in dialogue, and develop an adequate monitoring and evaluation system. Local resource persons and members of government agencies lent their expertise.

Third, following the 2002 elections and the new political environment, the Swedish embassy launched a project to put "equality for growth" on the public agenda, by working with civil society organizations, research bodies, the media, other donors, and decision makers in the executive and parliament. They looked specifically at gender, regional, and income inequalities. The project helped the Ministry for Planning and National Development share its poverty map with line ministries; the ambassador wrote in the press on inequality.

Sida found that it was able to successfully integrate an HRBA into development cooperation with Kenya because the Swedish cooperation strategy with Kenya for 2004–08 and 2009–2013 provided a clear mandate to tackle poverty reduction through work on democratic governance. These efforts were supported by stakeholders in the Kenyan government and civil society, who actively promoted democracy and respect for human rights and who saw the need for a new constitution (promulgated in 2010) that reflected these values (Sida 2012a).

efforts to integrate a human rights–based approach are well illustrated in its work on child protection (chapter 7), and Sida has made significant progress in mainstreaming a child rights perspective (box 2.3).

The reasons for their considerable success are attributable to a number of factors: first, that children's rights are often perceived as less controversial, although some areas, such as child participation or rights within the family can be particularly challenging. Second, the Convention has been nearly universally ratified for many years, creating opportunities for engagement in a wide range of countries, even in some where human rights language

Box 2.3 The Swedish International Development Cooperation Agency Mainstreams Children's Rights

Sida mainstreams child rights in all aid interventions as part of a long-term, sustainable development cooperation strategy, while also engaging in targeted interventions on child rights that have a more immediate impact. These efforts support the 2010 Swedish government policy on human rights and democracy, as well as Sweden's Policy for Global Development, both of which focus in significant part on the rights of the child. The latter policy states, "Children and young people should be regarded as competent and active individuals with civil, political, social, economic and cultural rights in their own right. They should be consulted to a greater extent in connection with both the planning and implementation of measures that concern them" (Government of Sweden 2003a).

In addition, Sida promotes and engages in policy dialogue on the rights of children. This dialogue is sought with multiple objectives in mind: to reduce the number of people who live in poverty; to minimize the risk of exploitation and abuse of children; and to fulfill states' legal obligations to respect the rights of children under national, regional, and international law. As part of a human rights dialogue kit, Sida produced four dialogue briefs on the importance and mechanics of dialogue on children's rights (Sida 2010h), young people's political participation (Sida 2010i), child protection (Sida 2010j), and public financial management for the rights of children and young people (Sida 2012b). One brief also mentions lessons learned from a 2010 dialogue on pregnant schoolgirls and corporal punishment in Tanzania, in which high-level political commitment from key ministers, persistent efforts to engage on the issue, and a strong relationship between development cooperation and political dialogue all contributed toward a constructive conversation (Sida 2010h).

In 2011, Sida and the Norwegian Agency for Development Cooperation (Norad) commissioned an evaluation of child rights work within the two agencies, including an analysis of four field studies in Guatemala, Kenya, Mozambique, and Sudan (Norad and Sida 2011). The evaluation concluded that mainstreaming child rights is feasible and worthwhile but requires greater commitment of resources, a more systematic approach to addressing child rights operationally, and improved reporting on results of mainstreaming work. Sida is working to address these issues by dedicating more human resources, developing methods for monitoring, evaluating, and reporting on results, and having Sida management take ownership over implementation.

is not well accepted. Third, the CRC provides a useful series of entry points for programming, as it covers social and economic rights as well as civil and political rights. Agencies have successfully put into practice the four CRC principles: best interests of the child; nondiscrimination; the right to life, survival, and development; and the right to participation. Finally, children's rights open the way to engage in a wide range of sectors by providing a clear target group. Examples include health (child mortality Millennium Development Goal); education and gender equality (girl child and gender parity Millennium Development Goal); and protection, juvenile justice, and child labor.

Women's Rights and Gender Equality

There is a considerable overlap between initiatives to promote gender equality and those to integrate human rights. Most donor agencies have adopted gender equality policies that call for both gender mainstreaming and interventions directly targeted at women. The approaches share a great deal at a normative and conceptual level: nondiscrimination, including gender equality, is a fundamental human rights principle. The Convention on the Elimination of All Forms of Discrimination against Women (CEDAW) provides a clear framework and monitoring mechanism aimed at eliminating gender-based discrimination, and the 1994 Beijing Declaration is the foundation for a wide range of national initiatives. The *DAC Guidelines for Gender Equality* (OECD 1999) explicitly refer to these frameworks.

Even at a programming level, interventions are often similar, and as a number of illustrations in this book demonstrate, although women's rights are central to the systematic integration of human rights in development assistance at a programming level more traditional development interventions targeting women will often look very similar, as a number of illustrations in this study demonstrate (box 2.4). For example, although the United Nations Development Fund for Women (UNIFEM) formally adopted an HRBA in 2004, it did not initiate a dramatic alteration of programming, as the organization's mandate had always been to advance gender equality and women's empowerment. This remains true of UNIFEM's successor agency, UN Women, created in 2010 (UN 2010b). It serves as a composite entity that consolidates four United Nations entities: the Office of the Special Adviser on Gender Issues and Advancement of Women, the Division for the Advancement of Women, the United Nations Development Fund for Women (UNIFEM), and the International Research and Training Institute for the Advancement of Women (INSTRAW). Although UN Women is currently developing its human rights mainstreaming policy, both its mandate (UN 2010b) and 2011–13 strategic plan (UN Women 2011b) make reference to the new agency's commitment to incorporate women's rights into all aspects of programming.

Box 2.4 Linking Human Rights and Gender

The 2002 review of the implementation of UNICEF's human rights–based approach (Moser and Moser 2003) found that although a number of country offices were trying to mainstream gender, there were few examples of that being done systematically. The majority of interventions responded to the needs of women, for example, in the area of safe motherhood, which is required by women as mothers rather than as rights-holders. The mantra "Children and women" was seen as unhelpful, as it did not necessarily entail programming for women's rights.

U.K. Department for International Development (DFID) programming in Bangladesh has evolved from the thematic objective "Improvements in the position of women in society" to "Girls and women first," as the organizing principle of the country strategy. As such, gender equality is now a strong current in all the country program's priority areas. DFID is fostering inclusion, helping women demand their rights more effectively, and calling upon government to be more responsive and accountable.

In 2009, Ireland launched a horizontal partnership with Liberia and Timor Leste to promote women's rights, peace, and security. Following an innovative trend of triangular cooperation, consistent with the Accra Agenda for Action Principle 19, on encouraging South-South cooperation, cross-sectoral events were held in each country to promote women's leadership and their role in conflict resolution and postconflict community building (Schulz 2010).

In Germany, a 2008 reorganization at BMZ led to the creation of a new unit responsible for human rights, gender equality, children's rights, and indigenous peoples' rights. Although cooperation with the governance unit (where these issues were previously hosted) continued, the creation of an independent unit fostered opportunities for more visibility and more synergy on strategic action for a human rights–based approach.

The European Commission frames gender inequality within the context of the denial of human rights. Its twofold approach includes both gender mainstreaming and specific measures for women. In 2003 an assessment examined how successfully gender had been integrated into its development cooperation (Braithwaite et al. 2003). It had a clear commitment to the rights of women and the girl child, Beijing principles, and specific targets, such as political participation and traditional practices. However, although the European Commission has created synergies between gender and other cross-cutting issues, especially human rights and democracy, specific objectives that link gender equality and human rights and development were yet to be developed. The report identified other challenges, such as a low level of awareness of the gender policy among staff and partners; insufficient resources, capacity, and institutional culture to support mainstreaming; and the absence of clear guidelines on undertaking a coherent approach to gender mainstreaming. Since the evaluation, the commission has implemented a number of measures to correct these weaknesses, in particular through the elaboration of a toolkit on mainstreaming gender equality in EC development cooperation, various guidelines on specific issues, such as sexual-based violence, and training for headquarters and delegation staff. It has also adopted a five-year European Union (EU) Plan of Action on Gender Equality and Women's Empowerment in Development (2010–15) that includes strengthened efforts on mainstreaming as an overarching objective (European Commission 2010a). The DAC Peers

(continued next page)

Box 2.4 (continued)

Review 2012 considered that good progress had been achieved in gender mainstreaming and set it as an example for other cross-cutting issues (OECD-DAC 2012).

The EU Instrument on Democracy and Human Rights (EIDHR; discussed in chapter 5) provides further support to actions on human rights issues covered by EU guidelines, including actions on violence against women and girls and combating all forms of discrimination against them. The EIDHR also mainstreams gender equality into its 2011–13 response strategy and in projects under all of its objectives. For example, its project to strengthen the judiciary in Cambodia aims to address gender issues through improvement of legal and judicial mechanisms and access to justice for Khmer Rouge victims. Likewise, the EIDHR mainstreams gender concerns into its election observation missions by including gender experts on its teams and watching for gender issues in the organization and implementation of elections (European Commission 2011a).

Gender equality activities are also an example of work on human rights in the absence of human rights policies. In 2011, the World Bank produced several key reports on gender equality, including "*Women, Business and the Law 2012: Removing Barriers to Economic Inclusion*" (World Bank and IFC 2011) and the *World Development Report 2012: Gender, Equality, and Development* (World Bank 2011g). At the same time, the Bank launched its "Think Equal" social media campaign, reiterating that "gender equality is a core development objective in its own right." USAID has undertaken a significant amount of work on women in development, including areas of antitrafficking, women's legal rights, trade liberalization, and education. The approach focuses on overcoming obstacles to opportunities rather than explicit human rights programming.

In some agencies greater opportunities exist for collaboration between human rights and gender equality work. For example, the gender experts at Sida were formerly part of the democratic governance division. Following the agency's reorganizations in 2008 and 2010, however, the gender equality experts became part of the same department and more recently, the same unit, as the democracy and human rights experts. A number of studies highlighted the difficulties of putting gender mainstreaming into practice (Sida 2002a; Braithwaite et al. 2003; Watkins 2004). Those lessons are also applicable in the field of human rights, and they underline the need for a substantial time frame to realize results from mainstreaming policies aimed at tackling power inequalities.

Rights of Minorities and Indigenous Peoples

When examining programming that links human rights standards to vulnerable or excluded groups, it is important not to overlook minorities and indigenous peoples. In May 2010, the OHCHR hosted its sixth meeting of the Inter-Agency Group on Minorities to discuss implementation of the 1992 Declaration on the Rights of Persons Belonging to National or Ethnic, Religious and Linguistic Minorities (UN 2010c). At that time, OHCHR highlighted the UN Development Program's (UNDP) recent report on the rights of minorities in development programming, which included a number of tools for program analysis, data collection, and evaluation (UNDP 2010a). An earlier review concluded that more progress has been achieved for indigenous peoples' rights than for those of other ethnic, religious, and linguistic minorities (box 2.5 and chapter 8). The politically sensitive nature of minorities' rights in some regions contrasts with the more successful advocacy for indigenous peoples in many parts of the world.

Box 2.5 Rights of Minorities and Indigenous Peoples

When Minority Rights Group International reviewed donor agency support to minorities (MRG 2004), it concluded that some agencies had made important progress toward considering indigenous peoples in policy and programming. However, much less work had been done on other ethnic, religious, and linguistic minorities, and the group called on donors to step up their capacity building and programming efforts. The report pointed to some solid examples: the Inter-American Development Bank's Action Plan for Combating Social Exclusion Due to Race or Ethnic Background (IADB 2002), Sida's good coverage of minorities in its Perspectives on Poverty (Sida 2002a), SDC's training on the inclusion of minorities in development cooperation through an HRBA and backstopping mandate on minority rights, and the UNDP's intention to elaborate and adopt a policy note on minorities.

In 2005, the World Bank issued an updated policy on indigenous peoples (World Bank 2005d). The policy requires the design of Bank-financed projects to avoid adverse impacts and provide culturally appropriate benefits. Design requires screening, social assessment by the borrower, consultation with affected communities, preparation of a plan or planning framework, and disclosure. It aims to ensure that financing is only provided where free, prior, and informed consultation results in broad community support, including broad support by the affected indigenous peoples for physical relocation in incidences where that is unavoidable. The Bank also established a Global Fund for Indigenous Peoples, which provides direct grants, as well as support to the UN Permanent Forum on Indigenous Issues.

Health

Human rights principles have relevance for the health sector in several ways. A significant number of health or HIV/AIDS policies make reference to human rights (e.g., discrimination of persons living with HIV/AIDS), although they do not always provide operational guidance to address those issues (for example, how to reconcile public health and human rights objectives in practice). Some agencies are developing innovative programs and tools that illustrate how a human rights–based approach to health can be implemented. For example, successful approaches to reproductive health and maternal mortality require that interventions examine the barriers women face in accessing services, in particular those related to gender discrimination, as well as sensitivity to cultural and religious factors (box 2.6). Germany has developed comprehensive guidance on how to implement human rights in the different areas of health programming and how to make health sector interventions inclusive for persons with disabilities. Likewise, the human rights focus of German support for health has led to more attention to Lesbian Gay Bisexual Transgender (LGBT) persons' access to health services. UNAIDS has developed a "people with stigma and discrimination index" to measure the situation of rights for people living with HIV (UNDG-HRM 2011).

In 2008, the DAC Human Rights Task Team undertook research on the links among human rights, aid effectiveness, and experiences in the health sector (OECD 2008a). The study concluded that applying human rights principles to the health sector supports the aid effectiveness principles contained in the Paris Declaration. For example, democratic ownership of the health sector was fostered by encouraging women and excluded groups to participate in discussions about health care policy and service provision. The report further explains how the human rights framework promotes the importance of accountability between a government and its citizens, as well as between a donor and country partners, through the use of administrative, judicial, and quasi-judicial processes at many levels. Through the use of human rights indicators and benchmarks, as well as disaggregated data, stakeholders can manage for results and better track how health policies affect different groups. Moreover, the human rights framework supports alignment and harmonization efforts by providing shared standards and norms on which projects can be organized.

Box 2.6 Gender and Health Outcomes

The maternal mortality Millennium Development Goal (MDG 5) is off-track. By moving to a human rights–based approach, UNICEF in Peru was better able to understand the gender, economic, and geographic barriers to poor indigenous women's using health care centers. Starting from the point of view of the women, UNICEF learned how to work with a range of government and nongovernment contacts to provide culturally appropriate health services and educate communities about safe motherhood practices.

Similarly, DFID has developed a how-to note to help staff program in a different way to address maternal mortality. DFID believes that approaches based on public health and health systems can be complemented by laws and policies that take women's rights into account, as well as by efforts that address inequalities in access to services and improve the quality of care, so that services are tailored to women's needs. DFID hopes to increase women's knowledge of their rights to health care, for example, through social mobilization or community-managed support systems (chapter 5).

At present the World Health Organization (WHO) is undergoing a reform process through which it is witnessing a renewed commitment to human rights. A recent report on the reforms, submitted to the UN by the WHO director-general noted, "The values of WHO continue to be grounded in a fundamental concern for equity and human rights; gender equality and the greater empowerment of women; and based on the principles of collective responsibility, shared vulnerabilities, sustained solidarity, and health as a global public good" (WHO 2011b). Although the WHO does not have an official human rights policy, a human rights team with mainstreaming responsibility within the agency is tasked with developing tools and providing examples of good practice. It has, for example, produced a guide to health and human rights and Poverty Reduction Strategy Papers, and it is working with the UN special rapporteur on the right to health. In 2011, WHO copublished a tool with OHCHR and Sida to support countries as they design and implement health sector strategies to ensure compliance with their legal commitments (WHO 2011a). WHO's *Medium-Term Strategic Plan for 2008–13* details its commitment to addressing the "underlying social and economic determinants of health through policies and programs that enhance health equity and integrate pro-poor, gender responsive, and human rights–based approaches." The plan states that the Secretariat will develop partnerships to advance health as a human right and the use of human rights as a tool to promote health and reduce inequities (WHO 2008).

By contrast, in 2004 the United Nations Population Fund (UNFPA) adopted a policy note on HRBA (complemented by an information note). UNFPA also issued a 2009 training manual, "Integrating Human Rights, Culture and Gender in Programming" (UNFPA 2009), and copublished with Harvard an implementation manual and training materials on incorporating a human rights–based approach to programming (UNFPA and Harvard School of Public Health 2010). With a mandate for reproductive rights and health, UNFPA is working within a particularly controversial area. Although cultural claims clearly cannot be used to justify the violation of human rights, UNFPA is committed to finding culturally sensitive ways to promote human rights. Innovative work is under way within its country programs to build partnerships with communities and faith-based organizations (chapter 5).

New partnerships are emerging as well. OHCHR has collaborated with UNAIDS and other partners on human rights–based advocacy on HIV and is pursuing partnerships with UNDP's Global Commission on HIV and the Law, as well as with the Global Fund to Fight AIDs, Tuberculosis, and Malaria, to maximize the impact of its efforts. The Global Fund itself provides funding for human rights programming and encourages programs that strengthen civil society (Global Fund 2011). Likewise, OHCHR has supported activities to strengthen the capacity of 35 national human rights institutions to integrate discrimination against people living with HIV into their work (OHCHR 2011).

Human rights budgeting is also a useful tool for analyzing health budgets. In 2005, the Central American Institute of Fiscal Studies (ICEFI) analyzed the budgets of every Central American country to determine whether it protects citizens' economic, social, cultural, political, and legal rights, particularly in light of the country's national and international commitments (such as the Millennium Development Goals, or MDGs). On the ground in Mexico, the NGO Fundar used a human rights framework to identify inequalities in the government's health budget, including lower per capita health spending in the poorer states of south and southeast Mexico. The results of that analysis enabled Fundar to advocate successfully for the inclusion of basic obstetric care in the government's poverty-focused popular insurance (OECD 2008b).

Education

Donor policies often refer to the right to education, and the range of experiences in adopting a human rights–based approach to education is increasing. In addition to putting into practice human rights principles such as participation, nondiscrimination, and accountability, an HRBA can encompass not only the right *to* education (access), but also rights *in* and *through* education, such as quality and relevance (SDC 2006b). Such a human rights–based approach would direct attention to the overall education framework (curricula, governance structure, distribution of resources in the education system), as well as to the social outcomes of education (box 2.7). Specifically, a human rights–based approach to education that emphasizes quality can promote social cohesion, as it includes a focus on respect for families, the values of local communities, and cultural diversity. It also builds respect for peace, supports empowerment of children and

Box 2.7 Right-to-Education Initiatives

Sida pioneered a human rights–based approach to education with its 2001 policy, "Education for All: A Human Right and Basic Need" (Sida 2001b) and its 2005 "Position Paper on Education, Democracy and Human Rights" (Sida 2005b). The concept of *rights to, in, and through education* has guided Sida's support to education. Since Sida began this work over a decade ago, the agency has observed significant changes in the landscape of rights. For example, education has been made mandatory for many boys and girls and is often free of charge at the primary level. In many countries corporal punishment in schools has been made illegal. In Tanzania, the law now ensures that pregnant schoolgirls can resume their education, and in Cambodia, with Sida's support, the government has decided to mainstream UNICEF's Child Friendly Schools initiative throughout the country.

In Pakistan, UNICEF and SDC have collaborated in a project to enhance skills for girls. The project promoted leadership and negotiation skills and succeeded in helping girls obtain their rights without inducing a negative reaction from their family and community. In Peru, UNICEF undertook a rights-based analysis to identify where children's rights were most at-risk: the Andean and Amazon regions. The Opening Doors to Education for Rural Girls program points to the need to identify and overcome cultural, economic, health-related, and in-school factors that have resulted in girls' exclusion from primary education. In Burkina Faso, a range of strategies improved access to and quality of education (e.g., communication for behavior change, a multi-sector approach, expanded partnerships, capacity building). The project also put forth complementary strategies, such as food aid and microcredit for families sending girls to school, and improvements in safety and privacy for girls. In Chile, a rights analysis showed that poor urban and rural adolescents were deprived of their right to education through low completion rates. By mobilizing duty-bearers (parents, teachers, faith-based groups), UNICEF helped draw up a new law giving the state responsibility for providing 12 years of free education for all.

SDC has also recognized the importance of education for adults and the severe shortage of access to adult education, based in part on the lack of skilled adult educators in places such as Burkina Faso, Benin, the Democratic Republic of Congo, Mali, Niger, Togo, and Haiti. As a result, SDC supported the launch of a course of study at Ouagadougou University for adult education specialists. Participants work in a range of professional disciplines such as health, education, literacy, and local development. SDC is working on having the university take over the coursework and incorporating the courses into its standard syllabus to give the project long-term sustainability.

In Vietnam, UNICEF is working with the ministry of education on a pilot program in three provinces to improve access to quality education for poor ethnic communities that do not speak Vietnamese. Children in these test areas attend preschools and primary schools where they can learn in their local language, and teachers are trained in bilingual education techniques. Early results in 2010 were promising, but the bilingual education pilots will continue to be monitored until 2015 (UNICEF 2011a).

In Burundi, a multisector approach to promoting the right to education for children living and working on the street was adopted, enabling more than 2,000 such children to attend primary schools as of 2007. The program involved a collaborative effort between government ministries, UN agencies, NGOs, and private companies to provide long-term pedagogical support and assistance for families (UNICEF and UNESCO 2007).

stakeholders to claim their rights, and develops the capacities of governments to fulfill their obligations (UNICEF and UNESCO 2007).

To better ensure children's right to education, increased attention has been placed on the creation of "child-friendly" schools that are accessible, welcoming, high-quality, gender-sensitive, and safe. Approaches that promote child-friendly schools require consideration of such factors as the location of schools, travel to and from school, and ensuring appropriate facilities for girls. One example was the UNICEF–supported "Building Child Friendly Schools and Communities Initiative," in Bosnia and Herzegovina, in 2008–09, which generated widespread professional assistance and promoted social unity and cultural diversity among 20,000 children. In addition, a child-to-child census was taken in Kenya as part of a child-friendly school approach to identify children who were not in school, to determine why they failed to attend, and to discuss and develop solutions at the community level. In one of the three pilot districts, approximately 7,000 of the 9,000 out-of-school children were brought back, half of them girls. A final example is found in Mozambique, where a UNICEF–supported Child Friendly Schools program is working to improve the quality of education by providing professional support and teacher resources to classroom educators (UNICEF and UNESCO 2007).

At the SDC's capitalization conference with Swiss and partner country staff, a working group on the right to education identified obstacles to adopting a human rights–based approach to education, including the fact that education can be culturally predetermined by communities in a way that perpetuates structural inequities and exclusion. As a result, it may be difficult to challenge power structures and identify those who have an interest in reform to build a more equitable society. Some powerful groups may appropriate the human rights discourse, which can lead to its being discredited (SDC 2006b).

Livelihoods

Integrating human rights in livelihood programs has been more challenging for donors, possibly because the relevance of human rights standards to this work requires more analysis. Some recent normative developments relevant to livelihoods are worthy of note; for example, the General Comment on the right to water issued by the UN Committee on Economic, Social and Cultural Rights in 2002.

The FAO adopted voluntary guidelines on the right to food in 2004, after 20 months of negotiations (FAO 2005).

Although they may share certain features and common goals, a sustainable livelihoods approach (SLA) is distinct from a human rights–based approach. Developed by DFID, the sustainable livelihoods framework is grounded in shifts in development thinking from the 1980s and 1990s that places a greater focus on human well-being and sustainability, rather than economic growth alone. The sustainable livelihoods approach puts people at the center of development and highlights their assets (natural, social, and human—not just financial or physical) rather than their needs. SLA and HRBA tend to be used in different circumstances, and in some instances a sustainable livelihoods approach can be appropriate where a purely human rights–based approach might meet political resistance (Foresti, Ludi, and Griffiths 2007).

There are nevertheless a number of positive examples of employing an HRBA in livelihood programs. UNIFEM adopted an HRBA to women's land rights in Central Asia, based on bridging analysis that links specific human rights commitments with policy-relevant recommendations. International NGOs have documented their experiences, which typically rely on the introduction of human rights principles (such as participation) into programming (box 2.8). DFID has undertaken considerable research comparing HRBAs and sustainable livelihoods. DFID concluded that human rights–based approaches draw attention to power relations and policy processes, encourage participatory planning, and help establish local accountability mechanisms. Inclusion, however, is more difficult to achieve.

Box 2.8 Food and Land Rights Interventions

In Kyrgyz Republic, UNIFEM supports a greater focus on women's rights as part of the land reform process. Achievements have included submitting draft amendments to the existing Land Code and related policies to the relevant government agencies and parliament, strengthening the capacity of local government officials and staff to better protect women's rights to land, and increasing the understanding of the general public (chapter 7).

Humanitarian assistance in Sierra Leone was distributed in collaboration with Village Development Committees, which often resulted in misappropriation of inputs. With DFID support, CARE has led dialogue on the need for community mechanisms to ensure the accountability of committee members and greater inclusion in the distribution of food aid.

Infrastructure

Human rights can make a substantial contribution to infrastructure programs, often through a human rights–based approach. By demanding rigorous political and social analysis, an HRBA can help ensure that interventions do not inadvertently reinforce existing conflicts and power imbalances, as was found in a WaterAid project in Tanzania (chapter 7).

Large infrastructure programs, such as the construction of dams, can also be a direct cause of human rights violations, for example, by resulting in forced displacements without compensation. A number of agencies are trying to introduce "do no harm" policies to prevent or mitigate negative impacts. For example, the World Bank's policy on involuntary resettlement (World Bank 2011l) recognizes the economic, social, and environmental risks and the need for safeguards to address and mitigate them (box 2.9).

Persons with Disabilities

Disability is a development issue because of its "bidirectional link to poverty": it can increase the likelihood of poverty, just as poverty can increase the likelihood of disability. More than one billion people in the world live with a disability (World Bank and WHO 2011), 80 percent of them in developing countries. UNESCO estimates that 98 percent of persons with disabilities in developing countries do not attend school, and access to health care services and public health information for those with disabilities is scarce (UNESCO 2008a). The Convention on

---

Box 2.9 World Bank Involuntary Resettlement Policy

The Bank's Operational Policy 4.12: Involuntary Resettlement is triggered in situations involving involuntary taking of land and involuntary restrictions of access to legally designated parks and protected areas. The policy aims to avoid involuntary resettlement to the extent feasible, or to minimize and mitigate its adverse social and economic impacts. It promotes participation of displaced people in resettlement planning and implementation, and its key economic objective is to assist displaced persons in their efforts to improve, or at least restore, their incomes and standards of living after displacement. The policy prescribes compensation and other resettlement measures to achieve its objectives and requires that borrowers prepare adequate resettlement planning instruments prior to Bank appraisal of proposed projects.

Source: World Bank 2011l. Originally issued in December 2001; updated in 2004, 2007, and 2011.

the Rights of Persons with Disabilities, adopted in December 2006, emphasizes nondiscrimination (e.g., Articles 3, 4(1), and 5) as well as equal access (e.g., Articles 3 and 9) to opportunities for fulfilling one's potential, including through development programs (UN 2006). Persons with disabilities are a key target group under MDG 1 (eradicating hunger and poverty) and for the realization of other development goals as well (UNESCO 2008a) (box 2.10).

Despite the fact that persons with disabilities are not mentioned in the Millennium Declaration or in any of the eight MDG 21 targets or 60 indicators (UN 2011d), UNESCO has concluded that the goals cannot be met without including persons with disabilities. The World Bank and WHO reached the same conclusion in the first-ever "World Report on Disability" (World Bank and WHO 2011), and the World Bank has examined the economic and social costs of neglecting disability in

---

Box 2.10 A Disability-Inclusive Australian Aid Program

AusAID has taken a lead in using human rights principles to affirm the rights of persons with disabilities. Its disability-inclusive development strategy, "Development for All: Towards a Disability-Inclusive Australian Aid Program 2009–2014," explains how disabilities are both a "cause and consequence" of poverty (AusAID 2008). The Convention on the Rights of Persons with Disabilities provides the guiding framework for this disability-inclusive development approach in Australia's aid program. The strategy promotes inclusion and participatory decision making by persons with disabilities. AusAID also created a Disability-Inclusive Development Reference Group in 2009 to help shape the implementation of its strategy. The majority of members of this group have a disability (AusAID 2009). AusAID's leadership and principle of inclusion of people with disability is demonstrated through its work with key regional stakeholders, such as the Pacific Island Forum Secretariat and the Pacific Disability Forum, to achieve goals set out in the Pacific Regional Strategy on Disability (2010–15).

Australia's disability-inclusive development strategy supports a variety of mainstream and disability-specific programs, such as education programs in Indonesia, Papua New Guinea, Samoa, and Laos. These programs contribute to the reduction of various barriers to education for people with disabilities, including physical, policy, or attitudinal barriers. Australia's support of the Pacific Disability Forum and the Disability Rights Fund enables people with disability to advocate within local communities and national governments and at international forums for their rights as citizens. In 2011 Australia provided $2 million to the UN Partnership to Promote the Rights of Persons with Disabilities, to assist states to join the Convention if they have not already done so, and to assist governments and disabled persons organizations to effectively implement the obligations under the Convention.

Source: AusAID.

the Bank's operational work (Posarac 2009). Argentina has developed 29 disability-specific indicators for monitoring progress on the Millennium Development Goals. UNICEF is currently planning a mapping on the integration of human rights into disability laws and principles (UNDG-HRM 2011). In 2011, the UNDP Bratislava Regional Centre for Europe also organized the first Regional Conference on Human Rights and Justice for Persons with Disabilities, in Turkmenistan, to address challenges to mainstreaming disability issues in development, including accessing the national human rights protection system.

The Global Partnership on Disability and Development (GPDD) evolved in 2008 as a global initiative focused on improving international cooperation to integrate disability issues into social and economic development efforts. GPDD includes government ministries, bilateral and multilateral donors, UN agencies, NGOs, and other development organizations, which collaborate on promoting a more inclusive society. Its work includes capacity building, knowledge building and sharing, and creating platforms for stakeholder dialogue. GPDD also seeks out opportunities to work with regional networks focused on social and economic development, such as Mercosur and ASEAN, to raise the issue of mainstreaming disability. One project focused on incorporating disability into Mozambique's Poverty Reduction Strategy Papers, building capacity and networking among stakeholders, and creating monitoring and evaluation mechanisms to measure long-term impact. A separate research study has focused on inclusive disaster preparedness and management by analyzing how disability issues were addressed and incorporated during natural disasters in Indonesia, Bangladesh, and the United States. The GPDD and the World Bank's Disability and Development Team also hosted a two-week-long e-discussion on women with disabilities in development (GPDD and World Bank 2009).

In April 2009, the Secretariat for the Convention on the Rights of Persons with Disabilities of the United Nations Department of Economic and Social Affairs (UNDESA) and the WHO organized the "Expert Group Meeting on Mainstreaming Disability in MDG Polices, Processes and Mechanisms: Development for All" to develop a road map for how disability can be included in the planning, monitoring, and evaluation of all MDG–related plans, programs, and policies in international development. The meeting identified data gaps on disability within the context of MDG evaluation and monitoring but also noted opportunities for mainstreaming disability using the current MDG framework and tools (SCRPD 2009). The next UN high-level meeting on disability and development is planned for September 2013.

The 10-year EU Disability Strategy (2010–20) identifies areas of action to empower people with disabilities, including accessibility, participation, equality, employment, education and training, social protection, health, and external action (European Commission 2010d). At an operational level, a 2004 "Guidance Note on Disability and Development" (European Commission 2004) provides a set of principles to guide EU delegations on how to address disability issues in development cooperation activities, but implementation can vary by location and program. The EU has supported partner countries' shifting from welfare to rights-based policies in places such as Morocco, where the first disability survey was conducted, and Chile, which performed a disability census to inform legislation and policy analysis. As budget support is increasingly used as the modality of EU development cooperation, however, incorporating or mainstreaming the rights of persons with disabilities becomes an integral part of policy dialogue with partner countries (Coleridge et al. 2010).

The Austrian Development Cooperation (ADC) supports a framework program, Light for the World, that provides support for inclusive development at community level in Ethiopia, Burkina Faso, or Mozambique. Instead of simply providing medical treatment and welfare aid, the program aims to ensure that persons with disabilities are integrated as actors at all levels of social activity. In community-based rehabilitation programs, helpers come into the house, plan individual assistance programs, and show relatives how they can help people learn critical skills. The primary aim is to enable people with special needs to take equal and self-determined part in development (ADC 2011).

Human Rights Dialogue and Conditionality

Human rights–based approaches and mainstreaming efforts offer comprehensive ways of connecting human rights and development. Yet, as noted by Uvin (2004),

When people first consider the relation between development and human rights, most spontaneously begin by thinking about conditionality. They argue that donors should threaten to cut off development assistance—and execute that threat—to recipients that consistently violate human rights.

However, the 1997 "Final Report of the Ad Hoc Working Group on Participatory Development and Good Governance" suggested that conditionality be used as a last resort:

> Development co-operation stresses positive measures for the promotion of participatory development and good governance. The withholding of assistance should be reserved for cases where persistent violations of men, women and children's basic rights are not being addressed by the government and no adequate basis of shared values and interests exists to permit a real partnership. (OECD 1997a)

Most bilateral agencies have explicit political conditionality policies which they apply more or less consistently (Piron and Court 2004; Piron and De Renzio 2005). Since the early 1990s, the European Union has introduced human rights clauses into its agreements, and it considers human rights, democracy, and the rule of law as "essential elements" of development cooperation. In 2010, the EU reaffirmed its policy of including human rights clauses in agreements with third countries; as of December 2011, the clause was included in agreements with over 120 countries (European Commission 2011f). If these clauses are not respected, aid can be suspended (box 2.11).

A wide range of dialogue approaches has been used to respond to systematic violations or weak commitment to human rights, at a technical (project) level, in the context of agreeing to overarching country strategies, or as part of diplomatic negotiations. The ways in which the EU dialogues are initiated and conducted are governed by EU guidelines promulgated in 2001 and updated in 2009. Four types of dialogue are identified:

1. Discussions of a general nature based on treaties or agreements dealing with human rights (such as the Cotonou Agreement);
2. Regular, institutionalized dialogues focusing exclusively on human rights between the EU and a third country or regional organization;
3. Ad hoc dialogues extending to Common Foreign and Security Policy (CFSP)–related topics, including human rights; and

Box 2.11 Examples of Human Rights Dialogue and Conditionality

The EU has a range of policies and experiences. For example, the Cotonou Agreement with Africa, Caribbean, and Pacific countries makes explicit reference to human rights and creates a mechanism for structured dialogue and eventual aid suspension if issues are not resolved. The EU undertakes dialogues focusing exclusively on human rights (e.g., with China since 1996 and Iran since 2002), as well as dialogues within the framework of joint commission meetings as part of trade and cooperation agreements. At the end of 2011, the EU had initiated approximately 40 dedicated human rights dialogues and consultations (European Commission 2011f).

Finland's position on conditionality is consistent with that of most other bilaterals. It is committed to long-term cooperation, but serious human rights problems may lead to a reduction or termination of aid. It pays attention to a country's commitment to improving human rights, democracy, equality, and corruption in its overall assessment of its commitment to development. In 2001, Kenya, Zambia, and Nicaragua failed to meet conditions relating to human rights, democracy, and good governance; since then, the situations have improved and cooperation is increasing. In 2004, Finland considered that instability and the poor human rights situation in Nepal meant there were no possibilities for increasing cooperation. German development cooperation policies are similar: Budget aid to Malawi was stalled in 2011 as a reaction to the criminalization of lesbian acts, and similar action was envisioned with respect to a draft law in Uganda.

4. Dialogues in the context of special relations with certain third countries on the basis of converging views with the possibility of cooperation with multilateral human rights bodies. (EU 2009)

Sometimes donors engage in both bilateral and multilateral dialogues on issues of human rights with the same countries simultaneously (for example, bilateral dialogues with China and Iran, as well as through the EU). The suspension of aid has usually been the exception and a measure of last resort. For instance, Spain has generally been opposed to using conditionality (FRIDE 2010). Anecdotal evidence suggests that such cases are usually linked to violations of democratic rights (e.g., coups, fraudulent elections) rather than economic or social rights.

Weaknesses in traditional approaches have been identified: they include ineffectiveness, lack of consistency in application, and ethical dilemmas.

In light of new ways of delivering and managing aid, some donors are revisiting common assumptions about addressing human rights through conditionality. Much can be learned from donor experiences, yet documenting and sharing those experiences in public forums is considered politically sensitive. More encouraging, an evaluation of Sida's engagement in human rights and democratic governance concluded that the agency effectively promoted human rights dialogue among stakeholders in places such as Colombia and Nicaragua (Sida 2008). Sida's focus is more on dialogue than conditionality, evidenced by its human rights dialogue kit (Sida 2010e) and other dialogue briefs on freedom of expression (Sida 2010g), the rights of the child (Sida 2010h), the rights of persons with disabilities (Sida 2010a), and the rights of LGBT persons (Sida 2010k). DFID also reviewed the application of political conditionality to general budget support in Africa. Earlier studies about dialogue and sanctions point to a number of lessons relevant for what is being called a "post-conditionality" approach in the Poverty Reduction Strategy Paper (PRSP) context of "process conditionality" and selectivity (Harrison 2001; Santiso 2003; Uvin 2004; Piron and de Renzio 2005).

DFID's conditionality policy works to strike a balance among accountability, partner country ownership, and predictability of aid flows. Although DFID does not use conditionality to micro-manage government reforms or force partner countries to make changes that they do not want, conditionality is used to support aid effectiveness and accountability (DFID 2009a). The UK policy on conditionality is based on three shared commitments with partner governments: (1) poverty reduction and meeting the MDGs; (2) respecting human rights and other international obligations; and (3) strengthening financial management and accountability and reducing the risk of funds being misused thorough weak administration or corruption (DFID 2011a). There have been suspensions of aid because of a breach of one of these commitments, often financial management.

Although the World Bank's mandate does not permit the institution to condition lending on human rights considerations, the Bank undertook a review and consultations from 2005 to 2007 that resulted in an alignment of its conditionality with five good practice principles: ownership, harmonization, customization, criticality, and transparency and predictability. Among the conditions applied to education funding for Ghana, for example, were completing a school mapping exercise in deprived districts to improve the targeting of budget resources; establishing incentives, such as scholarships, to improve girls' completion of primary school; and reducing teacher vacancies, which resulted in a significant increase in primary school and female student enrollment. The Council of Europe Bank (CEB) appears to stand alone among international financial institutions to the extent that its contracts are conditioned on respect for human rights and may be suspended by the CEB in the face of violations.

Human Rights Projects and Global Initiatives

Human Rights Projects

Traditionally, donors support human rights through projects that aim to build the capacity of human rights organizations, provide human rights training, or support the ratification of treaties and legal reform.

Human rights projects often focus on the promotion of specific rights, empowerment of specific groups (e.g., children, women, ethnic or minority groups, and persons with disabilities), or support to human rights organizations. Support to civil society organizations is one of the most common forms of direct intervention, working through them to build the capacity of rights-holders to claim and enforce their rights and to mobilize for social change. Recipients are usually local or international NGOs that receive resources through bilateral or multilateral human rights funds managed by embassies or donor agencies. Less often, sector programs may have civil society components that address the "demand side" of reform. In addition to targeted human rights funds, donor guidelines can create incentives for civil society organizations to work on human rights issues or adopt HRBAs (e.g., DFID program partnership agreements with UK-based international NGOs).

Human rights projects may stand alone or may be complemented by or related to other human rights–based approaches. Some human rights projects are strongly research based, providing analytical inputs and perspectives on a particular human rights issue. One such example is a Nordic Trust Fund grant that funded research as part the *2012 World Development Report* on gender. That research analyzed how state parties' commitments under the Convention on the Elimination of All Forms of Discrimination Against Women (CEDAW) and other international conventions reduced constraints to women's autonomy and decision-making capacities for income generation and economic development. Additional attention to human rights projects is provided in chapter 8.

Global Initiatives on Human Rights

Donors have promoted the integration of human rights and development well beyond country programs and direct interventions by funding international events, research, and networking at a regional or global level.

Bilateral agencies can count many successes in their funding of multilateral organizations. Examples in the UN system include the Global Human Rights Strengthening Program (box 2.12), the UN Development Group Human Rights Mainstreaming Mechanism (box 2.13),

---

Box 2.12 Bilateral Support for the Global Human Rights Strengthening Program and UNICEF

HURIST, the UNDP-OHCHR Global Human Rights Strengthening Program that operated from 1999 to 2005, received contributions from a wide range of bilateral agencies, demonstrating their commitment to mainstreaming human rights within the UN system: Finland, Norway, Sweden, the Netherlands, Canada, Ireland, Germany, Switzerland, and the United Kingdom. The program had a budget of US $8 million over six years and the objective of strengthening the work of the United Nations Development Program (UNDP) in the field of human rights. It funded UN volunteers working on human rights at the country level, the preparation of national human rights action plans, and country-level programming, as well as policy development, piloting, preparation of tools, and human rights program reviews. An evaluation concluded that HURIST had made significant contributions to creating a UN consensus on human rights–based approaches.

The human rights–based development work undertaken by UNDP is now guided by the 2008–11 Global Human Rights Strengthening Program (GHRSP). At the request of countries, UNDP provides assistance to strengthen the capacity of national systems and institutions that promote and protect human rights, encouraging the use of a human rights–based approach to development, and engages in dialogue with UN human rights offices and experts.

The Strengthening UNICEF Human Rights–Based Programming project was launched in 2000 and led UNICEF to revise programming guidelines, methodologies, and training materials; it provided support to regional and country-level staff and facilitated learning across the agency. By 2005, UNICEF had completed and analyzed 35 case studies, held two global consultations, completed a number of annual reviews of country programs, and conducted the Mid-Term Review of the Medium-Term Strategic Plan 2002–2005. These successes were thanks to DFID support, as well as to UNICEF regular resources, as the project was fully integrated in UNICEF's work at headquarters, regional, and country levels.

and funding for the Princeton (2001) and Stamford (2003) consultations, which elaborated the UN interagency common understanding of a human rights–based approach to development cooperation (see appendix 1). Bilaterals have also been working with development banks, which tend not to have explicit human rights policies. For example, the World Bank's strategy document on social development (World Bank 2005a) mentions support from Finland, Norway, and the Netherlands in building donor and client country capacity for social development, including greater cooperation within the Bank and with the UN; the Japan Social Development Fund, which has supported social accountability initiatives; and cooperation with GTZ and DFID on poverty and social impact analysis.

World Bank Nordic Trust Fund

Established in 2008 with a five-year, $17 million trust fund financed by the governments of Denmark, Iceland, Norway, Finland, and Sweden, the Nordic Trust Fund (NTF)'s objective is to help the World Bank

Box 2.13   United Nations Development Group Human Rights Mainstreaming Mechanism (UNDG-HRM)

The UNDG-HRM was established in 2009 at the request of the UN secretary-general to institutionalize the mainstreaming of human rights in the UN's development work. The mechanism works to strengthen coordinated UN responses to requests from member states for support in their efforts to fulfill international human rights commitments. The objectives of the UNDG-HRM are to strengthen systemwide policy coherence and collaboration and to support Regional UNDG Teams, UN country teams, and their national partners in mainstreaming human rights. These objectives are fulfilled through the development of guidance and tools on a human rights–based approach, documenting good practices, evaluating the impacts of the approach, delivering trainings, and expanding the UN HRBA practitioners' portal (http://hrbaportal.org/). UNDG-HRM also conducted a survey of UN country team needs in 2011 to better understand how it can best support the teams in the application of HRBA at the country level (UNDG-HRM 2011).

The UNDG-HRM is made up of 19 UN agencies, funds and programs. It is chaired by OHCHR, with a rotating vice chair, reporting to the full UNDG. Members and partners of the UNDG-HRM are DESA, FAO, ILO, OHCHR, UNAIDS, UNDP, UNEP, UNESCO, UNFPA, UN-HABITAT, UNHCR, UNICEF, UNIDO, UNSSC, UNODC, UNOPS, UN Women, WFP, and WHO (UNDG 2011c).

Source: UNDG; see http://mptf.undp.org/factsheet/fund/HRM00.

develop an informed view on human rights. This internal knowledge and learning program supports activities that generate knowledge about how human rights relate to the Bank's analytical activities and operations by identifying and tapping the Bank's comparative advantages and developing ways to systematize and improve existing involvement in the overall context of the Bank's core mission of promoting economic grown and poverty reduction (box 2.14).

Human Rights Research

Discrete human rights projects also include research into a wide range of thematic issues linking human rights and development; surveys of needs and capacity gaps within countries, institutions, and sectors;

Box 2.14 Nordic Trust Fund Grant Program

NTF activities primarily follow three tracks: research, analytical work, and training; fostering and building partnerships; and grants for pilot projects to help World Bank staff understand how human rights relate to the Bank's core work of economic growth and poverty reduction (NTF 2010). The NTF grant program provides support to task teams across the World Bank to integrate human rights perspectives into their projects, strategies, tools, or research. When evaluating grant proposals, the NTF consider two criteria: (1) whether the project has an explicit link to human rights and (2) whether the activities have "knowledge and learning potential." The Secretariat also confirms that the project fits with client country priorities and, where it might involve in-country activity, ensures that it has the express interest of the government. Between March 2010 and January 2011 financial support totaling $11 million (approximately US $400,000 each) was allocated to 27 pilot activities. Among its cross-cutting thematic areas are economic, social, and cultural rights; civil and political rights; discrimination and vulnerable groups; and capacity and institutions.

The NTF grant program includes work in several thematic areas: economic, social, and cultural rights; civil and political rights; capacity and institutions; and discrimination and vulnerable groups. These include pilot activities in analytic and operational work to generate and disseminate knowledge about how human rights relate to the Bank unit or team's work. One such project aims to better incorporate the right to health for Roma into health projects and health sector work in the Europe and Central Asia region. Another NTF pilot activity explores how the right to health can be implemented in Colombia by analyzing the fiscal and financial sustainability of eliminating disparities in services and insurance coverage, surveying the capacities of health facilities, designing a social communication and advocacy strategy, and monitoring the implementation of health rights, including doing so through constitutional litigation (chapter 7) (NTF 2011a).

Source: NTF 2010; 2011a.

analyses of indicators for measuring development outcomes using a human rights–based approach; and training materials on applying HRBAs. For example, with the support of a Nordic Trust Fund grant, the World Bank and International Finance Corporation (IFC) recently published, *Women, Business and the Law 2012: Removing Barriers to Economic Inclusion,* which examines how regulations and institutions in 141 economies distinguish between men and women in ways that affect one's capacity to work or to start or run a business (World Bank and IFC 2011). In collaboration with the Danish government, the NTF also supported publication of a 2010 World Bank study, *Human Rights Indicators in Development: An Introduction,* which considers the significance of human rights indicators for development processes and outcomes as they connect standards and obligations with empirical data (World Bank 2010b). In 2011, the NTF supported the World Bank's international law study, *Human Rights and Climate Change: A Review of the International Legal Dimensions,* comprising a literature review of human rights and environmental issues and a presentation of points of convergence and disconnect along with areas for future research (World Bank 2011a).

As part of its knowledge and learning mandate, the Nordic Trust Fund also engages in partnership building and takes the lead on research and training projects. To foster partnerships with academia, NGOs, the UN, EU, and OECD, it facilitates and participates in numerous learning events annually, such as peer-to-peer exchanges with the DAC Human Rights Task Team (HRTT) or UN and training courses on human rights and development for fund grantees (NTF 2010).

Institutionally, the UN System Staff College (UNSSC) is the primary provider of interagency training and learning within the UN system. It conducts a variety of training and learning activities in Turin, as well as at regional and country levels. Its work is organized around five areas, including human rights and development. The UNSSC, in close collaboration with OHCHR and other UN agencies, offers its services to the leadership of UN country teams and program staff alike, with a view to build capacity to integrate human rights into all policy and programming processes. In 2011 the college led the update of the HRBA Common Learning Package, resulting in the inclusion of results-based management elements and programmatically relevant information on the Universal Periodic Review process (chapter 6). UNSSC has conducted train-the-trainer workshops on the Common Learning Package and is developing a number of e-learning tools; upcoming research and training on human rights and HRBAs will focus on leadership development and evidence-based learning.

One of the unique features—actively supported by OHCHR, as co-chair of the UNDG-HRM—of UN engagement in mainstreaming human rights has been the process toward ensuring collective ownership of policy guidance and implementation support, particularly within the spirit of "One UN." HRBA learning tools for UN country teams are developed by the system for the system, and training teams are put together to reflect a variety of UN agencies. This internally owned process and approach has proved invaluable in deepening the system's collective engagement on the subject matter.

The UNDP Oslo Governance Centre conducts democratic governance assessments at the country level and of UNDP projects, including those of the UNDP Democratic Governance Thematic Trust Fund. In addition, it manages the Governance Assessment Portal, an online resource center for governance indicators, assessment frameworks, and country studies.

Over the past year, several multilateral donors and development banks have surveyed their members and peer institutions to better understand how human rights issues are being addressed. For instance, the UNDG-HRM engaged in a mapping of UN agency human rights mainstreaming policies and tools (UNDG-HRM 2011). In addition, EIB conducted a survey on human rights and the activities of the international financial institutions (EIB 2011). Finally, the DAC HRTT carried out a survey of how Human Rights Task Team members are implementing principles from the Paris Declaration on Aid Effectiveness and the Accra Agenda for Action (OECD-DAC 2011a).

Implicit Human Rights Work

Governance Interventions

Another lens through which to examine donor experiences is to look thematically at the content and objectives of donor interventions. As governance is seen as the sector most closely associated with human rights, most aid agencies locate the issue in the governance area. A wide range of civil and political rights projects have been undertaken, but little work has been done on integrating human rights into other governance areas, such as public sector reform or financial management.

Civil and Political Rights. Most direct human rights interventions have addressed civil and political rights issues, often under a governance heading, linked to democracy and the rule of law. Uvin (2004) estimated that this type of aid accounts for about 10 percent of aid budgets. Topics may include specific rights, such as freedom of expression (media projects, for example) or due process (rule of law programs). Options include investing in organizations (e.g., national human rights institutions), processes and procedures (e.g., democratization, including elections, parties, civic education), and structures (e.g., capacity building of state or civil society). Some examples include the European Instrument for Democracy and Human Rights and the EU Governance Initiative (chapter 5). In addition, CIDA has supported the creation of more than 22,000 Community Development Councils in Afghanistan, to strengthen community-level governance, and unprecedented involvement of women in rural community decision making (CIDA 2011a). However, as Carothers (1999; 2006) noted, there is little systematic knowledge in the area of democracy support and rule of law initiatives.

National human rights institutions (NHRIs) have a distinct role in supporting states in fulfilling their legal international obligations. These institutions can advocate for the removal of treaty reservations, encourage the government to pass legislation to implement international law where necessary, and argue that where case law is ambiguous, laws should be interpreted consistently with the state's international legal obligations. The prevalence of NHRIs is growing; they have more than tripled in number since 1993, and as of the end of 2010, there were 66 Paris Principle–compliant institutions in the world (UNDP and OHCHR 2010).

Access to Justice

The trend across a number of agencies to embrace an access to justice approach can be associated with a more strategic use of human rights. Traditional rule of law interventions have focused on building institutions by working with courts, prisons, ministries, and lawyers. These interventions can contribute to the achievement of specific rights and standards. Well-known examples include the provision of legal representation to defendants or reducing court delays and time on remand. Another example is USAID's provision of police training and organizational development to police forces in more than 20 countries (USAID 2011b). Such interventions also institutionalize the human rights principles of accountability and the rule of law. By including equal access to justice ("EA2J") in their policy documents and programs, donors have started to transform the way in which they analyze situations, set objectives, and provide assistance (Sida 2011c; see box 2.15 and chapter 8). This approach uses participatory research to identify poor people's priorities and tests new ways to overcome barriers. Instead of limiting interventions to enhancing the effectiveness of institutions, a people-centered perspective starts from the experiences of poor people themselves (for example, through perception surveys).

Access to justice links demand and supply activities. In particular, it focuses on the ability of poor and marginalized people to claim rights through the courts and the ability of the courts to deliver appropriate services to meet users' needs. It involves efforts to demystify the

---

Box 2.15 The Swiss Agency for Development and Cooperation and Equal Access to Justice in Peru

The Swiss Agency for Development and Cooperation (SDC) has adopted a more systematic human rights–based approach to justice reform. Inadequacies in the judicial system of Peru were hindering the socioeconomic development of the country and further marginalizing the poor and other vulnerable groups. Although the Constitution of Peru formally recognizes the role of traditional rural communities in the justice system, no implementing regulations existed to guide the coordination of traditional and formal jurisdictions, particularly with respect to the local justices of the peace, who often mediated conflicts. SDC has supported a group of NGOs working to create a basic local justice model, by promoting access to justice for rural people, strengthening the traditional justice system, and linking it to the formal justice system and the ongoing efforts to reform it. Working directly with the judicial authorities, the NGOs analyze the strengths and weaknesses of local judicial services and foster dialogue and cooperation between various stakeholders, with a view to improving access and promoting respect for human rights in informal and community-based judicial procedures.

Source: SDC 2008a.

law through rights awareness. It helps meet the needs of women, juveniles, isolated populations, minorities, or indigenous peoples, by looking at location, language used, simplification of procedures, cultural compatibility, or the best interests of the child. Explicit human rights or constitutional standards are used to set goals and benchmarks, such as diversion measures for juvenile offenders under the Convention on the Rights of the Child, or civil liberties contained in the International Covenant on Civil and Political Rights.

The shift does not necessarily require explicit reference to human rights mainstreaming or an HRBA. Although UNDP and Sida describe its policy in terms of implementing a human rights–based approach, DFID does not. For USAID and the World Bank, access to justice is one possible area of intervention. Either way, it is a resource-intensive approach. Lessons from UNDP Asia-Pacific point to substantial commitments of staff time and the need to identify new partners.

USAID rule of law projects aim to improve the independence and performance of the judiciary, increase effective criminal prosecution, and reduce delays, thereby contributing to civil rights objectives. The agency also has a number of access to justice programs, including the recent awarding of its first round of grants to law schools and civil society organizations in Iraq to provide legal aid to underserved and disadvantaged populations, such as women, widows, divorcees, orphans, internally displaced and undocumented populations, persons with disabilities, minorities, and others lacking state protections and services (USAID 2011c). In 2009, USAID also launched a one-month Women's Access to Justice Campaign in two provinces of Afghanistan to provide women in rural and urban areas a better understanding of gender equality, women's rights, and the legal system (USAID 2009). Likewise, the EU has supported access to justice for vulnerable and marginalized groups, such as women and juveniles in prison in Albania and those living in the townships and rural areas of South Africa (European Commission 2009b; 2010c).

Sida engaged in a mapping of international experiences promoting the rule of law and equal access to justice (Sida 2011c), which recounts the evolution from "law and development" to equal access to justice, describes obstacles people face in seeking justice, and outlines an equal access to justice approach. Based on this mapping, Sida produced a

"Guide on Equal Access to Justice" (Sida 2011d) which instructs Sida staff and others on identifying potential equal access interventions, while applying a human rights–based approach.

The World Bank's Justice for the Poor (J4P) Program takes a slightly different approach in that it "supports the emergence of equitable justice systems." Its focus is on enabling substantive justice outcomes rather than supporting predetermined institutional structures. Justice for the Poor works across several thematic areas: community-based paralegals; development effectiveness; gender; land and natural resources; legal pluralism; and local governance, anticorruption, and social accountability at the local level. In so doing, the program engages a range of justice institutions in each country, including formal/state, informal/nonstate, and hybrid systems. Its operational activities factor in user perspectives (particularly those of the poor and marginalized, such as women, youth, and ethnic minorities), capacity constraints, and the spectrum of justice institutions to ensure that dispute resolution is handled equitably and peacefully. Activities oriented around access to justice include, for example, legal empowerment programs that promote women's access to justice in Indonesia and support to legal aid services in Sierra Leone and Nigeria. Other activities support systems for addressing grievances around the provision of public goods and entitlements, such as the piloting of a grievance mechanism for a cash transfer program in Timor Leste and analysis to support the design of community-driven development programs in Papua New Guinea and Indonesia. Finally, J4P works to improve land and natural resource governance, for example, through a program to enable more inclusive and equitable engagement of customary landholders in the formal economy of Vanuatu by increasing their knowledge of land leasing (World Bank 2011j).

Other Governance Dimensions

In recent years, greater attention has been paid to the issues of corruption and corporate governance in the context of development. The impacts of corruption on human rights and development have been the subject of extensive research (see, for example, Sunga and Bottigliero 2007; Centre for Democratic Institutions 2001). International agreements have been signed (including an implementation monitoring mechanism agreed to in 2009 for the 2003 UN Convention Against

Corruption), corporate structures have been modified, and policies have been developed to address corruption. The World Bank adopted a new Governance and Anticorruption (GAC) Strategy in March 2007 (World Bank 2007b) and an Implementation Plan in October 2007 (World Bank 2007c), with progress reports presented to the Board in 2008 and 2009. An updated strategy was undergoing a review and consultation process in early 2012, with a final strategy expected at the end of March 2012.

Despite these efforts, much work remains to be done to combat corruption successfully. Human rights principles, such as participation, transparency and access to information, and accountability, however, could support anticorruption programs. As has been said, "Corruption is essentially an activity carried out by groups with power" (International Council on Human Rights Policy 2009), and a human rights–based approach would aid in addressing economic, political, and social factors that foster corruption, would legitimize the claims of marginalized populations, and would empower people to challenge the abuse of power (International Council on Human Rights Policy 2010).

Examples are emerging of agencies addressing governance and human rights issues. For example, the USAID Mobilizing Action against Corruption (MAAC) activity partnered with the International Council on Human Rights Policy (ICHRP) to publish the Armenian-language versions of the 2009 and 2010 ICHRP reports on anticorruption and human rights (USAID 2011d). With HURIST support, UNDP has prepared a wealth of new policies and practice notes on such areas as access to justice, parliaments, police, decentralized governance, national human rights institutions, and the right to information. OHCHR and UNDP organized an international seminar on human rights and governance in Seoul in 2004.

Documented examples also suggest that sometimes human rights principles have helped agencies move beyond civil or political rights projects in their governance portfolios. Though not always couched in a human rights language, more interventions are paying attention to institutionalizing participation (Gaventa and Barrett 2010), providing accountability and redress, and fostering a healthy relationship between the state and citizens, based on recognition of rights and duties. DFID work on tax reform in Peru illustrates this (box 2.16 and chapter 7).

Box 2.16 Political and Financial Accountability in Peru

DFID has strengthened political inclusion through the review of fiscal studies (notably tax reform and budget transparency) to encourage greater accountability and responsiveness to poor people. The program focused on the equity potential and accountability functions of fiscal policy (ensuring that resources reach excluded groups) on the expenditure side. It also promoted the perspective that when citizens pay taxes, not only is it a duty, but it also creates rights on the revenue-generation side. As such, the program introduced a focus on equity and accountability—rather than simply efficiency—into revenue policy and administration.

Source: DFID 2005b.

Findings and Issues for Further Consideration

Donors integrate human rights through direct projects, in their country programs and at a global level, supporting the work of international organizations. Most traditional interventions have been delivered through civil and political rights projects, often supported by civil society funds and closely associated with democracy and the rule of law. Some governance programming areas, such as access to justice, have begun to change as a result of the introduction of human rights–based approaches. Yet it is difficult to assess wider trends, in particular in governance areas where political dimensions have only recently been taken into account. The absence of an explicit application of a human rights perspective to the wider governance agenda is possibly one of the clearest limitations in donor experiences. This could be examined, for instance, with regard to the relationship between human rights and corruption (UNDP 2008a).

While at a policy level governments are committed to the indivisibility of all human rights, within development cooperation human rights work has tended to be narrowly construed around civil and political rights (OECD 2001). This narrow focus in part explains why there is limited evidence and advice to date on how governance interventions can strengthen the realization of all rights, including economic and social rights.

Nonetheless, significant efforts have been made to mainstreaming human rights across a number of nongovernance sectors. Possibly because they are perceived as less sensitive politically and due to the success of UNICEF in implementing its HRBA, child rights have been incorporated into a wide range of policies and programs. Mainstreaming human rights into health, education, or programming on gender and women in development is another growing trend. By comparison, donors seem to have less frequently linked human rights to other areas, such as minorities, infrastructure, or livelihoods.

Little research exists on the impacts of political conditionality, despite its use by bilateral agencies and the EU. As new aid approaches emerge, it will be important to conduct more open discussions about this issue and to find effective ways of handling political conditionality in the context of medium-to-long-term aid relationships, as well as in fragile and conflict-affected states.

Finally, there is scope for aid agencies to invest more in knowledge management across the board. Although almost all of the UNDG-HRM agencies have developed knowledge products (KPs) on operationalizing human rights, case studies and documents on lessons learned are still lacking. Few KPs are region specific, and nearly three-quarters are available only in English. Finally, most KPs are not specifically addressed to national counterparts, thereby missing an opportunity to strengthen the capacity of national partners (UNDG-HRM 2011). The UNDG-HRM has acknowledged this, and one priority for its work plan is to strengthen case studies, lessons learned, and knowledge sharing across the UN on human rights mainstreaming (see box 4.5, in chapter 4, on the UN HRBA portal.) The UN System Staff College is also presently working on the development of a Learning and Evidence Centre, capturing stories and experiences from within and outside the UN system and translating them into training and learning case studies for use in future skills development and leadership courses on human rights and development.

Additional issues for research and analysis that could be undertaken jointly include:

- Governance subareas where a demonstrable policy and programming shift has occurred (e.g., rule of law/access to justice or decentralization)
- Achievements of nongovernance interventions that have an explicit objective of human rights mainstreaming, or are based on an HRBA, to allow comparison among a small set of sectors (e.g., health and education)

- Human rights dialogue and the impact of conditionality used by bilateral donors and the EC, including the collaboration between development cooperation agencies and foreign ministries.

References

ADC (Austrian Development Cooperation). 2011. "Focus: Persons with Disabilities in ADC." May, Vienna.

AusAID (Australian Agency for International Development). 2008. *Development for All: Towards a Disability-Inclusive Australian Aid Program, 2009–2014.* Canberra: AusAID.

———. 2009. "Terms of Reference: AusAID's Disability Inclusive Development Reference Group." July, Canberra.

BMZ (German Federal Ministry for Economic Cooperation and Development). 2006. *Water Sector Strategy, Strategies 152.*Bonn: BMZ.

———. 2008. *Strategies 167, Development Policy Action Plan on Human Rights 2008–2010.* Bonn: BMZ.

———. 2009a. *Promotion of Good Governance in German Development Policy, Strategies 178.* February. Bonn: BMZ.

———. 2009b, *Sector Strategy: German Development Policy in the Health Sector, Strategies 187.* August. Bonn: BMZ.

———. 2010. *Human Rights in Practice: Fact Sheets on a Human Rights–Based Approach in Development Co-operation.* Bonn: BMZ.

———. 2011a. *Human Rights in German Development Policy.* Bonn: BMZ.

Braithwaite, Mary, 2003. "Thematic Evaluation of the Integration of Gender in EC Development Co-operation with Third Countries." Prepared for the European Commission, PARTICIP GmbH, Freiburg.

Carothers, Thomas. 1999. *Aiding Democracy Abroad: The Learning Curve.* Washington, DC: Carnegie Endowment for International Peace.

———, ed. 2006. *Promoting the Rule of Law Abroad: In Search of Knowledge.* Washington, DC: Carnegie Endowment for International Peace.

Centre for Democratic Institutions. 2001. "Human Rights and Corruption," prepared by Zoe Pearson. Canberra: Centre for Democratic Institutitons.

CIDA (Canadian International Development Agency). 2011a. *Development for Results, 2009–2010.* Québec: CIDA.

Coleridge, Peter, Claude Siminnot, and Dominique Steverlynck. 2010. "Study of Disability in EC Development Cooperation." November, European Commission, Brussels.

DFID (U.K. Department for International Development). 2005b. *Alliances Against Poverty: DFID's Experience in Peru 2000-2005.* London: DFID.

———. 2009a. "Implementing the UK's Conditionality Policy." How-to note, May, DFID, London.

———. 2011a. *Annual Report and Accounts, 2010–2011.* London: DFID.

European Commission. 2004. "Guidance Note on Disability and Development." July, Brussels.

————. 2009b. "List of Projects Financed under EIDHR 2009." Brussels.

————. 2010a. "EU Plan of Action on Gender Equality and Women's Empowerment in Development, 2010–2015." March, Brussels.

————. 2010c. "Partnership for Change: Development Cooperation with African, Caribbean and Pacific Countries," p. 31. European Commission, Brussels.

————. 2010d. "European Disability Strategy: 2010–2020." November 15, Brussels.

————. 2011a. "Adoption of the Annual Action Programme 2011 for the European Instrument for the Promotion of Democracy and Human Rights Worldwide (EIDHR)." March 29, Brussels.

————. 2011f. "Joint Communication to the European Parliament and the Council: Human Rights and Democracy at the Heart of EU External Action—Towards a More Effective Approach." COM (2011) 886 final, December 12, Brussels.

FAO (UN Food and Agriculture Organization). 2005. "Voluntary Guidelines to Support the Progressive Realization of the Right to Adequate Food in the Context of National Food Security." Adopted in November 2004, Food and Agriculture Organization of the United Nations, Rome.

Foresti, Marta, Eva Lude, and Roo Griffiths. 2007. "Human Rights and Livelihood Approaches for Poverty Reduction: Briefing Note." November, Swiss Agency for Development and Cooperation, Bern.

FRIDE (Fundacion para las Relaciones Internacionales y el Dialogo Exterior). 2010. "Democracy Assistance Factsheet: Spain." October 16, FRIDE, Madrid.

Gaventa, John, and Gregory Barrett. 2010. "So What Difference Does It Make? Mapping the Outcomes of Citizen Engagement." Institute for Development Studies (IDS) Working Paper 347, Brighton.

Global Fund to Fight AIDs, Tuberculosis, and Malaria, Global Fund Information Net. July 2011.

Government of Sweden. 2003a. "Shared Responsibility: Sweden's Policy for Global Development." Government Bill No. 2002/03:122, Stockholm.

GPDD and World Bank (Global Partnership on Disability and Development). 2009. "Women with Disabilities in Development: Intersecting Invisibility, Intersecting Realities: A Report on an E-Discussion on Women with Disabilities in Development." Prepared by Andrea Shettle, August 28, GPDD and World Bank, Washington, DC.

GTZ (German Organization for Technical Cooperation). 2009a. *The Human Rights–Based Approach in German Development Cooperation.* GTZ, Eschborn.

Harrison, Graham. 2001. "Post-Conditionality Politics and Administrative Reform: Reflections on the Cases of Uganda and Tanzania." *Development and Change* 32 (4): 657–79.

IADB (Inter-American Development Bank). 2002. *Action Plan for Combating Social Exclusion Due to Race or Ethnic Background, June 2002–December 2003.* Washington, DC: IADB.

International Council on Human Rights Policy. 2009. "Corruption and Human Rights: Integrating Human Rights into the Anti-Corruption Agenda: Challenges, Possibilities and Opportunities." Draft report, International Council on Human Rights Policy, Geneva.

————. 2010. *Integrating Human Rights into the Anti-Corruption Agenda: Challenges Possibilities and Opportunities*. Geneva: International Council on Human Rights Policy.

Moser, Caroline, and Annalise Moser. 2003. "Moving Ahead with Human Rights: Assessment of the Operationalisation of the Human Rights–Based Approach in UNICEF Programming in 2002." UNICEF, New York.

Norad and Sida (Norwegian Agency for Development Cooperation and Swedish International Development Cooperation Agency). 2011. *Supporting Child Rights: Synthesis of Lessons Learned in Four Countries,* by Arne Tostensen, Hugo Stokke, Sven Trygged, and Kate Halvorsen. Joint Evaluation 2011:1, Sida, Stockholm.

Nordic Trust Fund. 2010. *Knowledge and Learning for Human Rights and Development: Nordic Trust Fund Progress Report Sept. 2009–Oct. 2010*. November 25. Washington, DC: World Bank.

————. 2011a. *Knowledge and Learning for Human Rights and Development: Nordic Trust Fund Progress Report November 2010–October 2011*. Washington, DC: World Bank.

NZAID (New Zealand Agency for International Development). 2009. "NZAID Human Rights Mainstreaming Guideline." August 6, NZAID, Wellington.

OECD (Organisation for Economic Cooperation and Development). 1997a. "Final Report of the Ad Hoc Working Group on Participatory Development and Good Governance." OECD, Paris.

————. 1999. *DAC Guidelines for Gender Equality and Women's Empowerment in Development Co-operation*. Paris: OECD.

————. 2001. *Poverty Reduction*. DAC Guidelines. Paris: OECD.

————. 2008a. "Linking Human Rights and Aid Effectiveness for Better Development Results: Practical Experience from the Health Sector." Report for the Human Rights Task Team of the OECD DAC Network on Governance (GOVNET), prepared by Clare Ferguson, OECD, Paris.

————. 2008b. "Human Rights and Aid Effectiveness: Key Actions to Improve Inter-Linkages." Paris: OECD.

OECD-DAC. 2011a. "*Draft Results of the Human Rights Donor Survey*, May 2011. Final publication forthcoming, Paris.

————. 2012. "Review of the Development Co-operation Policies of the European DAC's Main Findings and Recommendations." March 28, OECD, Paris.

OHCHR (Office of the UN High Commissioner for Human Rights). 2011. "OHCHR's Human Rights Mainstreaming Work." Notes prepared by Saranbaatar Bayarmangai, August 2011. OHCHR, Geneva.

Piron, Laure-Hélène, and Julius Court. 2004. "SDC's Human Rights and Rule of Law Guidance Documents: Influence, Effectiveness and Relevance within SDC."

Independent evaluation commissioned by the Swiss Agency for Development and Cooperation, Bern.

Piron, Laure-Hélène, and Paolo de Renzio. 2005. "Empirical Study in the Application of Political Conditionality and PRBS in Africa 1999–2004." Report for DFID, Overseas Development Institute, London.

Posarac, Aleksandra. N.D. "Including Disability into Bank's Operational Work." Powerpoint presentation for the World Bank, Washington, DC.

SADEV (Swedish Agency for Development Evaluation). 2008. "Integrating the Rights Perspective in Programming: Lessons Learnt from Swedish-Kenyan Development Cooperation," prepared by Sara Brun, Karin Dawidson, Karolina Hulterström, and Susanne Mattsson. SADEV Report 2008:2, Karlstad.

Santiso, Carlos. 2003. "Responding to Democratic Decay and Crises of Governance: The European Union and the Convention of Cotonou." *Democratization* 10 (3): 148–72.

Schulz, Nils-Sjard. 2010. "Special Report: The Bogotá Spirit: South-South Peers and Partners and the Practice-Policy Nexus." *Development Outreach*, World Bank Institute, October 2010.

SCRPD (UN Secretariat for the Convention on the Rights of Persons with Disabilities). 2009. *Mainstreaming Disability in MDG Policies, Processes and Mechanisms: Development for All.* Report of the Expert Group Meeting. Organized by the Secretariat for the Convention on the Rights of Persons with Disabilities, Division for Social Policy and Development, Department of Economic and Social Affairs, in collaboration with the World Health Organization, New York.

SDC (Swiss Agency for Development and Cooperation). 2006b. *Human Rights and Development: Learning from Experiences.* Bern: SDC.

———. 2008a. "Rule of Law, Justice Sector Reforms, and Development Cooperation." SDC Concept Paper, SDC, Bern.

Sida (Swedish International Development Cooperation Agency). 2001b. *Education for All: A Human Right and Basic Need.* Policy for Sida's Development Cooperation in the Education Sector, Stockholm.

———. 2002a. *Perspectives on Poverty.* Stockholm: Sida.

———. 2005b. "Education, Democracy and Human Rights." Position paper, Sida, Stockholm.

———. 2008. *Experiences and Lessons Learnt from Sida's Work with Human Rights and Democratic Governance: Final Report,* prepared by Tom Dahl-Østergaard, Karin Schulz, and Barbro Svedberg. Sida Evaluation 2008:29, Stockholm.

———. 2009a. *Human Rights for Persons with Disabilities: Sida's Plan for Work.* October, Stockholm.

———. 2010e. *Disability as a Human Rights Issue: Conducting a Dialogue.* Stockholm: Sida.

———. 2010g. *Freedom of Expression: Dialogue.* Stockholm: Sida.

———. 2010h. *The Rights of Children and Young People: Conducting a Dialogue, Part 1.* Stockholm: Sida.

————. 2010i. *Young People's Political Participation: Conducting a Dialogue, Part 2.* Stockholm: Sida.

————. 2010j. *Child Protection: Conducting a Dialogue, Part 3.* Stockholm: Sida.

————. 2010k. *Human Rights of Lesbian, Gay, Bisexual and Transgender Persons: Conducting a Dialogue.* Stockholm: Sida.

————. 2011c. *Equal Access to Justice: A Mapping of Experiences,* prepared by Henrik Alffram. April, Sida, Stockholm.

————. 2011d. *A Guide to Equal Access to Justice Programmes.* April, Sida, Stockholm.

————. 2012a. *Resultat för rättvisa och utveckling: Resultatbilaga Till Sidas Årsredovisning 2011.* Stockholm: Sida.

————. 2012b. *Public Financial Management for the Rights of Children and Young People.* Stockholm: Sida.

Sunga, Lyal S., and Ilaria Bottigliero. 2007. "In-Depth Study on the Linkages between Anti-Corruption and Human Rights for the United Nations Development Program." Raoul Wallenberg Institute of Human Rights and Humanitarian Law, January 15, Lund, Sweden.

UN (United Nations). 2006. "Convention on the Rights of Persons with Disabilities." Resolution adopted by the General Assembly, December 13, 2006, entry into force 3 May 2008, A/RES/61/106, Annex I, New York.

————. 2010b. "System-Wide Coherence." Resolution adopted by the General Assembly, A/RES/64/289, New York.

————. 2010c. "Report of the United Nations High Commissioner for Human Rights: Rights of Persons Belonging to National or Ethnic, Religious and Linguistic Minorities." A/HRC/15/42, July 5, UN, New York.

————. 2011d. "Disability and the Millennium Development Goals: A Review of the MDG Process and Strategies for Inclusion of Disability Issues in Millennium Development Goal Efforts." Prepared by Nora Groce, Leonard Cheshire Centre for Disability and Inclusive Development, University College, London.

UNDG (UN Development Group). 2011c. "UNDG Fact Sheet: Mainstreaming Human Rights for Better Development Impact and Coherence." October 25, UNDG, New York.

UNDG-HRM (United Nations Development Group Human Rights Mainstreaming Mechanism). 2011. "Mapping of UN Agency Human Rights Mainstreaming Policies and Tools." April 18, UNDG, New York.

UNDP (UN Development Programme). 2008a. *Tackling Corruption, Transforming Lives: Accelerating Human Development in Asia and the Pacific.* Published for UNDP by Macmillan Publishers India Ltd., New Delhi.

————. 2010a. "Marginalised Minorities in Development Programming: A UNDP Resource Guide and Toolkit." May, UNDP, New York.

UNDP and OHCHR. 2010. "UNDP-OHCHR Toolkit for collaboration with National Human Rights Institutions." December, UNDP and OHCHR, New York and Geneva.

UNESCO (United Nations Educational, Scientific, and Cultural Organization). 2008a. "Follow-up to the World Summit for Social Development and the Twenty-fourth Special Session of the General Assembly; Emerging Issues: Mainstreaming Disability in the Development Agenda." E/CN.5/2008/6, February 6–15, Paris.

UNFPA (United Nations Population Fund). 2009. "Integrating Human Rights, Culture, and Gender in Programming: Participants Training Manual." UNFPA, New York.

UNFPA and the Harvard School of Public Health. 2010. *UNFPA: A Human rights–based approach to Development Programming; Practical Implementation Manual and Training Materials.* New York: UNFPA.

UNICEF. 2011a. *UNICEF Annual Report 2010.* New York: UNICEF.

UNICEF and UNESCO. 2007. *A Human Rights–Based Approach to Education for All.* NewYork: UNESCO and UNICEF.

UN Women (United Nations Entity for Gender Equality and the Empowerment of Women). 2011b. "United Nations Entity for Gender Equality and the Empowerment of Women Strategic Plan 2011–2013." UNW/2011/9, 27–30, June, New York.

USAID (U.S. Agency for International Development). 2009. "Success Story: Women Gain Access to Justice" April, USAID, Jalalabad. http://afghanistan.usaid.gov/en/USAID/Article/858/Women_Gain_Access_to_Justice.

———. 2011b. *A Field Guide for USAID Democracy and Governance Officers: Assistance to Civilian Law Enforcement in Developing Countries.* January, USAID, Washington, DC.

———. 2011c. "USAID's Access to Justice Program Awards First Round of Assistance Grants to Local NGOs and Vulnerable Populations of Iraq." Press release, September 14, Baghdad.

———. 2011d. "USAID/MAAC and ICHRP Discuss Report on Human Rights and Corruption." Press release, July 28, USAID, Yerevan, Armenia.

Uvin, Peter. 2004. *Human Rights and Development.* Bloomfield: Kumarian Press.

Watkins, Francis. 2004. "Evaluation of DFID Development Assistance: Gender Equality and Women's Empowerment. DFID's Experience of Gender Mainstreaming: 1995 to 2004." Report prepared for DFID, Glasgow.

WHO (World Health Organization). 2008. *Medium-Term Strategic Plan 2008–2013, Amended.* Draft, November, WHO, Geneva.

———. 2011a. *Human Rights and Gender Equality in Health Sector Strategies: How to Assess Policy Coherence.* Prepared by staff at WHO, OHCHR, and Sida, Geneva.

———. 2011b. "WHO Reforms for a Healthy Future: Report by the Director-General." EBSS/2/2, October 15, Geneva.

World Bank. 2005a. "Empowering People by Transforming Institutions: Social Development in World Bank Operations." January 12, World Bank, Washington, DC.

———. 2005d. "Indigenous Peoples." Operational Policy 4.10, July, World Bank, Washington, DC.

———. 2007b. "Strengthening World Bank Group Engagement on Governance and Anticorruption." March 21, World Bank, Washington, DC.

———. 2007c. "Implementation Plan for Strengthening World Bank Group Engagement on Governance and Anticorruption." September 28, World Bank, Washington, DC.

———. 2010b. *Human Rights Indicators in Development: An Introduction.* By Siobhán McInerney-Lankford and Hans-Otto Sano. Washington, DC: World Bank.

———. 2011a. *World Bank Study on Human Rights and Climate Change: A Review of the International Legal Dimensions,* by Siobhán McInerney-Lankford, Mac Darrow, and Lavanya Rajamani. Washington, DC: World Bank.

———. 2011g. *World Development Report 2012: Gender, Equality, and Development.* Washington, DC: World Bank.

———. 2011j. "Justice for the Poor." Washington, DC.

———. 2011l. "Involuntary Resettlement." Operational Policy 4.12, issued December 2001 and updated August 2004, March 2007, and February 2011, World Bank, Washington, DC.

World Bank and IFC (International Finance Corporation). 2011. *Women, Business and the Law 2012: Removing Barriers to Economic Inclusion.* Washington, DC: World Bank and IFC.

World Bank and WHO. 2011. *World Report on Disability.* Washington, DC: World Bank and WHO.

3

Preliminary Lessons: Integrating Human Rights Dimensions, Principles, and Obligations

Intrinsic Value: Human Rights as a Legal Obligation

A Coherent Normative and Analytical Framework

Human rights offer a coherent normative framework that can guide development assistance. This framework puts the human person at the center of the analysis, linked to state obligations as duty-bearers and citizen entitlements as rights-holders. It is a universal framework into which states enter freely, with a jurisprudence under human rights treaties to support decision making. Its grounding in a consensual global legal regime creates a normative legitimacy and consistency that may help guide development interventions.

Considerable convergence exists between the substance of human rights treaty provisions (such as the International Covenant on Economic, Social, and Cultural Rights, ICESCR) and areas of development activities, particularly as donors continue to expand cooperation into realms of social and human development. Moreover, several core principles that can be derived from international, regional, or domestic human rights instruments—participation and inclusion, accountability, equality and nondiscrimination, attention to vulnerable groups, and empowerment—are already part of the development discourse. Indeed, a human rights–based approach (HRBA) to development analyzes and addresses "the inequalities, discriminatory practices and unjust power relations which are often at the heart of development problems" (UNDG 2011b). This overlap of substance and principle can be illustrated by the principle of equality, which is central to many international human rights instruments, just as it is embraced by development actors in pursuit of equity, inclusion, or empowerment (McInerney-Lankford 2009).

Although a normative agenda is increasingly pursued under HRBAs, the approach does not necessarily emphasize human rights as legal obligations or the subject of binding treaty obligations under international law. This divergence results from legal constraints that put human rights beyond the reach of certain agencies' mandates, the political sensitivity of connecting human rights to the development context, the diversity of government interpretations of human rights in international contexts, or institutional or organizational arrangements that keep human rights and development separate.

Development agencies are recognizing the analytical value of human rights: changes to project cycle management and innovative tools have enabled agencies to ask new questions and analyze situations differently. The bridging analysis undertaken by UNIFEM, for example, helps define the meaning of relevant human rights standards for particular contexts; as such, it builds development partners' understandings of how human rights guidance can enhance existing work (box 3.1).

Legal Obligations

Human rights law obligations, like other international treaty obligations, are the voluntarily entered commitments of states, and as such, they potentially offer clear reference points and legitimacy. The human rights framework

---

Box 3.1 Women's Rights as an Entry Point to Analyze Land Reform

UNIFEM's bridging analysis in Central Asia has enabled project staff to use the international framework to identify priority areas in the land reform process. For example, analysis has pointed to the need to examine women's right to land; women's rights in relation to family; women's access to credit; and the impact of stereotypes, discriminatory customs, and religious laws on women's access to property.

offers a clear articulation of the responsibilities of duty-bearers and the entitlements of rights-holders, establishing a strong accountability paradigm. Depending on institutional and country context, human rights obligations may provide a relevant frame of reference for development where they relate substantively to development activities and objectives. Definitions of rights based on legal obligations benefit from the clarity of their definition in international treaties, as well as their elaboration in jurisprudence or the interpretations of expert bodies.

Even where states' development policy frameworks incorporate an explicit commitment to human rights, only a few explicitly incorporate human rights obligations. Notable examples include Canada's 2008 Official Development Assistance Accountability Act (ODAAA; see chapter 5), which provides that official development assistance can be provided only if it is consistent with international human rights standards (Canada 2008). Building upon the reference to human rights in the European Bank for Reconstruction and Development (EBRD) Articles of Agreement, the EBRD's 2008 Environmental and Social Policy precludes the institution from knowingly financing projects "that would contravene obligations under international treaties and agreements related to environmental protection, human rights and sustainable development." Similarly, the Council of Europe Bank's (CEB) human rights framework includes loan regulations that require projects to adhere to the Convention for the Protection of Human Rights and Fundamental Freedoms and the European Social Charter (CEB 2010a).

Operational Human Rights Principles

Many bilateral agencies, such as Swedish International Development Cooperation Agency (Sida) and the U.K. Department for International Development (DFID), have been successful in programming around operational human rights principles. With slight variations, these sets of operational human rights principles are a combination of the principles found in the UN Interagency Common Understanding of an HRBA (appendix 1). At the sector level, other principles derived from the comments of UN treaty-monitoring bodies about economic and social rights (e.g., accessibility, adaptability, acceptability, affordability of services) also offer concepts around which development programming can be effectively organized. German bilateral cooperation has demonstrated the use of these principles and published a series of promising practices (GTZ 2009b).

For agencies that have not adopted explicit human rights policies, operational principles also offer reference points for working on human rights in an implicit manner. That is the case with the World Bank's Social Development Strategy (box 3.2).

It is, however, important to distinguish operational principles that might be tangentially related to human rights from interventions specifically grounded in the human rights framework. There is a risk of "rhetorical repackaging" when every single intervention aimed at enhancing accountability, by using a participatory approach or channeling aid through civil society organizations, is described as "rights-based" or when it is argued that a donor is contributing to social and economic rights simply because of investments in schools, health, or job creation, for example. Such interventions need to be related to specific state obligations in order to be categorized as contributing to the realization of human rights. Nevertheless, there may also be a risk of understating the indirect, positive human rights impact of projects undertaken with an implicit human rights approach. For instance, an independent review found that the Australian aid program is rich in activities that advance Australia's commitment to human rights. However, the review also found that the program should more clearly communicate the interconnection between it and human rights (Government of Australia 2011).

Box 3.2 World Bank Social Development Strategy

In 2005, the World Bank adopted a new social development policy (World Bank 2005a). Although not grounded in the international human rights framework, it is based on commitments found in the UN 1995 Copenhagen Social Development Summit and the 2000 Millennium Declaration. It describes similarities to related frameworks, such as Sen's work on capabilities (1999) or Japan's endorsement of "human security" as an overarching framework.

The strategy presents three operational principles (closely related to other agencies' human rights principles), built on inclusion, nondiscrimination, and accountability: inclusive institutions to promote equal access to opportunities, enabling everyone to contribute to social and economic progress and share in its rewards; cohesive societies, to enable women and men to work together to address common needs, overcome constraints, and consider diverse interests; and transparent, accountable institutions that respond to the public interest in an effective, efficient, and fair way (World Bank 2010a). As a result, the Bank has increasingly involved indigenous communities in its environmental, agricultural, and educational projects over the past decade.

The UN Interagency Common Understanding of an HRBA offers a useful framework for distinguishing between elements that are *unique* and clearly linked to the human rights framework, and others that are *essential* but shared with other perspectives and more commonly found in development. Unique elements include using the recommendations of international human rights bodies and mechanisms, assessing the capacity of rights-holders to claim their rights and of duty-bearers to fulfill their obligations, and developing strategies to build those capacities. Essential elements include, for example, recognizing people as key actors in their own development (rather than as passive recipients of commodities and services) and valuing participation, empowerment, and bottom-up processes, generally considered good programming practices.

Meaningful Participation

HRBAs are often associated with the adoption of participatory techniques. DFID, for example, invested in Participatory Rights Assessment Methodologies, which were piloted in Peru and Malawi. UNICEF has adopted a participatory community development strategy in parts of Africa. In addition to approaches that aim to contribute to the empowerment of poor and vulnerable populations, the integration of human rights calls for free, informed, and meaningful participation that can be institutionalized and can affect public policy choices (box 3.3). More traditional human rights projects in support of civic education or election processes have also contributed to this process.

Box 3.3 Work of the Canadian International Development Agency on Child Participation

Child rights programming by donors and NGOs such as Save the Children has emphasized child participation. For example, CIDA funded child participation pilot projects as part of the implementation of its 2001 Action Plan on Child Protection (CIDA 2001). CIDA has also supported the participation of children in research, international conferences, and policy dialogue.

In some cases, this has led to outcomes that were not anticipated. In CIDA's Egypt pilot, it was observed that child labor often benefited children and their families. (Save the Children has also come up with the same finding.) Rather than calling for abolition, the project supports working children, to improve their learning and working conditions. They are taught to identify labor hazards and to design healthy responses. At the national level, the Egyptian government has asked the CIDA project for expertise on a methodology for a participatory, rights-oriented national strategy for children (chapter 8).

Instrumental Value

Apart from the intrinsic value that human rights may bring to development practices, they may be instrumentally useful in promoting good governance, managing risk, reducing poverty, and improving aid effectiveness.

Governance

Governance issues and human rights are mutually reinforcing. Good governance is defined by a transparent and accountable environment in which individuals can claim and exercise their rights. Human rights principles and frameworks can support improved governance—since they highlight the demarcations between institutions, and their constituents, underscore lines of responsibility and promote transparency, so that individuals are empowered to hold their governments accountable.

Focusing on the Links between the State and Its Citizens Donor interventions tend to work either on the supply side (for example, reforming state institutions to make them more effective) or on the demand side (for example, civil society advocacy campaigns that promote responsive governance). HRBAs help to break this artificial distinction by linking demand and supply through the conceptual lens of rights-holders, duty-bearers, and citizenship (box 3.4).

Accountability, Redress, and Legitimacy Strengthening state legitimacy is fundamental to the governance agenda: respect for human rights standards itself offers a source of legitimacy. Institutional channels for domestic accountability are becoming an important development concern, not only in the context of improved aid effectiveness (e.g., in relation to general budget support and financial management) but also as a spur to pro-poor domestic reform (e.g., encouragement of parliamentary involvement in poverty reduction strategies). Human rights provide an accountability framework at the international, regional, and national (constitutional) levels, which emphasizes the need to document and monitor practices and progress regularly and provides recommendations and opportunities for compensation or redress. This channel of accountability can be used to hold states, but also aid agencies, accountable for their performance (chapter 4).

Box 3.4 Combining Citizen Awareness with State Ability to Deliver

Claiming citizenship rights requires that citizens be registered in the first place, so that they can legitimately demand their entitlements. In Bolivia, DFID and other donors are funding a project designed to provide identification documents to undocumented Bolivians (in particular, the poor, women, and indigenous people) and raise awareness about citizen rights among civil society, registration officials, and members of the electoral court. The project has also worked with the supply side by developing the capacity of the court and the registration service to handle the referendum and municipal elections during 2004–05.

In Peru, DFID has also supported mechanisms of citizen participation and the formal institutions of representative democracy. It worked with a coalition of state and civil society organizations to facilitate electoral education and oversight during presidential, congressional, regional, and municipal elections. The project helped strengthen citizenship by involving the poor in the electoral process. At the same time, DFID helped transform the institutional/legal framework in which the political parties operated, by bringing together state and civil society actors to seek consensus on a new Law of Political Parties and a reform of the electoral code. It also worked directly with parties (see chapter 7; DFID 2005b).

A World Bank Nordic Trust Fund grant is exploring how efforts to strengthen the capacity of the government of Vietnam to guarantee the rights of its citizens can be reinforced by activities supporting citizens with rights awareness (Nordic Trust Fund 2010; 2011a). The NTF grant enables Bank staff to work with the government of Vietnam to (1) raise awareness of rights through the media; (2) work with People's Councils, which represent citizens, in holding the administration accountable; (3) support public awareness and capacity-building activities that enable citizens to use new legal instruments that improve access of poor and vulnerable groups to the formal justice system; and (4) train local civil servants through the Institute of Human Rights of the Ho Chi Minh Political Academy.

German-funded participatory complaint surveys in Indonesia resulted in improved service delivery by the public sector. Citizens became more aware of their rights, and civil society organizations acted as watchdogs and responsible partner at the local level. Local decision makers and service providers learned to be accountable to citizens but also experienced the benefits of regular feedback. This helped them to seek improvement and prioritize actions and gave local authorities leverage when requesting more resources from the central government (GTZ 2009b).

Various initiatives foster accountability processes and institutions, for example, around the rule of law (chapter 7), but also around democracy and political participation (chapter 6). Denmark supports domestic accountability through several of its development cooperation programs. Examples include programs aimed at strengthening democratic institutions and their accountability and facilitating the development of pluralist political systems based on accountable and legitimate political parties (e.g., Uganda, Nepal). Other examples include providing support to parliamentary development as a key domestic mechanism of democracy (e.g., Mozambique, Bangladesh, Mali), promoting a democratic culture in which institutions, civil society, and political actors interact, supporting free and fair elections, supporting free and diverse media as a watchdog and platform for democratic debate (e.g., Tanzania, Burkina Faso), promoting the equal participation and voice of women and men (e.g., Niger), strengthening justice institutions (e.g., Mozambique, Vietnam, Mali), promoting autonomous and independent national human rights institutions (e.g., Bangladesh), and supporting civil society organizations to assist people in formulating their demands, to carry out advocacy, and to provide legal assistance to poor and disadvantaged groups (in most partner countries).

"Do No Harm" and Risk Mitigation

The "do no harm" principle is one of the 10 key principles identified in the DAC Action-Oriented Policy Paper on Human Rights and Development (AOPP), given that donors can "inadvertently reinforce societal divisions, worsen corruption, exacerbate violent conflict, and damage fragile political coalitions if issues of faith, ethnicity and gender are not taken fully into consideration" (OECD 2007a). In this connection, the human rights framework can provide a normative baseline mandating nonretrogression and a legal grounding for the principle of "do no harm." The AOPP encourages donors to respect human rights principles in their policies and programming, to identify practices that are potentially harmful, and to develop strategies for mitigating such potential harm.

Some agencies have development policy frameworks that embody a principle of "do no harm" without explicitly relying on the international human rights framework. For instance, the World Bank has environmental and social safeguard policies to prevent and mitigate undue harm to people and the environment in the development process. These policies provide guidelines for Bank and borrower staffs in the identification, preparation, and implementation of investment lending projects and programs. They have substantially increased the effectiveness and development impact of projects and programs supported by the Bank. Safeguard policies frequently provide a platform for stakeholder participation in project design and promote ownership of projects among local populations.

To improve enforcement of the Bank's policies, the Inspection Panel was created in 1993 as an "independent, 'bottom-up' accountability and recourse mechanism" to investigate complaints and report findings directly to the Board of Directors. This step was followed by the creation of a separate Quality Assurance and Compliance Unit in 1999 for additional oversight (World Bank–IEG 2010). The World Bank safeguard policies reflect certain human rights considerations implicitly rather than explicitly. One exception is the Bank's safeguard policy on indigenous peoples, which makes explicit reference to human rights in its preamble, stating that it "contributes to the Bank's mission of poverty reduction and sustainable development by ensuring that the development process fully respects the dignity, human rights, economies, and cultures of Indigenous Peoples" (World Bank 2005d). (For a discussion of the World Bank's involuntary resettlement policy, see box 2.9 in chapter 2.) The World Bank is currently undertaking a two-year process of updating these safeguard policies.

In 2010, the World Bank Group's private sector arm, the International Finance Corporation (IFC), launched a revised version of its Guide to Human Rights Impact Assessment and Management (HRIAM) (IFC et al. 2010) at the UN Global Compact Leaders Summit. This online tool is designed to help companies engaged in a range of development and industrial activities to understand and manage human rights risks and impacts, particularly in countries with weak governance, fragile and postconflict states, and areas inhabited by vulnerable local populations. The Web-based guide includes a number of interactive tools, such as scenarios, human rights identification, due diligence mapping, and a human rights management system, as well as online resources and performance indicators. The Nordic Trust Fund is supporting dissemination of the guide and associated capacity building for IFC staff and clients (NTF 2010).

Conducted for the IFC and the UN Representative of the Secretary-General on Business and Human Rights by an independent expert, a 2009 study was published on the human rights impact of stabilization clauses. In certain circumstances, such clauses can operate to insulate a company from compliance with laws that change during the course of an investment contract (Shemberg 2009). Human rights advocates have expressed concerns that stabilization clauses protect companies from having to meet legal obligations to respect human rights or discourage enforcement by the state if the clause requires the host country to compensate for a company's compliance costs. The study identified good practices, particularly in contracts by OECD countries, which limit the scope of stabilization clauses to only the most arbitrary and discriminatory conduct by the host country.

Most recently, IFC released an update of its Policy and Performance Standards on Environmental and Social Sustainability and Access to Information Policy, which took effect in January 2012 (IFC 2011). This update followed implementation of the 2006 Sustainability Framework and was based on a three-year review presented in 2009, as well as extensive public consultations. The updated policy increases access to information throughout the IFC project cycle, resulting in further disclosure of project-level information on environmental, social, and development outcomes. The policy and performance standards now recognize the private sector's responsibility to respect human rights and the need to undertake additional due diligence in some high-risk circumstances. The update addressed gaps identified in the earlier version of the performance standards (which define clients' roles and responsibilities for managing their projects and the requirements for receiving IFC support), particularly in regard to human trafficking, forced evictions, and community access to cultural heritage. Finally, the policy has been revised to require that free, prior, and informed consent (FPIC) be obtained in certain circumstances affecting indigenous peoples. (For a discussion of the IFC Voluntary Principles on Security and Human Rights, see box 5.6, chapter 5.)

Poverty Reduction

Identifying the Root Causes of Poverty   The lessons put forward under a "governance" heading also contribute to those related to poverty reduction, especially in the areas of participation, empowerment, and the transformation of state–society relations. Many studies highlight the analytical value of human rights for identifying the structural and root causes of poverty. Instead of a needs-based framework, programming based on a human rights analysis looks at states' ability to meet their obligations, as well as at their capacity and political will constraints.

CIDA develops country development program frameworks, and country programs must do a human rights analysis that takes into account human rights commitments. Such analysis also examines citizens' ability to claim their rights and the cultural and social barriers that may exist. For example, DFID recognized that inequality and exclusion represented major barriers to poverty reduction in Latin America and required tackling in new ways (chapter 7).

Exposing Power Relations and the Inertia of Social Norms Identifying root causes of poverty requires understanding structural factors that perpetuate it, such as the roles of elites, abuse of state power, or gender discrimination. Donors are not always comfortable examining such issues explicitly, or they may not have the social or political skills to do so. A human rights analysis can enable such an approach (box 3.5).

A number of studies point to the limitations of any approach that aims to respond only through legal or institutional change. Social norms and values (or informal power networks) are among the most difficult challenges faced in realizing human rights (and pro-poor development outcomes more generally), as illustrated by the difficulties in achieving gender equality objectives.

Paying Attention to the Excluded and Marginalized Agencies have also found human rights programming more effective in tackling disparities directly. Human rights principles of universality, equality, and non-discrimination require that aid programs pay attention to individuals and groups who are harder to reach through normal channels. They must take into account the institutional, political, economic, and social

---

Box 3.5 Water Rights in Tanzania

In the Kileto District, Tanzania, WaterAid launched a project to improve water access for residents. By integrating human rights principles—in particular participation, nondiscrimination, equality, and empowerment—into the programming process (and including these as explicit program goals), WaterAid was able to identify and eliminate underlying obstacles to equitable access to water. The participatory approach and analysis revealed that because of power imbalances, lack of land rights, and exclusion from national policy decisions, two main ethnic groups were denied access to water. Project members worked with the communities to overcome the intergroup conflict.

factors that lead to exclusion and discrimination. Not least, this calls for greater use of disaggregated data (box 3.6).

Aid Effectiveness

While human rights may themselves constitute important development goals, they may also have instrumental value as "critical objectives of aid effectiveness" (Ferguson 2008). This understanding was reflected in the DAC AOPP as well as the five principles of the Paris Declaration: ownership, mutual accountability, alignment, harmonization, and managing for development results. The linkages between human rights and aid effectiveness are being explored in a number of settings. In the health sector, Ferguson recommends that partner countries use the human rights framework to support legislation, regulations, and policies; to identify citizen entitlements; to open up dialogue on critical issues; and to institutionalize quasi mechanisms for engaging civil society and monitoring the fulfillment of rights. She further argues that donors can improve aid effectiveness by developing coherent positions within agencies and between donors on human rights issues, acknowledging the importance of partner and donor countries' international human rights commitments, and ensuring that their programs, at a minimum, do no harm (Ferguson 2008).

Box 3.6 UNICEF's and Nepal's Use of New Data

UNICEF's review of the implementation of an HRBA provides many examples of efforts to reduce disparities and reach the most excluded. The review highlighted the use of disaggregated data to analyze the situation of women and children to reduce discrimination (Bangladesh); use of school drop-out rates, rather than enrollment, to shift policies and budgets toward adolescents excluded from the education system (Chile); and a polio eradication campaign targeting poor Muslim children under the age of two to reach the last 5 percent to 15 percent. This required specially adapted inclusive strategies, including a new communication strategy to reach the most marginalized families (India).

The OECD reported that Nepal's Ministry of Health and Population piloted a system to collect disaggregated data from hospitals and other health facilities on the basis of sex, age, caste, ethnicity, and regional identity to collect data on which groups and regions are benefiting from the abolition of fees for basic health services and other health policies. In so doing, the ministry is helping to ensure that resources are addressing underlying inequalities and are being used effectively to improve overall health outcomes.

Source: OECD 2008b.

Paragraph 13(c) of the Accra Agenda for Action (2008) lends further support to the link between human rights and aid effectiveness, committing donors and partner countries to "ensure that their respective development policies and programs are designed and implemented in ways consistent with their agreed international commitments on gender equality, human rights, disability and environmental sustainability." Similarly, the outcome document of the Fourth High-Level Forum on Aid Effectiveness, in Busan (2011), explicitly preserves the commitments of the AAA, and like the Accra agenda, it contains important provisions on human rights. It also provides explicitly for the right to development and confirms the "common principles which consistent with our agreed international commitments on human rights, decent work, gender equality, environmental sustainability and disability— form the foundation of our cooperation for effective development" (Busan Outcome Document, paragraph 11).

Alignment and Harmonization "Alignment" refers to donor commitments to base support on partner countries' national development strategies, institutions, and procedures. It requires strengthening of partner countries' sustainable capacity, in particular in the areas of public financial management and procurement, as well as increased use of partner country systems on the part of donors. Harmonization requires donor actions to adopt common arrangements, simplified procedures, a more effective division of labor, more collaborative behavior, and greater transparency.

In recent years, a greater focus has been placed on alignment and harmonization in reference to integrating human rights into development. The Paris Declaration and the Accra Agenda for Action encourage donors to harmonize their approaches to cross-cutting issues, and the 2011 Busan Outcome Document confirms human rights among the shared principles that should guide donors and partners to achieve common goals. The 2007 AOPP further elaborated 10 principles to guide donors in areas where harmonization is critical (OECD 2007a; see also box 1.1, in chapter 1, and chapter 8). Human rights, given their role in states' domestic legal and policy frameworks, play a part in setting national development priorities, which donors can assist in implementing. In addition, there is a strong congruence between, on the one hand, building partners' capacity and ensuring that aid does not undermine national capacities and, on the other, the fundamental principle that states are the main duty-bearers and that aid can be used to assist them in meeting their human rights obligations.

Work continues in several donor agencies on how to integrate human rights in various areas of development cooperation. A number of examples illustrate how capacity development can be undertaken through a human rights–based approach (boxes 3.7 and 3.8).

The DAC conducts in-depth, periodic peer reviews of all 24 member states to examine the effectiveness of their development systems and strategies and to share good practices in light of their commitments under the Paris Declaration, the Accra Agenda for Action, and the Busan Outcome Document. Every four years, each member country submits to a six-month review by two other member states. The DAC also publishes lessons learned about aid management challenges from across the collected peer reviews. The peer reviews focus on members' development programs overall and do not necessarily address how human rights issues are being integrated. For instance, the over-100-page

---

Box 3.7 Public Expenditure and Rights Programming

UNICEF and UNIFEM have supported a number of initiatives to develop capacity for budget preparation and monitoring from a rights perspective, for example, through gender (UNIFEM 2006) or children's budgets, bringing together ministries of finance and social movements.

DFID has supported the Uganda Debt Network in its monitoring of the Poverty Action Fund, through which a significant amount of donor resources is channeled to local levels. In Peru, DFID-supported taxation reform was linked to citizens' rights and duties.

Box 3.8 Positive Complementarity

Denmark's policy and strategic framework for support to democratization and human rights, developed in 2009–10, has increased emphasis on a coherent approach to its normative human rights agenda in the support it provides both in multilateral forums and in bilateral aid. One example is Denmark's promotion of "positive complementarity," which strengthens domestic jurisdictions to conduct national investigations and trials of crimes included in the Rome Statute of the International Criminal Court—through support for capacity development provided by bilateral donors, multilateral organizations, and civil society.

Source: Ministry of Foreign Affairs of Denmark 2011.

reviews of the Portuguese and U.S. programs each include only three brief references to the term "human rights" (OECD 2010; 2011a).

Results-Based Management The Paris Declaration includes a commitment to manage aid in a way that focuses on the desired results and uses information to improve decision making. This commitment was affirmed by the Accra Agenda for Action and in the Busan Outcome Document, which articulated these in terms of eradicating poverty, reducing inequality, sustainable development, and building developing countries' capacity. The literature on results-based management rarely touches upon the role of human rights in conceptualizing and achieving results. The reason may be a perception that human rights give attention to processes, qualitative measures, and normative standards, rather than focusing on measurable outcomes. For example, agencies such as UNICEF have found that the lack of disaggregated data has constrained their ability to target and monitor progress in equality and nondiscrimination.

A number of agencies have, however, worked to integrate human rights within their results-based management frameworks (box 3.9). There have been attempts to use national and international reporting on human rights commitments as part of country performance assessment frameworks, as well as investments in disaggregated data or tracking qualitative impact, and a focus on structures and processes as well as outcomes.

Mutual Accountability "Mutual accountability" refers to the individual and joint accountability of donors and partner governments to their citizens and parliaments for their development policies, strategies, and performance. The Paris Declaration requires that partner governments use participatory processes to develop and monitor national strategies and involve their parliaments, that donors provide transparent information on aid flows to promote public accountability, and that both parties jointly assess progress in meeting aid effectiveness commitments. These mutual accountability principles are fully compatible with the human rights principles of accountability and transparency—which were reiterated in the Accra Agenda for Action and the Busan Outcome Document—and which require access to information as well as participation in decision making.

Box 3.9 Denmark's and UNIFEM's Approaches to Results-Based Management

With the adoption of a new strategy for Danish development cooperation, "The Right to a Better Life," in 2012, Denmark has committed to taking a human rights–based approach to development cooperation (Ministry of Foreign Affairs of Denmark 2012). In already-existing programs the Ministry of Foreign Affairs actively supports the inclusion of human rights–related indicators in Poverty Reduction Strategy Paper (PRSP) performance assessment frameworks, when it is deemed relevant. For example, in Mozambique, one of several justice or law-and-order indicators was concerned with a gradual increase in the percentage of criminal cases processed within the limits established by law. Separately, in Niger, a support program aimed at promoting gender equality and equity includes results indicators that, in effect, work to remove Niger's reservations to the Convention on the Elimination of All Forms of Discrimination against Women (CEDAW) and encourage ratification of its additional protocol. In Zambia, an indicator of improved access to justice is expressed as a decreased ratio between prisoners on remand versus ones convicted. In November 2011, Denmark was planning to launch an international research program with the purpose of improving the documentation of results, with a focus on the five pillars of the overall strategy for Danish development cooperation: freedom, democracy and human rights, growth and employment, gender equality, stability and fragility, and environment and climate.

UNIFEM's Multi-Year Funding Framework set four rights-based goals: reduce feminized poverty and exclusion, end violence against women, reverse the spread of HIV/AIDS among women and girls, and achieve gender equality in democratic governance in times of peace and in recovery from war. UNIFEM issued a guide for measuring results from a human rights perspective. It included recommendations on how to measure progress in building the capacity of duty-bearers and rights-holders. It used CEDAW as the source of indicators, and adopted a participatory approach to planning and reporting (chapter 5).

Human rights norms and standards can be an explicit part of this mutual accountability framework. It would require not only that partner governments demonstrate progress in implementing their human rights commitments but also that donors be held accountable for their contribution to the realization of human rights in partner countries. There are several examples of governments and agencies' specifying human rights as a shared value underpinning their aid partnerships (for example, Finland, Netherlands, Sida, DFID, the UN system, or Germany, which in 2011 committed itself to assess the possibility of setting up a human rights accountability mechanism; box 3.10). However, disagreements also exist regarding the extent to which the international human rights framework requires donors to be legally accountable for the human rights impacts of their policies and activities.

Accountability can also be fostered through community participation. UNDP Sri Lanka launched the AIDWATCH initiative in 2005 to empower civil society in an effort to ensure that recovery and

---

Box 3.10 Human Rights and Mutual Accountability

DFID's policy on conditionality (DFID 2005a), which remains in place, mentions both that human rights commitments form the basis of the aid partnership and that significant human rights violations can be used as a justification to suspend aid. It is the latter aspect which has caused the most discussion. The Memorandum of Understanding (MoU) with Rwanda is one example of a mutual accountability framework. Rwanda has signed four MoUs (with the UK, the Netherlands, Sweden, and Switzerland). The UK MoU included references to human rights as a shared commitment of the UK and Rwanda, a wider set of commitments on the part of the UK than other donor governments (to meet aid effectiveness principles), and explicit references to the government of Rwanda's human rights commitments. Of note, DFID has recently modified its analysis for making decisions about budget support by adding to the existing three commitments (poverty reduction and the MDGs, respecting human rights, and improving public financial management and promoting good governance) an additional prong: strengthening domestic accountability. Assessment of this new criterion will entail an evaluation of the partner government's commitment to making government information transparent, to engaging citizens, and to answering calls to justify its actions (DFID 2011d).

The OECD reported on two missions to Uganda, performed by the UN Special Rapporteur on the Right to Health, to report on the government of Uganda's action on neglected diseases and on the health program of SIDA's Ugandan office. The missions, which were facilitated by the OHCHR, the WHO, and the Uganda Human Rights Commission, strengthened public accountability and ownership of the national health strategy by enabling the engagement of Ugandan civil society organizations and the ministry of health in the strategy review process. As a result of these missions and the broad stakeholder engagement, the ministry of health has included gender equality and human rights assessments in the mid-term review of the sector strategy, helping to ensure that the strategy is addressing the underlying causes of ill health in Uganda (OECD 2008b).

---

development take place in an environment of increased accountability, transparency, and participation. A representative sample of beneficiaries was chosen and given basic rights awareness training, as well as advocacy and negotiation skills. They were also given access to local authorities and grievance redress mechanisms (UNDP 2008a). In a UNDP housing project, for example, AIDWATCH participants were encouraged to discuss the project with field staff, ask questions, share grievances, and make recommendations (OECD 2008b).

Other Operational Benefits

From Direct Service Delivery to Capacity Development

Human rights highlight the importance of states' and citizens' respective capacity to deliver and claim their rights. All too often, aid agencies and international NGOs have attempted to fill in capacity gaps, and deliver services directly, or advocate for policy change in the place of domestic actors. The various case studies of HRBAs, in particular those commissioned by UNICEF, consistently find that such an approach helps donors and NGOs understand the need to move away from direct delivery and work at the level of the overall legal and policy framework, institutions, and programs. This approach is more sustainable, as it requires capacity to be developed beyond donor or NGO interventions (box 3.11).

Holistic and Integrated Approaches

Linking the principles of interdependence and interrelatedness of all human rights with development programming, a number of studies have found that an HRBA produces operational benefits. It encourages more integrated programming (as opposed to a "silo" approach) by examining the range of factors that constrain the realization of particular rights. This includes, for example, linking the lack of security at school with girls' school attendance, rather than the availability or quality of education per se. This approach often calls for collaboration with other agencies within a sector, between different sectors, or across state and civil society actors (box 3.12). In a UNICEF survey, 36 percent of country offices said that they had engaged in multisector programming as a result of applying a human rights–based approach (Raphael 2005).

Box 3.11 Irish Aid's Role in Aid Effectiveness

Although Irish Aid is a relatively small organization of fewer than 300 people, Ireland has been considered a leader in implementing the aid effectiveness principle (Agulhas 2010). Irish Aid has been a strong advocate of local ownership, harmonization, and alignment both at policy and at field level (OECD 2009). Ireland's 2008 Civil Society Policy commits Irish Aid to (1) create an enabling environment for NGOs to organize and engage with their own broader constituencies; and (2) support the role of NGOs in promoting participation and good governance, pro-poor service delivery and growth, and building a constituency for development, human rights, and social justice (OECD 2009).

Irish Aid's Fellowship Training Programme (FTP) has been a critical part of its capacity-building efforts. The program awards approximately 60 fellowships annually to students from Ireland's program countries (public services or nongovernmental sector) to come to Ireland for postgraduate studies. Irish Aid also provided substantial inputs for a 2007 workshop that it hosted on applying the Paris Declaration principles on gender equality, environmental sustainability, and human rights. Ireland's efforts at aid effectiveness have become increasingly important since the financial crisis of recent years has forced aid agencies to scrutinize, optimize, and reduce aid budgets (Irish Aid 2009).

Box 3.12 The "Justice Chain"

UNDP's access to justice policy focuses on the various stages and capacities needed for citizens to move from grievance to remedy, going through recognition of a grievance, awareness of rights, claiming, adjudication, and enforcement. This allows the justice system to be analyzed from the perspective not just of institutions, but also of citizens and the barriers they need to overcome. Responses may require collaboration across justice institutions; in the Asia-Pacific region, they included working with traditional justice.

Box 3.13 New Partnerships

Sida's mainstreaming project in Kenya has worked with a network of local partners (government, NGOs, and UN) acting as resource persons for its sector programs. The project also contributed to a national process around the Kenya National Human Rights Commission.

When UNICEF wanted to ensure accountability in Costa Rica, it joined forces with the Catholic Church, public universities, chambers of commerce, and political leaders and came up with new social, economic, and political proposals. In Jordan, when it found limited material available in Arabic on the Convention on the Rights of the Child (CRC) and CEDAW for legal experts, UNICEF opened discussions with the country's law school. The school now provides a mandatory course on human rights for all students, as well as courses on CRC and CEDAW.

In Peru, the DFID country team cultivated new alliances for change and nurtured existing networks. For example, it brought together human rights organizations working on civil and political rights with more traditional development and poverty reduction organizations. It supported coalitions between the state and civil society at election times. It also supported networks of health professionals and umbrella bodies to work with government on health policy.

Building New Partnerships

Uvin (2004) notes, "One of the major—and by now totally evident—consequences of a human rights–based approach to development is that it encourages development actors to identify different partners." This trend encourages donor agencies to work with wider sets of actors, often in a facilitative way, to support domestic change processes in partner countries (box 3.13). CIDA's Aid Effectiveness Plan directs CIDA to delegate greater authority to the field level as well as use partner countries' public systems as much as possible (CIDA 2009b).

Explicitly Recognizing the Political Dimensions of Aid

A human rights–based approach to poverty reduction is inherently political because it attempts to change power relations within society. Recognizing that donors themselves can be political actors raises difficult issues regarding the legitimacy of donor action, the practice of power, and lines of accountability. DFID realized these consequences in Peru, which also meant that the potential existed for conflict between DFID and the state (box 3.14). Although few aid agencies would be able to act in an explicitly political manner, a number of studies, including political economy analytic work such as "Lessons Learned on the Use of Power and Drivers of Change Analyses in Development Co-operation" (Dahl-Østergaard et al. 2005), recognize the political dimensions of poverty reduction and the political role of donors promoting pro-poor change.

Reinforcing "Good Programming Practices"

Some of the contributions of human rights presented above can be described without using a "rights language." That is the reason behind the UN Interagency Common Understanding's distinction between unique and essential elements of a human rights–based approach (see appendix 1), specifying what is found across good programming in general and the specific value of the human rights normative framework.

Why have some agencies preferred to maintain references to human rights (box 3.15)? They argue that a foundation in a coherent, normative framework helps to make these good programming approaches non-negotiable, consistent, and legitimate. They create the potential to transform some of the more traditional, technical, and beneficiary-oriented or needs-based approaches to aid.

Box 3.14 Political Party Reform in Peru

To start tackling exclusion and inequality, DFID Peru supported reform of the legal and institutional framework but also worked with political parties themselves to help them think more about poverty and how to tackle it—clearly a sensitive area for a donor. The Agora project brought together militants from a wide range of parties to examine how to strengthen party governance. It emphasized inclusiveness by facilitating the participation of all parties; for example, meetings were held outside Lima to encourage the involvement of local party activists.

> **Box 3.15 Spain's "Africa Plan 2009–2012"**
>
> Spain's Agency for International Development Cooperation (AECID) retains an explicit focus on human rights, with a concentration on social and economic rights as well as women's rights (FRIDE 2010). It has shifted its geographic focus from middle-income countries to fragile and least-developed countries. Building on its new Human Rights Plan (Government of Spain 2008), Spain's Ministry of Foreign Affairs and Cooperation and AECID published "Africa Plan 2009–2012," which includes among its three mainstreaming objectives human rights, gender equality, and environmental sustainability and adaptation to climate change (AECID 2010).

Adaptability to Different Political and Cultural Environments

Aid agencies and their partners are sometimes concerned that programming in this area is simply too difficult, for example, because of conflicts between human rights and local religion or culture, or certain political contexts. Yet some agencies have been able to use human rights as a tool to influence harmful and discriminatory practices that might otherwise remain unchallenged. For example, in the area of health and reproductive rights, United Nations Population Fund (UNFPA) has been able to identify culturally sensitive ways of promoting human rights, drawing on Islamic sources in Muslim countries and distinguishing between culture at large and harmful practices that violate women's rights (chapter 5). Other agencies have adopted approaches tailored to individual country situations. For example, UNICEF focuses on policy, legal, and institutional reforms in Latin America, community-level work in parts of Africa, and a progressive approach to human rights engagement in Vietnam that underlines the importance of the time factor and nonconfrontational strategies (box 3.16 and chapter 7).

Findings and Issues for Further Consideration

Development agencies integrate human rights in the international human rights framework to varying degrees. Some, such as BMZ, Sida, or the UN, are explicit about the foundation of this work in international human rights agreements and obligations, whereas others, such as CIDA or USAID, adopt a much more implicit approach, integrated

Box 3.16 UNICEF's Work in Vietnam

This country program demonstrates the results of long-term engagement using a nonconfrontational language and high-level political dialogue in centralized socialist political systems. When UNICEF first introduced child rights principles in its analysis and planning, explicit rights language would have been too sensitive. By broadening the range of its state and party counterparts, UNICEF was able to raise awareness of children's rights in a number of areas. As a result, UNICEF has made progress in legal reform, juvenile justice, and child protection.

at an operational level. Ultimately, the integration of human rights into development has to be related to the international framework that is the main source of legitimacy of the approach. This framework continues to evolve, making it important for development agencies, partner countries, and civil society groups to continue to interact with human rights actors such as UN bodies, human rights academics and lawyers, or NGOs. At the same time, human rights organizations should become more familiar with development concepts and approaches to be able to participate effectively in the mainstream of development debates.

The 2005 World Summit reaffirmed member states'

> solemn commitment to fulfill their obligations to promote universal respect for and the observance and protection of all human rights and fundamental freedoms for all in accordance with the Charter, the Universal Declaration of Human Rights and other instruments relating to human rights and international law. (UN 2005a)

It resolved to strengthen the UN human rights machinery, the OHCHR, and the treaty-monitoring bodies, further mainstreaming within the UN, and establishing a Human Rights Council. Members should continue to support initiatives aimed at strengthening the human rights system and mainstreaming human rights within the UN.

States should ensure that human rights standards and the general comments of the treaty-monitoring bodies are well known and more should be done to enhance the usefulness and relevance of the recommendations of these bodies (O'Neill 2004; Alston 2004). Development agencies should step up their capacity to interact with human rights bodies and organizations and the capacity for "translation" between the development and human rights communities.

References

Accra Agenda for Action. 2008. Third High-Level Forum on Aid Effectiveness. September 4, Accra.

Agulhas Consulting. 2010. "Joint Evaluation of the Paris Declaration—Phase 2; Donor HQ Study—Irish Aid." July. Prepared by Nigel Thornton, Anne Barrington, and Kevin Carroll. Irish Aid, Limerick.

Alston, Philip. 2004. "A Human Rights Perspective on the Millennium Development Goals." Paper prepared for the Millennium Project Task Force on Poverty and Economic Development, UN, New York.

Busan Outcome Document. 2011. Busan Partnership for Effective Development Cooperation, Fourth High-Level Forum on Aid Effectiveness, November 29–December 1.

Canada. 2008. *Official Development Assistance Accountability Act*, June 28, 2008, S.C. 2008, c. 17. Québec: Minister of Justice.

CEB (Council of Europe Bank). 2010a. "Policy for Loan and Project Financing." Adopted in June 2006 under Administrative Council Resolution 1495, Paris.

CIDA (Canadian International Development Agency). 2001. *CIDA's Action Plan on Child Protection: Promoting the Rights of Children Who Need Special Protection Measures.* Québec: CIDA.

Dahl-Østergaard, Tom, Sue Unsworth, Mark Robinson, and Rikki Ingrid Jensen. 2005. "Lessons Learned on the Use of Power and Drivers of Change Analyses in Development Co-operation." Review commissioned by the OECD-DAC Network on Governance (GOVNET), September 20, OECD-DAC GOVNET, Paris.

DFID (U.K. Department for International Development). 2005a. "Partnerships for Poverty Reduction: Rethinking Conditionality." A UK Policy Paper, DFID, London.

———. 2005b. *Alliances Against Poverty: DFID's Experience in Peru 2000–2005.* London: DFID.

———. 2011d. "Implementing DFID's Strengthened Approach to Budget Support: Technical Note." July 8, DFID, London.

Ferguson, Clare. 2008. "Linking Human Rights and Aid Effectiveness for Better Development Results: Practical Experience from the Health Sector." Report for the Human Rights Task Team of the OECD-DAC Network on Governance (GOVNET), May 14. OECD, Paris.

Government of Australia. 2011. *Independent Review of Aid Effectiveness.* Canberra: Government of Australia.

GTZ (German Organization for Technical Cooperation). 2009b. "Compilation—Promising Practices on the Human Rights–Based Approach in German Development Cooperation." GTZ, Eschborn.

IFC (International Finance Corporation) et al. 2010. *Guide to Human Rights Impact and Assessment Management.* Washington, DC: International Finance Corporation, United Nations Global Compact, and International Business Leaders Forum.

Irish Aid. 2009. "Plan of Action to Implement Commitments under the Accra Agenda for Action, Internal Working Document." October, Irish Aid, Limerick.

IFC (International Finance Corporation). 2011. "Update of IFC's Policy and Performance Standards on Environmental and Social Sustainability and Access to Information Policy." April 14, IFC, Washington, DC.

McInerney-Lankford, Siobhán. 2009. "Human Rights and Development: A Comment on Challenges and Opportunities from a Legal Perspective." *Journal of Human Rights Practice* 1 (1): 51–82.

Ministry of Foreign Affairs of Denmark. 2011. *Road Map for the Implementation of the Strategy for Denmark's Development Cooperation in 2011: Freedom, Democracy and Human Rights.* Copenhagen.

NTF (Nordic Trust Fund). 2010. *Knowledge and Learning for Human Rights and Development: Nordic Trust Fund Progress Report September 2009–October 2010.* Washington, DC: World Bank.

———. 2011a. *Knowledge and Learning for Human Rights and Development: Nordic Trust Fund Progress Report November 2010-October 2011.* Washington, DC: World Bank.

OECD (Organisation for Economic Co-operation and Development). 2007a. "DAC Action-Oriented Policy Paper on Human Rights and Development." February, OECD, Paris.

———. 2008b. "Human Rights and Aid Effectiveness: Key Actions to Improve Inter-Linkages." OECD, Paris.

———. 2009. "DAC Peer Review of Ireland." March 24, OECD, Paris.

———. 2010. "DAC Peer Review of Portugal." October 13, OECD, Paris.

———. 2011a. "DAC Peer Review of the United States." June 23, OECD, Paris.

O'Neill, William G. 2004. "Human Rights–Based Approach to Development: Good Practices and Lessons Learned from the 2003 CCAs and UNDAFs." Review prepared for the Office of the UN High Commissioner for Human Rights, December, OHCHR, Geneva.

Raphael, Alison. 2005. "HRBAP Program Review 2003: Implementation of Human Rights Approach to Programming in UNICEF Country Offices. 1998–2003." UNICEF, New York.

Sen, Amartya. 1999. *Development as Freedom.* Oxford: Oxford University Press.

Shemberg, Andrea. 2008. "Stabilization Clauses and Human Rights." Research project conducted for IFC and the United Nations Representative of the Secretary-General on Business and Human Rights, March 11.

UN (United Nations). 2005a. "2005 World Summit Outcome." Resolution adopted by the General Assembly, A/RES/60/1, New York.

UNDG (UN Development Group). 2011b. "Human Rights–Based Approach to Development Programming (HRBA)." www.undg.org/index.cfm?P=221 (accessed December 14, 2011).

UNDP (UN Development Programme). 2008a. *Tackling Corruption, Transforming Lives: Accelerating Human Development in Asia and the Pacific.* Published for UNDP by Macmillan Publishers India Ltd., New Delhi.

Uvin, Peter. 2004. *Human Rights and Development.* Bloomfield: Kumarian Press.

World Bank. 2005a. "Empowering People by Transforming Institutions: Social Development in World Bank Operations." Operational document approved by the World Bank Board of Executive Directors January 12, World Bank, Washington, DC.

————. 2005d. "Indigenous Peoples." Operational Policy 4.10, July, World Bank, Washington, DC.

————. 2010a. *Demanding Good Governance: Lessons from Social Accountability Initiatives in Africa.* Ed. Mary McNeil and Carmen Malena. Washington, DC: World Bank.

World Bank–IEG. 2010. "Safeguards and Sustainability Policies in a Changing World: An Independent Evaluation of World Bank Group Experience." IEG Study Series, World Bank, Washington, DC.

4

Challenges and Opportunities

Institutionalization

Institutionalization remains an important internal challenge facing aid agencies. Agencies that are committed to applying a human rights–based approach internally need to take a systematic look at their procedures and operations to identify required changes and to strengthen staff capacities and incentive structures. Organizational culture plays a role in this process, potentially impeding an institution's ability to adopt or adapt to new ideas. For agencies committed to working on human rights in a more selective fashion (such as at the level of projects or in their dialogue) it has been important to provide guidance to staff on how and why to undertake that work more effectively.

A synthesis of documented experiences, along with a large number of interviews, suggests that the following elements are important for effective institutionalization: external environment, senior leadership, staff capacity and incentives, new tools and guidance on changes to project cycle management, and adapting to working in a more decentralized context.

International and Domestic Political Context

Chapter 1 reviewed some of the legal and political constraints to inte-grating human rights. Opportunities created in the post-Cold War international environment included the Vienna (human rights), Beijing (women), Copenhagen (social development), and Durban (racism) conferences. These were reflected in the Millennium Declaration and again reaffirmed in the 2005 and 2010 World Summit Outcome Docu-ments (UN 2005a; 2010d). Such international statements, and the pol-icies, agendas, and action plans derived from them, such as the DAC AOPP (OECD 2007a) and the AAA (2008), can create strong incentives for agencies to review the extent to which they have put their human rights policies into practice.

Domestic political contexts have also created opportunities and challenges for aid agencies. For example, studies point to the domes-tic commitment to human rights in Nordic countries. As is illustrated by Sweden's Policy for Global Development (Government of Sweden 2003a), domestic commitments can then be extended into interna-tional action, including aid. In the United Kingdom, the 1997 elections brought into power politicians committed both to an ethical foreign policy in the Foreign and Commonwealth Office and to paying greater attention to economic and social rights within aid provision (DFID 1997). Although a more recent change of government in the country in 2010 has not affected the country's human rights policy, the focus of development aid has shifted more toward demonstrating deliver-ables and tangible results (DFID 2011a). Similarly, Switzerland's human rights policy remains intact, but several activities were placed on hold as the Swiss Agency for Development and Cooperation (SDC) underwent a 2008 reorganization to establish thematic networks, including one on conflict and human rights.

Constitutional and Legislative Initiatives

Donors and partners often work together on domestic legal initiatives related to human rights that aim to support sustainable development. These initiatives sometimes draw from the international human rights framework or from international human rights initiatives. The right to water provides an example of this potential for interplay between the domestic and international law spheres.

At the international level, the right to water is considered to be protected under Articles 11 and 12 of the International Covenant on Economic, Social, and Cultural Rights (ICESCR), which provide for the "right to an adequate standard of living" and the "right of everyone to the enjoyment of the highest attainable standard of physical and mental health," respectively. The right to water and sanitation was explicitly recognized in 2010 by UN General Assembly resolution 64/292, which acknowledged that clean drinking water and sanitation are critical to the fulfillment of all human rights (UN 2010f).

At the national level, constitutional provisions explicitly requiring the protection or provision of clean water are found in at least 17 nations, including Kenya. Consultations were supported by a project funded by the German Federal Ministry for Economic Cooperation and Development (BMZ) to promote good governance; the project was implemented by Germany's GIZ. The Kenyan-German water program, also implemented by GIZ, continues to support efforts to further incorporate Kenya's human rights obligations related to the right to water into national law, policy, and regulation aligned to the new constitution. In South Africa, the right to water is also explicitly enshrined in its 1996 constitution and is enforceable in the courts. In addition to these constitutional provisions, several countries have incorporated the right to water in their national laws and policy, making it easier to enforce (Boyd 2011; box 4.1; see also box 7.3, chapter 7).

Box 4.1 Enforcing the Right to Water in Argentina

In many instances where there is no explicit constitutional right to water, courts have found that the right to water is implicitly included as a fundamental prerequisite to enjoying other explicitly protected rights. In one instance, the drinking water in a poor community in Argentina (Chacras de la Merced) was being contaminated by inadequate wastewater treatment. An NGO filed a lawsuit against the upstream municipality and the province, alleging a violation of the local residents' constitutional right to a healthy environment. The court found that there was a violation of the right and ordered the government to upgrade the treatment plant and provide clean water to the local residents in the interim. The government met its obligations, and the municipality subsequently passed a law requiring all future sewage and sanitation tax revenue to be invested in improvements and maintenance of the sewage system.

Source: Boyd 2011.

In some instances, development cooperation of a technical sort can be seen to result in human rights–relevant legal initiatives at the domestic level. For instance, a review of the Australia-China Human Rights Technical Cooperation Program found that the All China Women's Federation attributes the passage of new laws on domestic violence by the local level People's Congress to domestic violence workshops sponsored by the program (AusAID 2006). Since 2004, CIDA has also supported the UNIFEM CEDAW Southeast Asia Program (CEDAW SEAP) to support governments, civil society organizations, and partners within the UN system and international community to facilitate better implementation of the Convention on the Elimination of All Forms of Discrimination against Women (CEDAW) to advance women's rights in Cambodia, Indonesia, Lao People's Democratic Republic, the Philippines, Thailand, Vietnam, and Timor-Leste.

A range of initiatives is taking place within multilateral organizations to analyze, catalogue, and support domestic laws that integrate human rights. In 2011, UNICEF planned a mapping of the integration of human rights into domestic laws and policies on disability. WHO is developing a database on national constitutions and case law relevant to the right to health and other health-related human rights. The UN Office on Drugs and Crime (UNODC) plans to review model laws on criminal justice systems and juvenile justice, to ensure consistency with human rights norms and standards. The UN Population Fund (UNFPA) plans to conduct an assessment of legal obstacles to sexual and reproductive health and an assessment of international, regional, and national human rights standards related to older persons. Finally, the Food and Agricultural Organization (FAO) has published a number of documents that review laws on the right to food (UNDG-HRM 2011). The challenge of enforcing such laws remains (box 4.2).

Senior-Level Commitment, Accountability, and Communication

Resistance to policy change is common among agencies. However, reviews indicate that senior-level managers and other policy champions (in agencies such as UNICEF, BMZ, and Sida) have taken steps to ensure that new policies are effectively developed, communicated, and

Box 4.2 Justiciability of Economic, Social, and Cultural Rights (ESCR)

One obstacle to the full realization of economic, social, and cultural rights is their justiciability and legal enforceability. Most recently, the 2008 Optional Protocol to the ICESCR created a mechanism for individuals to file individual communications (complaints) for violations of economic, social, and cultural rights (ESCR) under the ICESCR with the Committee on Economic, Social, and Cultural Rights (UN 2008b). However, the protocol will not enter into force until 10 parties have ratified it and so far only three states have done so.

At the national level, similar challenges have been raised about the justiciability of ESCR enshrined in a national constitution. The Grootboom decision (*Government of Republic of South Africa and Others v. Grootboom and Others* 2000 (11) BCLR 1169 (CC)) by the South African Constitutional Court in 2000 was the first to recognize that such economic, social, and cultural rights were justiciable and that remedies could be found to compensate victims for violations. The decision also confirmed the obligations of the state to provide for ESCR regardless of budgetary or other limitations (UNDP and OHCHR 2010). Basing its decision on Section 26 of the South African Constitution, the High Court held:

> Everyone has the right to have access to adequate housing; and the state must take reasonable legislative and other measures, within its available resources, to achieve the progressive realisation of this right.

The court held that "Section 26 imposed a negative duty on states not to prevent or impair the access to housing, as well as a positive obligation to create an enabling environment for the fulfillment of this right."

In late November 2011, the Kenyan High Court issued an important decision on the justiciability of ESCR, highlighting that the need to recognize the "interdependence [of human rights] is out of the realization that people living without the basic necessities of life are deprived of human dignity, freedom and equality." The decision was grounded in the new constitution, as well as in provisions of the ICESCR and the African Charter on Human and Peoples' Rights. The Kenyan NGO Hakijamii had filed a petition on behalf of local community members in the Medina Location of Garissa, Kenya, who were violently evicted and had dwellings destroyed with little notice and no due process. Affirming that any treaty ratified by Kenya is part of Kenyan law, the court found violations of many economic, social, and cultural rights, among them the rights to life, adequate housing, sanitation, clean and safe water, and education. The High Court issued a permanent injunction, ordering the state to return petitioners to their land and reasonable residence, and awarded damages to the petitioners (*Ibrahim Sangor Osman v. Minister of State for Provincial Administration and Internal Security and Others*, High Court of Kenya at Embu 2011).

Efforts to engage judicial systems in the enforcement of ESCR can be expected to continue, with institutions offering training and capacity building in relevant areas. For example, the Global School on the Enforcement of Social and Cultural Rights, a consortium of institutions coordinated from the University of Oslo, offers international, regional, and national trainings on litigation of ESCR, including one on litigating health-related rights.

implemented in their organizations. Making staff accountable to senior management has been a useful approach (box 4.3). The UN Systems Staff College has recognized the need to develop strong leadership on human rights issues and is developing new trainings aimed at strengthening senior-level commitment. Similarly, one of the priorities for

Box 4.3 Senior-Level Directives

In 1998, UNICEF issued an executive directive introducing its human rights–based approach to programming (UNICEF 1998). It assigned responsibilities for dissemination and implementation to heads of offices, regional directors, and division directors. The new approach was not made a separate thematic area; instead, every staff member and country office was given responsibility for implementation. Both the Vietnam case study and the evaluation of UNICEF's HRBA emphasize the important role played by senior staff in this transformation (chapter 5).

NZAID translated ministers' commitments to human rights mainstreaming into an implementation plan (NZAID 2004). An implementation team, including senior managers, met monthly to review progress and reported to ministers after a few years. The implementation plan targets not only strategy, planning, and programming, but also organizational capacity and cultural transformation within NZAID. It called for data capture on human rights programming, staff recruitment and training, a process for responding to staff concerns about human rights abuses (within the agency or in partner countries), and a review of contracting procedures and the agency's communication strategy (chapter 5). The agency is now called the New Zealand Aid Program. Human rights continue to be a cross-cutting issue that is mandatory in all New Zealand Aid Program policies, processes, and activities, for which management is clearly accountable. Human rights considerations are appraised in all project designs, included in implementation, tracked through monitoring, and reported in results for all aid initiatives.

the UNDG-HRM is to strengthen the capacity of Resident Coordinator and UNCT leadership to drive mainstreaming efforts by providing them with enhanced learning support and guidance.

Staff Capacities and Incentives

Agencies generally had little staff expertise when they first adopted their human rights policies. To put the policies into action, most have created new focal point positions, and some have recruited experts externally. The newly formed EuropeAid-DEVCO (formed by a January 2011 merger of the EuropeAid Cooperation Office [AIDCO] with the Directorate General for Development and Relations with ACP States [DEV]), which manages European development policy, has a unit dedicated to Governance, Democracy, Gender, and Human Rights. The European Union has also created a Directorate on Human Rights and Democracy within the European External Action Service (EEAS; launched in December 2010) and assigns a human rights focal point in all EU delegations around the world (European Commission 2011f).

More often, however, staff numbers remain small, often with only one or two persons responsible for human rights (e.g., Austrian

Development Agency [ADA] Department on Human Rights, BMZ) and related issues at headquarters (usually located within governance units). In those instances, capacity development initiatives are particularly important (box 4.4). Some agencies have given responsibility to a professional cadre with country programming responsibility (e.g., DFID social development advisers). Other agencies have launched training programs in headquarters and the field, targeted to audience and level of expertise, to mainstream expertise across the agency (e.g., UNICEF, BMZ, Sida, ADA, and Dutch development cooperation). A number of agencies have promoted outside networking opportunities and exchanges of information within the agency (e.g., DFID's social development retreats and Sida's democratic governance events).

Box 4.4 Capacity Development Initiatives

Shortly after NZAID was created, its Human Rights Policy Statement (NZAID 2002) was the second document issued by senior management. As most staff were newly recruited, they were instructed about the human rights policy. Similarly, most UNICEF staff members undergo human rights training as part of their induction training. These examples contrast with agencies where staff have been in post for longer, are already familiar with existing approaches and frameworks, and are not offered training. Despite a major organizational restructuring and the development of new business processes in the past year, human rights continue to be one of three cross-cutting thematic issues for the New Zealand Aid Program (formerly NZAID), along with gender and the environment (New Zealand Ministry of Foreign Affairs and Trade 2011).

DFID's significant policy and programming developments can be credited to its professional network of social development advisers (about 70 out of 2,500) who ensure that a social perspective (including human rights considerations) is applied to all DFID activities. Individual advisers have championed the approach in specific projects and programs, as well as in the development of country strategies or new policy initiatives. This contrasts with most other bilateral agencies, where human rights have been seen primarily as a governance concern or where there are fewer professional advisers working on these issues.

UNIFEM, along with UNAIDS and UNFPA, produced a training manual for community-based AIDS workers, *Gender, HIV, and Human Rights: A Training Manual* (2000). It includes comprehensive background information and statistics on HIV/AIDS, step-by-step training materials and questionnaires about misconceptions, case studies about the dangers of limited knowledge, and references to background material. The manual incorporates a gender-responsive human rights–based approach to learning about, and devising solutions to, the challenges posed by HIV/AIDS (UNIFEM et. al. 2000). This training manual is complemented by the subsequent publication *Turning the Tide: CEDAW and the Gender Dimensions of the HIV/AIDS Pandemic* (2000), which explains to women, governments, and organizations working with women how women's rights standards set forth in CEDAW can be used to address HIV/AIDS.

The Danish Institute for Human Rights (DIHR) held a three-day training course for World Bank teams receiving grants from the Nordic Trust Fund to familiarize the staff with human rights law, HRBA, and human rights in development programming and practice (NTF 2010).

Implementation guides, such as SDC's "Implementation of Governance as a Transversal Theme with a Human Rights–Based Approach," makes it easier for an agency's development practitioners to apply HRBA to programs and projects (SDC 2008b).

There are many examples of agencies learning from one another. The Danish Ministry of Foreign Affairs invited Sida, GIZ, and UN staff colleagues to share experiences with Hrbas in January 2012. In September 2011, Minority Rights Group (MRG) Europe, which published a guide on the integration of a human rights–based approach, held a two-day seminar in Budapest and invited both old and new EU member state development agencies to share their experiences working with an HRBA. Similarly, the Austrian Development Cooperation looked to AusAID's leadership as it developed its focus paper on persons with disabilities (ADC 2011).

Multilateral donors have a large role to play in this kind of information sharing. Since its establishment in 2008 the Nordic Trust Fund (NTF) at the World Bank has supported exchanges across an informal network of interested Bank staff and sponsored learning events with international, regional, and national partners as part of its knowledge and partnership program (Nordic Trust Fund 2011a). In February 2010, the NTF hosted a two-day peer-to-peer exchange among 50 Bank staff and members of the DAC Human Rights Task Team. A similar exchange on human rights and development took place in June 2011 between Bank staff and the UNDG-HRM, and another such exchange took place in September 2012 between UN, EC, and World Bank staff. The UN HRBA portal is an excellent, albeit underutilized, online resource where agencies can share and seek information about HRBA programming (box 4.5).

New Tools and Procedures

A detailed review of the impact of SDC's human rights and rule of law documents illustrated that new policies need to be accompanied by practical advice to facilitate implementation (Piron and Court 2004). UNICEF and Sida report that staff are now familiar with the concept of a human rights–based approach but want concrete tools and examples illustrating how value can be added. As a result, agencies have produced documents to help with mainstreaming. Some are sector specific (e.g., health, education) or thematic (e.g., children). Denmark produced

Box 4.5 The UN HRBA Portal

With the support of the Action 2 Global Program on Human Rights, the UN Practitioners' Portal on Human Rights–Based Approaches to Programming ("HRBA portal") was created in 2009—http://hrbaportal.org/. It is a centralized forum for UN practitioners to pool their knowledge and experience in mainstreaming human rights into their work. It has a database of resources, including virtual access to reports, handbooks, guides, and case studies on HRBAs, as well as training and learning materials on integrating a human rights–based approach into development programming. The materials are organized into 17 thematic areas, but based on the recent UNDG-HRM mapping exercise of knowledge products, it will be expanded to 28 specific topics and further subcategories.

The UN HRBA portal also offers access to the HuriTALK corner for e-discussions about experiences, lessons learned, and examples of good practice shared by UN members of the Human Rights Policy Network. This includes the periodic HuriTALK Insight Series, an online publication that looks at emerging issues in the field of human rights and development in greater depth. The portal is supported by the UNDG-HRM and is primarily for UN staff, with only 10 percent of participants being non–UN (including former UN staff, consultants, civil society organizations, and academics). The 2011 UNDG-HRM mapping of UN agency human rights mainstreaming indicated that many UN focal points are unaware of the UN HRBA portal and that a communications strategy is needed to increase staff awareness about it (UNDG-HRM 2011). The portal was expanded and relaunched on Human Rights Day, December 10, 2011.

four how-to notes (on justice sector reform, informal justice, political parties, and parliaments) to help translate its strategic priorities into programming choices, particularly for thematic programs focusing on democratization and human rights. Sida recently drafted a how-to note to assist its staff and the Ministry for Foreign Affairs in integrating HRBA into a program-based approach (Sida 2011a). Germany also produced a number of how-to notes on human rights and gender equality (BMZ 2010; 2011b) plus a series of "promising practices," which illustrate how programs adopted a human rights–based approach and the value added (GTZ 2009b). In addition, its human rights desk produces brief human rights updates for country teams, including information from the treaty body recommendations and the Universal Periodic Review (UPR).

Several agencies have made changes to project cycle management procedures to help integrate human rights at all levels of design, implementation, monitoring, and evaluation of regional and country strategies, programs, and projects. In some cases, these have been compulsory. Within the UN system, reviews of UNICEF's work, common country assessments, and the United Nations development assistance framework show the impact of this mandatory approach on country strategies and activities (box 4.6).

Box 4.6 UN Country Assessment and Programming

In 2007, the UN issued new guidelines for preparing common country assessments (CCAs) and UN development assistance frameworks (UNDAFs) that employed a human rights–based approach. The guidelines were supported by a guidance note that gave additional technical advice on applying indicators for HRBA programming. Further clarity on the human rights–based approach was provided in the 2009 updated guidelines. These documents now explicitly state that human rights form the basis of their analysis and programs. The documents contain a more thorough analysis of the root causes of poverty and take a more sophisticated approach to advocacy. They point out data inadequacies in identifying discrimination and inequities and provide greater clarity in their capacity analyses of both duty-bearers and rights-holders (UN 2007; 2009).

Two more recent assessments of UNDAFs were conducted in 2011. For the first study, the UN Development Operations Coordination Office (UN-DOCO) developed a matrix of variables to evaluate UNDAFs and their success applying an HRBA (UN-DOCO 2011a). The UNDG-UNDAF Programming Network (UPN) also assessed how an HRBA, among other programming principles, has been applied to development assistance frameworks. The study concluded that a human rights–based approach was one of the best, most uniformly integrated principles across the development assistance frameworks (UNDG-UPN 2011; see also chapter 6).

Since 2006 agencies have continued to make the most changes at the level of strategy and program appraisal and design. New approaches have included the following:

- Human rights situation analyses contribute to country strategies by identifying national human rights constraints and opportunities to strengthen capacities of both state and nonstate actors (chapter 5).
- Bridging analysis looks at a country's existing international, regional, and constitutional human rights obligations and identifies gaps in legislative frameworks, policies, and programs. The analysis then describes measures recommended by the human rights system to fill the gaps, thereby identifying programming priorities (e.g., UNIFEM in Tajikistan, chapter 7).
- Participatory approaches used at all stages (e.g., DFID's Participatory Rights Assessment Methodologies or the joint UNDP-OHCHR rights-based municipal assessment and planning project in Bosnia-Herzegovina).

One of the core human rights principles applied to project cycle management is "do no harm," but there seem to be few approaches to monitoring this, particularly in the implementation of donor-funded activities. In the humanitarian field, the Sphere Project and the

Humanitarian Accountability Partnership are initiatives to improve the quality of disaster relief and to enhance the accountability of the humanitarian system. The revised Standards of Conduct for the International Civil Service (International Civil Service Commission 2002) identify human rights as one of the values that must guide international civil servants in all their actions. Although many donors have human resources policies to improve staff diversity and gender equality, the policies do not deal with the direct accountability of staff to the public or the impact of donor activities on beneficiaries.

In general there is a dearth of instruments to hold donors accountable for implementing their human rights policies. This was a conclusion of a HURIST lesson-learning workshop in March 2005, which recommended the establishment of mechanisms at the country level to support the UNDP in implementing its HRBA—an approach piloted in Kenya with indigenous people. Through capacity development, donor agencies can bring partner country governments and civil society actors into a better position to hold both donors and partners accountable, thereby creating momentum to improve collective performance. Last year, UNICEF introduced the Equity Tracker, a tool for monitoring progress made by country offices and the organization at large on its refocus on equity (UNICEF 2011a). Based on annual reporting, however, it seems that although most staff members appreciate the value of human rights, no accountability system is operating, and much depends on individual interest in mainstreaming (UNDG-HRM 2011).

Human rights monitoring and evaluation continue to be a weakness across most agencies and at all stages in the programming cycle. This applies to human rights projects, mainstreaming efforts, and dialogue initiatives, as well as to country program impacts and the overall institutionalization of human rights policies within agencies. For example, at the level of projects and country programs, the Norwegian Agency for Development Cooperation developed a human rights impact assessment tool (Norad 2001), but it does not appear to have been systematically used. Human rights indicators are being developed to assess overall country performance and influence aid allocations, but they remain controversial. Metagora—an international project implemented under the auspices of the OECD-hosted consortium Paris 21 and concluded in 2008—aimed at enhancing evidence-based assessment and monitoring in the areas of human rights, democracy, and governance.

Its main objective was to develop tools based on well-established statistical methods to obtain data and create indicators upon which policies can be formulated and evaluated (see also box 1.5 and box 4.13 on the Millennium Challenge Corporation). It is too soon to know whether the new complaint procedures made available through the 2008 Optional Protocol to the ICESCR will prove helpful in monitoring human rights commitments and projects (UN 2008b).

Adapting to Decentralized Working

The increasing decentralization of most aid agencies, which fosters closer interaction with national partners and country-based aid coordination, poses a challenge to the institutionalization of human rights and other policies. These policies have tended to be developed at headquarters and need to be applied in specific country contexts. That has presented a challenge to agencies such as the World Health Organization, whose decentralized structure has complicated its ability to offer consistent interpretations and approaches on human rights-based policies (UNDG-HRM 2011). Other agencies have used their decentralized structure more opportunistically. As illustrated in SDC and DFID reviews, decentralization has enabled some country offices to experiment with a HRBA, even when central policies and procedural changes lagged behind.

The reviews have identified a range of techniques to ensure improved links between policy and implementation. Some agencies ensure field representation in the development of human rights policies and guidance (e.g., SDC consultation process), decentralize expertise to country offices (e.g., Sida's regional democracy and human rights advisers, DFID's social development advisers) or include human rights in the terms of reference for a wider range of field positions (e.g., UNIFEM). Other techniques include providing headquarters advice to targeted country programs (e.g., GIZ country programs draw on headquarters human rights expertise, HURIST reviews of UNDP country programs; see box 4.7) or adding questions about progress on human rights programming in annual planning instructions and country office reports, such as UNICEF annual reviews.

Organizations are documenting their experience with country-level piloting of new approaches to feed into institutional learning (e.g., DFID's Participatory Rights Assessment Methodology initiatives in Peru

Box 4.7 HURIST—Global Human Rights Strengthening Program—Country Reviews

HURIST facilitated 14 human rights–based UNDP country program reviews (well beyond the original five pilots). The aim was not to rate individual country programs, but to strengthen and share best practices with the help of a checklist. Programming benefits have included, for example, encouraging country offices to pay greater attention to participation and vulnerable groups. This initiative has brought country offices into UNDP's mainstreaming process and gained institutional support from regional bureaus. In some cases, a HURIST review mission was the first event in which human rights were firmly put on the agenda of a UNDP country office. The last reviews capitalized on the staff capacity-building opportunities that the process created (see also box 2.2, in chapter 2).

and Malawi), or even with the application of a HRBA across a full country program (e.g., UNICEF case studies, Sida Kenya program, and DFID programs in Peru, Bolivia, and Brazil). In addition, they are establishing region-based, multiagency communities of practice to share lessons about human rights in a region- or country-relevant way (e.g., OHCHR Lessons Learned Project on HRBA in the Asia-Pacific region or UNDP's lesson-learning work on rights and justice in the same region).

Development Partnerships between Donors and Partner Countries

Integrating human rights into development assistance is not simply a technical matter resolved by adequate training or better tools and procedures. In some contexts, aid agencies have found engagement with partner governments around human rights issues particularly difficult because these issues highlight the political dimensions of poverty reduction or because of weak capacity (box 4.8). Two overarching challenges face donors at this level: understanding and addressing the links between fragile states and human rights, and reconciling human rights with the national ownership and leadership of strategies on which aid is increasingly based.

State Fragility and Capacity Limitations

Donors realize that they need to find better ways of engaging in difficult environments or fragile states, defined by the DAC as "countries where there is a lack of political commitment and/or weak capacity to develop

> **Box 4.8   Challenges for UNICEF Staff**
>
> UNICEF identified a number of contextual challenges that its staff members face in implementing a human rights–based approach. Constraints include the operations of government structures in partner countries, in particular when they operate in a highly centralized manner with limited public accountability. Some country contexts present greater challenges: war-torn societies, widespread poverty, or extremely weak capacity, where basic survival or institution building is seen as a priority. Human rights can also encounter open political resistance, for example, in the context of sharp ethnic divisions, where collecting disaggregated data or providing education in native languages is not politically acceptable. Resistance to human rights goes beyond governments and can include social norms and values, such as opposition to child and adolescent participation and a preference for seeing aid as charity.

and implement pro-poor policies, suffering from violent conflict and/or weak governance" (OECD 2005b). Acute human rights violations and the fear of being seen as complicit with human rights–abusing governments are among the most important factors impeding a stronger role for donors in fragile states (World Bank 2011b).

In 2007, the OECD Development Assistance Committee (DAC) brought attention to the challenges of working with and within fragile states by identifying that as a new focus area in the Action-Oriented Principles on Human Rights and Development (OECD 2007a; see also box 1.1, chapter 1) and soon thereafter in the Principles for Good International Engagement in Fragile States and Situations (OECD 2007c; box 4.9). The latter laid out 10 principles to guide donor engagement in fragile states, including several references to human rights. For example, when donors consider suspending or continuing aid in the context of human rights violations in the recipient country, the DAC's "do no harm" principle reminds donors to consider what impact such decisions may have on circumstances in-country. It also encourages a focus on state building, so that state institutions can safeguard human rights. Yet the theoretical and practical links between the human rights and fragile states agendas are underdeveloped and tend to be implicit. Few agencies have developed policy statements or strategies in these areas; when they have, human rights are not given much prominence. One notable exception is Denmark's policy on fragile states established in 2010 (Ministry of Foreign Affairs of Denmark 2010a). It lists the promotion of democratic development, good governance, and human rights among its five priority areas for working in fragile situations.

Box 4.9 Development Assistance Committee Principles for Good International Engagement in Fragile States and Situations

At the DAC's High-Level Forum in April 2007, ministers and heads of agencies endorsed the DAC Principles for Good International Engagement in Fragile States and Situations to maximize engagement in fragile states and minimize potential harm:

1. Take context as the starting point.
2. Do no harm.
3. Focus on state building as the central objective.
4. Prioritize prevention [of conflict and other crises].
5. Recognize the links among political, security, and development objectives.
6. Promote nondiscrimination as a basis for inclusive and stable societies.
7. Align with local priorities in different ways in different contexts.
8. Agree on practical coordination mechanisms between international actors.
9. Act fast . . . but stay engaged long enough to give success a chance.
10. Avoid pockets of exclusion.

Concerns remain as to whether these principles are applied in practice and what mechanisms exist to monitor their implementation.

Source: OECD 2007c.

Weak capacity to realize human rights can result from a range of factors, such as limited resources to meet minimum standards or lack of awareness of human rights duties and claims. The positive approaches examined in chapter 2 and the key role given to capacity development of rights-holders and duty-bearers in the UN Interagency Common Understanding of an HRBA (appendix 1) are the strategies most commonly adopted to overcome the problem. For example, Danish support to human rights is centered around the strengthening of the capacity of relevant national institutions to promote the rule of law and human rights, such as support to ministries of human rights (e.g., Burkina Faso), national human rights commissions (e.g., Uganda and Bangladesh), and ministries of justice (e.g., Mozambique). For its part, the International Finance Corporation (IFC) focuses on the role of private sector actors in fragile and conflict-affected states. With support from the Nordic Trust Fund, International Committee of the Red Cross, extractive industry trade associations, and others, the IFC launched an Implementation Guidance Tool for IFC's Voluntary Principles of Security and Human Rights in September 2011.

In weak or fragile states, state capacity may be so limited that the realization of some human rights obligations may not be realistic: for example, holding states accountable for meeting most basic obligations, such as security or access to services. However, human rights may help to identify what is required for effective nation or state building: An HRBA can highlight how to move progressively to a situation where states can meet their basic obligations, reconstructing the social contract between rulers and ruled. This echoes the current focus of the DAC's fragile states approach, which prioritizes state core functions such as basic security, justice, economic and service delivery functions, legitimacy and accountability, and an enabling environment (OECD 2005b 2007c). Likewise, the World Bank's 2011 *World Development Report* emphasizes that institutional legitimacy is key to breaking the cycle of violence, conflict, and poverty (World Bank 2011b).

Partner Country Ownership and Political Resistance to Human Rights

Aid agencies have often been reluctant to engage in human rights programming because they fear that official partners may reject the human rights agenda, for example, on grounds of political interference in domestic sovereignty or cultural relativism (box 4.10). The recent UN World Summit Outcome Document is useful here: It reaffirms the universality

---

Box 4.10 Promoting a Human Rights–Based Approach and Cultural Sensitivity

The 2011 UNDG-HRM mapping of UN agency human rights mainstreaming policies and tools highlights the challenge of advocating a human rights–based approach in politically sensitive contexts (UNDG-HRM 2011). The report points to a recently produced programming manual for UNFPA country staff and national partners with modules on how to apply an HRBA to its work (UNFPA and Harvard 2010). The manual distinguishes between promoting human rights with cultural sensitivity and using "culture" as an excuse to disregard or violate human rights. It refers back to a 2004 policy note by then-UNFPA Executive Director Thoraya Ahmed Obaid:

> By adopting culturally sensitive approaches to promote human rights standards and principles, UNFPA is not making value judgments on any cultural values held by communities or groups; rather it is addressing harmful practices that represent violations of international standards of human rights. For example, campaigning to end female genital cutting is a judgment that the practice denies the right to freedom from discrimination on the basis of gender and the right to health. A human rights perspective affirms that the rights of women and girls to freedom from discrimination and to the highest standard of health are universal. Cultural claims cannot be invoked to justify their violation. (UNFPA 2004a)

of human rights and commits member states "to integrate the promotion and protection of human rights into national policies" (UN 2005a).

Strategies to overcome political resistance have included progressive engagement (UNICEF in Vietnam), bypassing state actors (EIDHR), the use of dialogue, and the possibility of applying conditionality, such as sanctions and aid suspension. Case studies of DFID in Peru and Sida in Kenya suggest that opportunities for engagement are greater at certain times, for example, during political transitions, although resistance will also be found at other levels in government and society (such as resistance to equal gender relations).

When state fragility is more clearly linked to a lack of will than capacity, human rights can play an important role in donor engagement. They can provide a tool to analyze power relations and state capacity issues behind that lack of will. They offer an entry point for dialogue based on an international, rather than bilateral, approach. Special human rights procedures can be used as part of fact-finding and guiding an international response (e.g., human rights missions could have been listened to prior to the 1994 genocide in Rwanda). When the political environment permits, a human rights–based approach to aid can support social change processes to demand more effective and accountable states, or focus on the core rights required for change (e.g., freedom of expression and association or a move to more equitable services).

Partner governments often claim that human rights are an externally imposed agenda. This would seem to conflict with the principle of national ownership, where partner countries exercise effective leadership over their development policies and strategies and coordinate development actions. In response, agencies refer to fundamental rights entrenched in national constitutions and domestic legal standards, as well as the (freely entered into) international human rights obligations: Aid can help partner countries to meet those commitments, primarily through capacity development support.

Donors may support partner country actors' participation in poverty reduction strategy processes, thereby allowing wider constituencies to engage and supporting domestic accountability. In Uganda, for example, DFID has funded participatory processes, including a focus on pastoralist communities. UNDP has supported the Uganda Human Rights Commission in policy debates, and a coalition of civil society organizations has advocated for a human rights–based approach to the Poverty Eradication Action Plan revisions, leading to greater emphasis on equity considerations. More lessons about the integration of human rights in poverty reduction strategies may emerge from research on poverty and human rights by the Geneva-based International Council on Human Rights Policy. Lessons may also be drawn from current OHCHR efforts, such as the application of the Draft Guidelines on a Human Rights Approach to Poverty Reduction Strategies (OHCHR 2003) and the piloting of the approach by HURIST in a limited set of countries.

Despite these strategies to overcome resistance and encourage partner country ownership challenges remain. In some countries gaps persist between the improved frameworks and their actual implementation, leading to impunity gaps and lack of access to justice for all. In other countries certain groups remain the subject of systemic discrimination (e.g., homosexuals in some African countries). Standstills or setbacks can occur, despite continued donor support (including training and study tours, for example) and sustained diplomatic pressure at country and multilateral levels.

Key International Reference Points

A number of key international reference points guide agencies in integrating human rights into development policies, including the Millennium Development Goals (MDGs) and aspects of the aid effectiveness agenda. Since 2006, such reference points have become increasingly explicit about the centrality of human rights to the attainment of the MDGs and about aid effectiveness. While progress has been slow, and while challenges persist, agencies have continued to work to meet the MDGs and to explore how human rights might advance that work and support the goals of aid effectiveness.

Millennium Development Goals and the 2010 Summit Outcome Document

Poverty reduction and the MDGs are now at the center of most agencies' policies and strategies; progress toward the MDGs is being used to plan and monitor agency performance. The 2000 Millennium Declaration (UN 2000) and the 2010 MDG Summit Outcome Document

(UN 2010d) make explicit references to human rights, but the MDGs themselves (box 4.11) are not identical to the existing human rights framework (table 4.1). In fact, some have argued that certain MDGs may undermine international human rights law standards (Darrow 2012). For a number of agencies, however, the MDGs and human rights

---

Box 4.11 Millennium Development Goals

The eight Millennium Development Goals are:

1. Eradicate extreme poverty and hunger.
2. Achieve universal primary education.
3. Promote gender equality and empower women.
4. Reduce child mortality.
5. Improve maternal health.
6. Combat HIV/AIDS, malaria, and other diseases.
7. Ensure environmental sustainability.
8. Develop a global partnership for development.

The MDGs are accompanied by 18 targets to be reached mostly by 2015 and are measured with 60 indicators (UN 2000). At the September 2010 UN Summit on the MDGs, donors reaffirmed their commitment to meeting the goals by 2015 and refocused their attention on the countries and goals that were most off-track. For example, although the right to water and malaria control was found to be on-track, maternal and child mortality, as well as sanitation, were identified as significantly off-track (UN 2010d).

Source: UN 2000, 2010d.

Table 4.1 Possible Links between the Millennium Development Goal Targets and Human Rights

MDG 1. Eradicate extreme poverty and hunger.

- Target 1.A Halve, between 1990 and 2015, the proportion of people whose income is less than $1 a day.
  - *Right to adequate standard of living*
- Target 1.B Achieve full and productive employment and decent work for all, including women and young people.
  - *Right to work*
- Target 1.C Halve, between 1990 and 2015, the proportion of people who suffer from hunger.
  - *Right to food*

MDG 2. Achieve universal primary education.

- Target 2.A Ensure that, by 2015, all children everywhere, boys and girls alike, will be able to complete a full course of primary schooling.
  - *Right to education*

(cotinued next page)

Table 4.1 (Continued)

MDG 3. Promote gender equality and empower women.

- Target 3.A Eliminate gender disparity in primary and secondary education, preferably by 2005, and in all levels of education no later than 2015.
  - *Women's rights to equality*

MDG 4. Reduce child mortality.

- Target 4.A Reduce by two-thirds, between 1990 and 2015, the under-five mortality rate.
  - *Right to life*

MDG 5. Improve maternal health.

- Target 5.A Reduce by three-quarters, between 1990 and 2015, the maternal mortality ratio.
  - *Women's right to life and health*
- Target 5.B Achieve, by 2015, universal access to reproductive health.
  - *Women's right to life and health*

MDG 6. Combat HIV/AIDS, malaria, and other diseases.

- Target 6.A Have halted by 2015 and begun to reverse the spread of HIV/AIDS.
  - *Right to health*
- Target 6.B Achieve, by 2010, universal access to treatment for HIV/AIDS for all those who need it.
  - *Right to health*
- Target 6.C Have halted by 2015 and begun to reverse the incidence of malaria and other major diseases.
  - *Right to health*

MDG 7. Ensure environmental sustainability.

- Target 7.A Integrate the principles of sustainable development into country policies and programs and reverse the loss of environmental resources.
  - *Right to environmental health*
- Target 7.B Reduce biodiversity loss, achieving, by 2010, a significant reduction in the rate of loss.
  - *Right to environmental health*
- Target 7.C Halve, by 2015, the proportion of people without sustainable access to safe drinking water and basic sanitation.
  - *Right to water and sanitation*
- Target 7.D By 2020 to have achieved a significant improvement in the lives of at least 100 million slum dwellers.
  - *Right to adequate housing*

MDG 8. Develop a global partnership for development.

- Targets 8.A–D Cover aid, trade, debt, landlocked, and small island states.
  - *Right to development*
  - *Economic, social and cultural rights*
- Target 8.E In cooperation with pharmaceutical companies, provide access to affordable essential drugs in developing countries.
  - *Right to health*
- Target 8.F In cooperation with the private sector, make available the benefits of new technologies, especially information and communications.
  - *Economic, social and cultural rights*

Source: OHCHR 2008a.

are fully compatible frameworks, given that the MDGs are derived from the UN conferences of the 1990s, which included human rights and social development objectives.

During a midterm review of progress toward meeting the MDGs, the OHCHR concluded that human rights had not yet played a significant role in MDG development planning (OHCHR 2008a). Concerns were expressed that the MDG targets do not focus enough on the poorest of the poor or on inequality within a country—several MDGs require only the halving of a certain poverty indicator. Similarly, some commentators point to the limited nature of obligations under the MDGs, in that they ignore civil and political rights and can be achieved without reaching the most vulnerable and excluded groups (UN Women 2011a). Furthermore, OHCHR has stated that some MDG targets are not consistent with human rights and could diminish gains enshrined in international human rights treaties. For example, MDG 2 calls for universal primary school education but does not require that such education be free, consistent with human rights obligations under the ICESCR. Finally, the special adviser to the UN High Commissioner for Human Rights on the MDGs found that there was a wide discrepancy between the treatment of human rights in reporting on MDG progress and actual program content (Alston 2005; OHCHR 2008a). Alston's earlier work (2004) applies a human rights perspective on the MDGs, providing a detailed review of the debates and recommendations.

A 2010 UNDP review of progress concluded that the MDGs have led to unprecedented commitments, partnerships, and progress in combating poverty and hunger, improving school enrollment, fostering gender equality, and extending equal access to health care. Nevertheless, progress was found to be uneven across sectors and within countries. The review does not emphasize how HRBAs are contributing to the achievement of the MDGs; although it acknowledges that the legal empowerment of women catalyzes progress across all the MDGs and that weak governance and a lack of respect for the rule of law are development challenges (UNDP 2010b).

In addition to the use of indicators, some agencies are looking at legal tools, such as public interest litigation, to help ensure that the

MDGs are met. For example, UNDP Turkey is working with Turkey's National Bar Association on possible strategies for litigating human and constitutional rights in Turkey's administrative courts. That would involve filing lawsuits when failure to make progress on the MDGs is associated with violations of corresponding human rights. By drawing explicit legal links between MDGs and human rights through litigation, UNDP Turkey hopes to promote this link in theory and practice (UNDP 2007).

In September 2010, world leaders came to the UN headquarters in New York for an MDG summit to examine ways to accelerate progress on meeting the MDGs by 2015. The result of the summit was a document entitled "Keeping the Promise: United to Achieve the Millennium Development Goals" ("MDGs Summit Outcome document"; UN 2010d). The document contains numerous human rights references and commitments and gives broad support to the linkages between human rights and the MDGs. Particular emphasis was placed on the principles of equality and nondiscrimination, and gender equality principles in particular, while the principles of participation and accountability were featured less prominently (Darrow 2012). Overall, the Summit Outcome document "reads like a checklist for a human rights approach to achieving the MDGs" (OHCHR and CESR 2011).

Agencies have responded to the challenges surrounding the MDGs in a variety of ways by:

- Linking the MDGs to specific human rights standards and indicators (box 4.12; table 4.1).
- Highlighting the Millennium Declaration (as well as the MDGs) in their policy statements, so as to keep the full range of human rights standards and principles to the fore. For example, SDC has highlighted its contribution to human rights in Switzerland's national report for the Millennium Summit.
- Illustrating how a human rights–based approach to meeting the MDGs can be adopted. For example, DFID has developed a tool to promote an HRBA to maternal mortality. Its social exclusion policy aims to ensure that efforts to meet the MDGs also reach excluded individuals and groups. UNDP and OHCHR have also provided

Box 4.12 Linking the Millennium Development Goals and Human Rights Indicators

As a cross-cutting concern for the achievement of all the MDGs, gender equality is not well reflected in the global targets and indicators. In its biennial reports on the status of the world's women and girls, UN Women and its predecessor, UNIFEM, analyzed progress made, or lack thereof, under each of the MDGs—not only those that explicitly mention women and children (goals 2 through 5) (UNIFEM 2008; UN Women 2011a). In so doing, the agency works to ensure that progress made on reaching the MDGs does not mask gender inequalities that remain. For example, MDG 1 calls for the eradication of extreme hunger and poverty. In areas where households report a decrease in poverty, figures often do not account for the distribution of income *within* households. In Malawi, household surveys indicate that among the small percentage of married women who earn a cash income, only a third have any input in how that money is spent. As a result, sex-disaggregated household income data are needed to know whether such women are indeed living in poverty.

CEDAW and the Beijing Platform for Action set further-reaching obligations than the MDGs. In cooperation with the German Federal Ministry for Economic Cooperation and Development (BMZ) and GTZ, UNIFEM has developed a tool to show how the MDGs can be used as a vehicle for Beijing and CEDAW implementation at the national level. In *Pathway to Gender Equality* (UNIFEM 2004b), each goal is accompanied by an analysis of the gender issues it raises and an identification of CEDAW and Beijing commitments to inform national MDG reporting and implementation strategies.

In March 2006, the UN Special Rapporteur on the right to health submitted to the Commission on Human Rights a report containing a human rights–based approach to health indicators covering structural factors, processes, and outcomes and linking human rights norms to duty-bearers and the principle of nondiscrimination. These indicators were developed to make it easier to measure progress in meeting the health MDGs and to promote the right to health, including dimensions ignored in the MDGs, such as mental health (UNESCO 2006).

some strong guidance on applying HRBA to the MDGs (UNDP 2007; OHCHR 2008a).

- Integrating perspectives, such as gender, in the MDGs to ensure that vulnerable groups are not left behind (UN Women 2011a).

Looking ahead, the international community is debating the development framework that will succeed the MDGs after 2015 and the role that human rights principles and obligations might play in that. OHCHR is encouraging the global community to focus on accountability gaps in the MDGs and to use the international human rights standards, principles, instruments, and mechanisms to fill them. Along with the Center for Economic and Social Rights (CESR) the OHCHR will be launching a joint publication on the relevance of the human rights framework for the purpose of meaningful and effective MDG accountability.

The 25th Anniversary of the Right to Development

December 2011 marked the 25th anniversary of the U.N. Declaration on the Right to Development, which in 1986 reoriented development to be centered around people. In anticipation of this anniversary, 18 intergovernmental organizations and specialized agencies of the United Nations issued a joint statement that reaffirmed the commitments made in the 2010 MDG Outcome document and that the right to development is "an inalienable human right by virtue" (UN 2011b). It stated that their work is guided by the human rights principles of nondiscrimination, equality, participation, transparency, and accountability. They further emphasized that:

> this Declaration has provided normative underpinnings for a human-centered approach to development. Human development and human rights are embedded and reinforce each other conceptually and in practice, helping to secure the well-being and dignity of all people. (UN 2011b)

This interagency statement was preceded by a July 2011 joint statement of nine chairpersons of the U.N. treaty bodies that reflects on the interdependence and indivisibility of civil, political, economic, social, and cultural rights. The chairpersons resolved to "promote a development-informed and interdependence-based reading of all human rights treaties so as to highlight and emphasize the relevance and importance of the right to development in interpreting and applying human rights treaty provisions and in monitoring compliance with these provisions."

In 2004, on the recommendation of the Working Group on the Right to Development, the UN Commission on Human Rights established a high-level task force on the implementation of the right to development. The task force's primary focus has been to help achieve Millennium Development Goal 8 by developing and applying criteria for evaluating global partnerships for development to make them more effective. The task force concluded its mandate by submitting to the Working Group a report that enumerates criteria and operational subcriteria developed to assess progress on implementation of the right to development and to evaluate the human rights implications of development activities and trade policies (UN 2010e).

Aid Effectiveness

Aid effectiveness has been a global policy issue of growing importance over the past decade, and the potential relevance of human rights to aid effectiveness has begun to be recognized. Following the September 2000 Millennium Summit, where world leaders issued the UN Millennium Declaration establishing the MDGs framework, a number of critical global gatherings have taken place. In March 2002, the UN International Conference on Financing for Development was held in Monterrey, Mexico, leading to the Monterrey Consensus, which enumerated the actions needed to promote a global partnership for development to accelerate progress toward the MDGs. The Monterrey Consensus includes several references to rights, particularly in the context of good governance, noting:

> Sound economic policies, solid democratic institutions responsive to the needs of the people and improved infrastructure are the basis for sustained economic growth, poverty eradication and employment creation. Freedom, peace and security, domestic stability, respect for human rights, including the right to development, and the rule of law, gender equality, market-oriented policies, and an overall commitment to just and democratic societies are also essential and mutually reinforcing. (UN 2003b)

Following regional preparatory workshops in Jamaica, Vietnam, and Ethiopia, the OECD organized the first of four high-level forums on aid effectiveness in February 2003: the High-Level Forum on Harmonization, in Rome, Italy. More than 40 bilateral and multilateral development institutions and 28 partner countries agreed to the Rome Declaration on Harmonization, a common set of principles to improve the management and effectiveness of aid. The Rome declaration focuses exclusively on commitments by *donors* and addresses the issue of harmonization of donor procedures and practices to reduce transaction costs for partner countries. It marked the first time that principles for aid effectiveness were outlined in a political declaration.

In 2005, the DAC organized the Second High-Level Forum on Aid Effectiveness, in Paris, France. Its outcome document, the Paris Declaration on Aid Effectiveness (OECD 2005a), set out a road map to improve the quality of aid and increase its impact on development. At least 136 donor and partner countries and 28 multilateral organizations currently adhere to the declaration, which enumerates five fundamental principles for making aid more effective:

1. Ownership. Partner countries exercise effective leadership over their development policies and strategies and coordinate development actions.
2. Alignment. Donors base their overall support on partner countries' national development strategies, institutions, and procedures.
3. Harmonization. Donor countries coordinate, simplify procedures, and share information to avoid duplication.
4. Managing for results. Developing countries and donors shift focus to development results and results are measured.
5. Mutual accountability. Donors and partners are accountable for development results.

In the years immediately following the Paris Declaration, the DAC Human Rights Task Team has explored the connection between aid effectiveness and human rights principles, ultimately adopting the Action-Oriented Paper on Human Rights and Development (AOPP) (OECD 2007a). Among the 10 principles elaborated in the AOPP (box 1.1, chapter 1), several underscore the connections between human rights and aid effectiveness:

• Consider mutual reinforcement between human rights and aid effectiveness principles (Principle 7). DAC members should consider human rights principles, analysis, and practice in the roll-out of the Paris Declaration's partnership commitments. The Paris Declaration principles should be followed in designing and implementing human rights programs.
• Consider human rights in decisions on alignment and aid instruments (Principle 6). It is important to take the inclusiveness of government strategies, and their responsiveness to the perspectives of different interest groups and actors in a country—including the

marginalized and most vulnerable—into consideration when assessing ownership and making decisions on alignment behind government strategies. The human rights context should also inform—in part—donors' choice of aid instruments and the appropriate balance of support to state and non-state actors. A range of instruments that can help strengthen accountability and ensure that resources reach those who have difficulty in accessing services and exercising their rights should be considered.

- Ensure that the scaling up of aid is conducive to human rights (Principle 10). In an era of scaled-up aid, it is important to avoid the perception that the provision of additional resources is an endorsement of poor human rights performance. Moreover, it is vital to avert the risk of negative effects on accountability and governments' willingness to tackle deep-rooted problems. Efforts to increase aid should therefore move in tandem with the strengthening of human rights institutions, accountability mechanisms, and related capacities (OECD 2007a; 2007b).

A diverse group of stakeholders came together in Accra, Ghana, in September 2008 for the Third High-Level Forum on Aid Effectiveness. In addition to charting progress made in implementing the Paris Declaration, the forum yielded the Accra Agenda for Action (AAA) (2008). The AAA encouraged developing countries to take ownership of their own development by exercising leadership in development policies and in setting economic, social, and environmental goals. The AAA also encouraged South-South partnerships, dialogue at the country level, and capacity building of country systems. The AAA noted that progress had been made on overall development indicators but also that challenges, such as rising food and fuel prices, as well as climate change, could threaten those gains.

As a follow-up to the forums held in Rome, Paris, and Accra, more than 3,000 delegates came together for the Fourth High-Level Forum on Aid Effectiveness (HLF4) in late 2011 in Busan, Korea, to review implementation of the Paris Declaration, including the results of the 2011 Survey on Monitoring the Paris Declaration. It found that at the global level only one out of the 13 targets established for 2010 had been met: coordinated technical cooperation on capacity development.

The progress report on implementation of the Paris Declaration noted substantial progress in two areas: the number of developing countries that have established sound national development strategies has more than tripled since 2005, and high-quality, results-oriented frameworks are increasingly in place (OECD 2011b).

The event concluded with the Busan Partnership for Effective Development Cooperation, a framework for development cooperation that includes established and emerging donors, South-South partnerships, civil society organizations, and private funders. The process was guided by the DAC Working Party on Aid Effectiveness, which includes representatives of more than 80 nations and organizations. The Busan declaration underscores the importance of human rights in development cooperation, making several references to human rights. Paragraph 11 of the Busan declaration notes that developed and developing countries "share common principles which—consistent with our agreed international commitments on human rights, decent work, gender equality, environmental sustainability and disability—form the foundation of our cooperation for effective development." The declaration further emphasizes the role that civil society organizations play in "enabling people to claim their rights, in promoting human rights–based approaches, in shaping development policies and partnerships, and in overseeing their implementation." Finally, paragraph 28 calls on developed and developing countries to "rethink what aid should be spent on and how, in ways that are consistent with agreed international rights, norms and standards, so that aid catalyzes development" (OECD 2011c). Also significant at the Busan meeting was the thematic session held on HRBAs, entitled "Better Integration of a Rights-Based Approach into the Aid Effectiveness Agenda: Towards Inclusive Development." The event brought together government officials and human rights experts to debate the importance of human rights for development effectiveness and in particular to explore how human rights principles such as empowerment, inclusion, and participation strengthen the application of aid effectiveness principles, such as ownership, accountability, and transparency, as acknowledged in the Paris Declaration and paragraph 13(c) of the AAA. Through the presentation of evidence and operational examples, the session sought to explore the role of a human rights–based approach in advancing aid effectiveness and development results, as well as to encourage concrete political action to better integrate rights-based approaches into development cooperation.

Sustainable Development

A recent international event highlighted the importance of human rights in the context of sustainable development: the UN Conference on Sustainable Development—"Rio + 20"—was held in Rio de Janeiro, Brazil, in June 2012. The purpose of the conference was to take stock of progress on commitments made at the 1992 UN Conference on Environment and Development, which resulted in the Rio Principles and "Agenda 21." The outcome document of Rio + 20 reaffirms the importance of all human rights, including the right to development (paragraph 8), as well as the importance of the Universal Declaration of Human Rights and other international law instruments relating to human rights, emphasizing states' obligations to respect, protect, and promote human rights and fundamental freedoms for all (paragraph 9). The outcome document further affirms that green economy policies, in the context of sustainable development and poverty eradication, should "promote sustained and inclusive economic growth, foster innovation and provide opportunities, benefits and empowerment for all and respect all human rights" (paragraph 58).

Aid Allocations and Aid Modalities

Assessments of whether human rights are being met and of the kind of additional resources needed to allow partner governments to better respect, protect, and fulfill human rights, are already contributing to aid allocation decisions. This is a sensitive area, as it is closely related to the use of political conditionality and the withholding or suspension of aid in certain circumstances. Some agencies are using publicly available sets of human rights and governance indicators to identify and reward good performance (box 4.13). The assessment of good governance, including "a minimum respect for human rights, a free press, pluralistic democracy and rule of law, including independence of the judiciary," is an established step in the assessment of whether to provide Danish budget support to partner countries.

Box 4.13 The U.S. Millennium Challenge Corporation

The U.S. Millennium Challenge Corporation (MCC), created in 2004, aims not to use U.S. political or foreign policy objectives to select beneficiary countries. Instead, it first identifies a set of countries based on their per capita income. It then uses 17 third-party indicators, in three categories, to measure candidate countries:

- Ruling justly (civil rights, political rights, control of corruption, government effectiveness, rule of law, voice, and accountability);
- Investing in people (immunization rates, public expenditure on health, girls' primary education completion rate, public expenditure on primary education, and natural resource management); and
- Encouraging economic freedom (business start-up, land rights and access, trade policy, regulatory quality, inflation, and fiscal policy) (MCC 2011).

It explicitly uses governance indicators and draws on the six dimensions of the World Bank Institute's database, which itself uses a range of human rights indicators. Countries then become eligible to submit proposals for Millennium Challenge Account funding. The board can exercise discretion in the selection process, to consider data weaknesses, additional qualitative information, or if a country performs very poorly on any indicator. However, care must be taken that use of discretion does not lead to a repoliticization of the selection process. USAID recently commissioned an independent evaluation of MCC and concluded that the agency is largely aligned with the Paris declaration principles (USAID 2011a).

Chapter 2 illustrated how, traditionally, human rights were addressed through stand-alone projects or are now being mainstreamed in sector programs. A number of donor agencies are concerned that, in the current shift to program aid modalities (such as general budget support or sectorwide approaches), a focus on human rights is being lost. Some agencies are, for example, cutting down on nonprogram aid interventions, such as support to civil society organizations or grassroots activities, as the activities are perceived as more difficult to design and manage. Yet they are considered a central element of integrating human rights into development cooperation, by supporting the ability of rights-holders to become aware of, claim, and enforce their rights.

Agencies are responding to this dilemma. For example, the German Development Bank (KfW) commissioned a study and portfolio analysis of the relevance of HRBAs for financial cooperation (Heinz 2006). Some agencies have already developed tools to ground their choice of aid modalities based on country analysis, including human rights and governance (box 4.14). Research suggests that a mix of aid instruments is desirable (Booth and Curran 2005). Program aid needs to be seen in the context of a range of options: appropriate policy dialogue, technical advice, and capacity development support to enable governments to identify and implement their national priorities. Finally, donors and governments need to build more effective accountability mechanisms, which can help integrate human rights into aid initiatives.

Policy Coherence

Legal and Policy Considerations

In the development context, policy coherence can be understood as "strengthening synergies and weeding out inconsistencies between non-aid policies and development objectives" (European Commission 2011e). It can promote effectiveness and efficiencies in aid allocations, as it minimizes duplication and ensures that policy efforts are not contradictory; it can also serve to uphold a principle of "do no harm" in development. The pursuit of policy coherence is consistent with core aims and principles of the Paris Declaration and the AAA. The pursuit of coherence is a useful exercise in assessing the impacts that a policy may have on other policies or individuals. It can also add value—coherence across both related and diverse policy arenas maximizes the potential for synergies at an operational level (McInerney-Lankford 2009).

International treaties may provide a relevant reference point for policy coherence. The DAC noted that:

> The fact that both donor and partner countries have ratified the international human rights treaties provides a uniquely valuable reference

point for harmonization efforts. A mutually agreed, universal normative framework already exists, supported not only by political commitment, but also by the force of legal obligation. As well, at the operational
level, there is growing convergence on the integration of human rights in
development. (OECD 2007b)

The integration of human rights within development assistance is
consistent with the need for donors to improve the coherence of their
aid with their other policies, an issue already firmly on the DAC agenda.
Indeed, human rights have traditionally been part of foreign policy, and
in a number of countries, ministries of foreign affairs have the overall lead on human rights. They often lack leverage over other ministries
that implement policies of immediate relevance for overseas countries
(e.g., defense or external trade). Initiatives that use aid to pursue human
rights objectives, and to ensure that aid does not contribute to human
rights violations overseas, may promote policy coherence.

The coherence challenge has been easier to overcome for agencies already working closely with (or integrated into) the ministries of
foreign affairs (box 4.15). Other agencies have been developing closer
relationships and worked more strategically with ministries of defense,
trade, or interior. The Austrian Development Agency, for example, had
organized a training workshop on the protection of children's rights
in emergency situations with the Austrian Ministries of Defense and
Foreign Affairs.

Policy coherence has a role to play at the national level as well as at
the international level. For example, DFID distinguishes between two
types of policy coherence: "coherence across UK government policies

---

Box 4.15 Swedish and Dutch Models for Aid Policy Coherence

In 2003, the Parliament of Sweden unanimously adopted a policy on global development, requiring that the "perspectives of the poor" and a "rights perspective" be
systematically adopted (Government of Sweden 2003a). Sida is working through
the implications of this policy, which requires significantly greater coherence internally within Sida and also across the ministry of foreign affairs and other ministries.
Coherence is facilitated in the Netherlands by the fact that the aid program is developed and implemented through the ministry of foreign affairs and its embassies. This
has made it easier to integrate human rights with development cooperation and other
responsibilities of the embassies. A handout was produced to guide dialogue.

and coherence within multilateral institutions such as the European Commission" (McInerney-Lankford 2009). Likewise, Sweden reported that its policy for development cooperation "was not only aiming to empower partner countries with increased budget support but was also promoting overall coherence among policies within its own boundaries as well as in the recipient countries with a view to contribute to the promotion and protection of human rights both domestically and internationally" (Salomon 2007).

WHO, OHCHR, and Sida recently developed a tool for supporting countries to ensure policy coherence between the design and implementation of national health sector strategies and their legal obligations and commitments. The tool employs three assessment levels:

- Assessment Level 1. State obligations and commitments made on human rights and gender equality.
- Assessment Level 2. Translating human rights and gender equality obligations and commitments in the national legal, policy, and institutional framework.
- Assessment Level 3. Identifying human rights and gender equality obligations and commitments in national health sector strategies (WHO 2011a).

In the Council of Europe, a recent initiative can also be considered in policy coherence terms, albeit domestically focused on member states' internal social and poverty reduction policies. In 2011 the Parliamentary Assembly of the Council of Europe issued a recommendation that its 47 member states should be guided by OHCHR's 2006 Principles and Guidelines on a Human Rights Approach to Poverty Reduction in their policy making and budget decisions; member state progress will be assessed by the Assembly in 2013 (Council of Europe 2011; see box 4.16).

Fragmentation of Public International Law

Despite the convergence between development cooperation objectives and human rights principles, policy coherence faces significant challenges. Development policy frameworks and human rights obligations have generally evolved on parallel tracks. Where integration has occurred, it more frequently entails the loose application of human

> **Box 4.16 Policy Coherence for Development in the European Union**
>
> Policy coherence is a long-established priority for EU development cooperation. This was reiterated in the 2006 European Consensus on Development and affirmed in Article 208 of the Lisbon Treaty, which requires the European Union to "take account of the objectives of development cooperation in the policies that it implements which are likely to affect developing countries."
>
> To that end, the 2009 European Commission Impact Assessment Guidelines require an assessment of proposed new policies' coherence with the objectives of EU development policy, as well as an assessment of their potential impact on developing countries (European Commission 2009c).
>
> In May 2010, the European Parliament created the Standing Rapporteur on Policy Coherence for Development, responsible for facilitating more interaction between the parliamentary committee on development and other committees (European Parliament 2010a). Policy coherence for development focal points have also been appointed within the European Commission Directorates-General and the External Action Service. This is supported also by a 2010 European Parliament resolution that mandates the respect of human rights and social and environmental standards in international trade agreements. It also requires that those standards take precedence over respect of the rules of the WTO and encourages greater cooperation at the multilateral level between the WTO and the main UN human rights institutions (European Parliament 2010b).

rights principles and language rather than legal obligations under internationally agreed upon instruments (McInerney-Lankford 2009).

This divergence is further complicated by the diverse array of international regulatory regimes that exist, many with potential relevance for development—the international human rights framework being just one. Trade and regional economic integration and cooperation represent a second set of regimes with distinct objectives and regulatory instruments. A third category of international regime pertains to development issues, such as economic growth, poverty reduction, and sustainable development through lending and technical assistance. International oversight of the environment and the protection of natural resources occupy a separate realm. A fifth regime applies to security, cooperation, and humanitarian affairs (NTF 2011b). While there are thematic overlaps among these regimes, each possesses its own normative frameworks, procedures, institutions, and approaches. Understanding and reconciling these multiple frameworks and their relevance to development for the purposes of coherence may present considerable challenges.

Even where the convergence appears to be more intuitive, disconnects are evident. For instance, although the Millennium Declaration makes reference to human rights, the MDGs and their targets contain no reference to human rights. Similarly, poverty reduction strategy papers (PRSPs), descriptions of policies and programs that a country will pursue to promote growth and reduce poverty, rarely incorporate rights language or references to international human rights treaties (Stewart and Wang 2005).

Budgetary Challenges

Donor agencies have faced an additional challenge in recent years due to the 2008 financial crisis. Some foreign aid budgets have been reduced, and an stronger focus has been placed on demonstrating the value of aid. Austria's overseas development budget fell to 0.3 percent of GNP, instead of continuously rising toward the expected 0.5 percent in 2010, and 0.7 percent in 2015, the target year for reaching the Millennium Development Goals (Global Responsibility 2011). As a result, Austria's Ministry of Foreign Affairs, which develops the Austrian Development Cooperation (ADC) strategies and programs that are implemented by the Austrian Development Agency (ADA), has had to move out of several partner countries and programs. Likewise, the Canadian International Development Agency (CIDA) announced in its recent Aid Effectiveness Action Plan that it would be focusing 80 percent of its resources in 20 countries, down from approximately 34, and on five priority themes, in an effort to make its assistance more focused, effective, and accountable (CIDA 2009b). These concentrations of activities in more limited areas and sectors may ultimately help ADA and CIDA harmonize programming with other donors in line with the Paris Declaration principles.

In some instances however, the global financial crisis has coincided with a continued increase in aid and emphasis on demonstrating its effective use. For example, in 2011 Spain unveiled its new Fund for the Promotion of Development (FONPRODE). It has kept its aid budget on a steadily rising trajectory, with a goal for overseas development assistance to reach 0.7 percent in 2012. To ensure that these funds are well spent, a working group was recently created to establish a new focus on the quality and efficacy of Spanish aid distribution as a horizontal priority (FRIDE 2010). Similarly, Australia's aid budget has doubled over the last six years. By 2016–17 the annual aid figure is estimated to reach around $8 billion to $9 billion (0.5 percent of Gross National Income). The Office of Development Effectiveness, established in 2006, conducted a thorough independent review of aid effectiveness in 2011, making recommendations on how the program could be less fragmented and could improve its performance management system. The review is introduced with the explanation that "Australians want their contribution to be effective. They want to know that there is value for money; that it is having a real impact on the lives of people" (Government of Australia 2011). Likewise, Canada's prime minister of international cooperation remarked that "Canadians want to know that their tax dollars are spent wisely and effectively" (CIDA 2011a). But when such value is demonstrated, it can also have positive effects.

With a number of initiatives to merge into their existing development initiatives (e.g., gender mainstreaming), in addition to integrating human rights principles, agencies are being asked to do more with less. Successes with information sharing and joint reporting, however, are being reported, such as UNHCR's collaboration with UNICEF on presenting input to expert committees on refugee children (box 4.17).

Findings and Issues for Further Consideration

Donors face several challenges in further integrating human rights: institutionalizing the approach internally within agencies; working on human rights issues positively with partner governments, particularly in fragile states; and making sure that a human rights–based approach influences the manner in which key issues on aid effectiveness and new aid modalities are framed and understood. Moreover, questions remain about what lessons can be learned from the MDG process and applied to the post-2015 development agenda.

With regard to the institutionalization of human rights policies, donors could more regularly share tools and guidance documents and undertake joint training, rather than investing in them separately:

- A knowledge management (and possibly advisory) center for interested agencies would provide a helpful mechanism to enable agencies to learn more systematically from one another. Although the UN HRBA portal (box 4.5) is a useful online repository for documents,

Box 4.17 European Union Development Policy: An Agenda for Change

The European Union (including member states plus commission-managed funds) is the largest donor of official development aid worldwide. In 2010, it provided €53.8 billion, or more than 50 percent of global aid. The European Commission is responsible for the management of €11 billion of aid per year, putting it in second place among donors globally. In the context of the current economic crisis facing Europe, EU officials have been under increasing pressure to defend aid program expenditures (Tran 2011).

Following consideration of two green papers published by the European Commission in 2010, one on the future of development policy and the other on the instrument of budget support, two new policies emerged in October 2011. The first, "Increasing the Impact of EU Development Policy: An Agenda for Change," seeks to focus aid on fewer countries and fewer sectors, while prioritizing two thematic areas: human rights, democracy, and other elements of good governance; and inclusive and sustainable growth for sustainable development (European Commission 2011c). The second paper, "The Future Approach to EU Budget Support to Third Countries" (European Commission 2011d), reiterates the linkage between human rights and development, indicating that its proposed approach "would lead to enhanced importance of human rights, democracy and good governance trends in determining the mix of instruments and aid modalities at country level." These linkages would present conditions for partner countries to meet at the outset of an agreement as well as during its execution. The budget support policy recommends,

> The EU should assess whether pre-conditions exist to entrust Good Governance and Development Contracts to a partner country, i.e., whether fundamental values of human rights, democracy and rule of law or a clear path towards international standards exist and whether such a Contract could clearly act as a driver to accelerate this movement. (European Commission 2011d)

According to the Agenda for Change, if a client country were to "loosen its commitment to human rights and democracy" during the lifespan of the development contract, the "EU should strengthen its cooperation with non-state actors and local authorities and use forms of aid that provide the poor with the support they need. At the same time, the EU should maintain dialogue with governments and non-state actors. In some cases, stricter conditionality will be warranted" (European Commission 2011c). The EU hopes that by focusing its aid in targeted ways and tying budget support to progress made in good governance, the EU can leverage its impact and demonstrate the effectiveness of the aid it is disbursing.

On December 12, 2011, the Commission and the High Representative of the EU for Foreign Affairs and Security Policy issued a joint communication to the European Parliament and the Council to explore how European institutions can help make the EU's external human rights and democracy policy more effective and coherent (European Commission 2011f). Recalling that the EU has been committed to mainstreaming human rights and democracy throughout its development cooperation, the commission recommends that these issues "run as a 'silver thread' throughout EU external policies." The communication further states that country human rights strategies and a human rights–based approach should ensure that human rights and democracy are reflected across the entire development cooperation process and ensure continuity between political and policy dialogue on human rights issues and development cooperation.

and HuriTalk provides a platform for discussion about HRBA, nei-
ther presently performs any analysis of case studies or has produced
a common template to facilitate comparative learning, potentially
limiting their use by practitioners.

- Identification and documentation of examples of "do no harm" policies, possibly including past negative impacts and how they can be
overcome, would demonstrate the value of that approach.
- To enhance donor accountability, codes of conduct for staff and project implementers could be developed. Complaint and redress mechanisms would allow beneficiaries to hold agencies to account.
- The area of human rights related monitoring and evaluation requires more comprehensive review. It would be helpful to see further
work providing more evidence of the impact of human rights on the
achievement of development objectives (UNDG-HRM 2011) such as
poverty reduction. This process might include application of human
rights indicators linked to the MDGs developed by organizations
such as OHCHR (2008b), UNDP (2006b), and UNFPA (UNFPA
and Harvard 2010) that are suitable to help document experiences,
to measure the impact of human rights projects and mainstreaming
initiatives, and to inform aid allocation and aid modality decisions
(UNDG-HRM 2011).

To further promote human rights as part of nationally owned strategies, wider consultative processes are needed. Parliamentarians (e.g.,
parliamentary human rights committees), national human rights
institutions (NHRIs), national civil society organizations, and international NGOs should be included to build wide ownership and draw on
considerable country-based experience.

With regard to the ways of delivering and managing aid, donors
could document existing approaches to using human rights to inform
decisions on aid allocations and modalities. This should not be reduced
to the use of selectivity and conditionality and should go beyond
project-based aid. There is much potential cross-fertilization with the
fragile states agenda here.

Responding to paragraph 42 of the Paris Declaration and paragraph 13(c) of the AAA, donors should continue to harmonize their
approaches to human rights. DAC members could also think about

examining the implementation of human rights policies in peer reviews so as to encourage the application of existing commitments and share good experiences.

The application and impact of conditionality have not been well researched; new approaches to aid effectiveness and aid modalities create opportunities to revisit this area. Agreement on a set of principles for the design and application of conditionality, along with improved understanding of partner countries' political trajectories and how internal forces may respond to external pressures, would enhance donor approaches when dealing with governance crises. Clear aims and objectives will make it easier to be consistent and predictabile—in line with partnership commitments. Conditions found in existing partner governments' commitments should be used as far as possible. This refers to constitutions, poverty reduction strategies, and other national frameworks, as well as the relevant international and regional human rights instruments. Maintenance of minimum bottom lines, based on public commitments set in overall aid agreements, is a prerequisite for principled actions by donors if all else fails. Experience also suggests that, for consistency of message and likelihood of impact, coordinated donor action and the use of multilateral channels are essential.

It is increasingly recognized that donors can make better efforts to explore ways in which human rights can be more explicitly linked to the important fragile states agenda. There are various entry points, linked to the "Principles for Good International Engagement in Fragile States" (OECD 2007c), to demonstrate where and how human rights could be made explicit and relevant. One promising approach could be to use human rights analysis as part of "understanding the context" and to adopt a "prevention mode" by focusing on the root causes of state fragility. Use of the "do no harm" principle could be extended to apply to both state capacity and the fundamental rights of the populations.

"Civilian protection" already offers a way of responding to humanitarian crises or violent conflict. A new entry point is the "responsibility to protect," as recently agreed by UN member states at the 2005 World Summit (UN 2005a). Another fruitful option could be to consider the concept of human security (Commission on Human Security 2003) in relation to fragile states and security agendas, as it integrates a focus on human dimensions and therefore human rights.

To promote more harmonized approaches, donors might wish to pilot human rights programming, including policy dialogue, in a selected number of countries, for example, where UN and bilateral agencies have made most progress. It could range from collaborating more closely on ongoing initiatives and documenting joint work, to a more ambitious approach in which new work could be undertaken in the context of enhanced harmonization of work towards human rights at country level.

References

Accra Agenda for Action. 2008. Third High-Level Forum on Aid Effectiveness, September 4, Accra.

ADC (Austrian Development Cooperation). 2011. "Focus: Persons with Disabilities in ADC." May, Vienna.

Alston, Philip. 2004. "A Human Rights Perspective on the Millennium Development Goals." Paper prepared for the Millennium Project Task Force on Poverty and Economic Development, UN, New York.

———. 2005. "Ships Passing in the Night: The Current State of the Human Rights and Development Debate Seen through the Lens of the Millennium Development Goals." *Human Rights Quarterly* 27 (3): 755–829.

AusAID (Australian Agency for International Development). 2006. "China Australia Development Cooperation Program: Review of Human Rights Technical Cooperation Program." Report, AusAID, Canberra.

BMZ (German Federal Ministry for Economic Cooperation and Development). 2010. "Human Rights in Practice: Fact Sheets on a Human Rights–Based Approach in Development Co-operation." November, BMZ, Bonn.

———. 2011b. "Gender Equality in Development Policy. Fact Sheets on Gender Equality in Development Co-operation." September, BMZ, Bonn.

Booth, David, and Zaza Curran. 2005. "Aid Instruments and Exclusion. Developing the Empirical Evidence for DFID's Strategy on Exclusion." London: Overseas Development Institute.

Boyd, David R. 2011. "The Right to Water: A Briefing Note." Presented at the Inter-Action Council High-Level Expert Group Meeting, "The Global Water Crisis: Addressing an Urgent Security Issue," Toronto, March 21–23.

CIDA (Canadian International Development Agency). 2009b. "CIDA's Aid Effectiveness Action Plan. 2009–2012." CIDA, Québec.

———. 2011a. *Development for Results, 2009-2010.* Québec: CIDA.

Commission on Human Security. 2003. *Human Security Now.* New York: Commission on Human Security.

Council of Europe. 2011. "Parliamentary Assembly Recommendation 1963 Combating Poverty." Council of Europe Parliamentary Assembly, Strasbourg.

Darrow, Mac. 2012. "The Millennium Development Goals: Milestones or Millstones? Human Rights Priorities for the Post-2015 Development Agenda." *Yale Human Rights and Development Law Journal* 15 (March): 55–127.

DFID (U.K. Department for International Development). 1997. "Eliminating World Poverty: A Challenge for the 21st Century." White Paper on International Development, DFID, London.

———. 2011a. *Annual Report and Accounts, 2010–2011.* London: DFID.

European Commission. 2009c. "Impact Assessment Guidelines." SEC 2009(92), January 15, Brussels.

———. 2011c. "Increasing the Impact of EU Development Policy: An Agenda for Change." October 13, Brussels.

———. 2011d. "The Future Approach to EU Budget Support to Third Countries." October 13, Brussels.

———. 2011e. "EU 2011 Report on Policy Coherence for Development." Commission Staff Working Paper, SEC, 1627 final, December 15, Brussels.

———. 2011f. "Joint Communication to the European Parliament and the Council: Human Rights and Democracy at the Heart of EU External Action— Towards a More Effective Approach." COM(2011) 886 final, December 12, Brussels.

European Parliament. 2010a. "Report on the EU Policy Coherence for Development and the 'Official Development Assistance Plus' Concept." A7-0140/2010, (2009/2218/(INI)), May 5, Brussels.

———. 2010b. "European Parliament Resolution of 25 November 2010 on Human Rights and Social and Environmental Standards in International Trade Agreements." (2009/2219(INI)), Brussels.

FRIDE (Fundacion para las Relaciones Internacionales y el Dialogo Exterior). 2010. "Democracy Assistance Factsheet: Spain." October 16, FRIDE, Madrid.

Global Responsibility, Austrian Platform for Development and Humanitarian Aid. 2011. "Universal Periodic Review Austria," January, Vienna.

Government of Australia. 2011. "Independent Review of Aid Effectiveness." Commonwealth of Australia, Canberra.

Government of Sweden. 2003a. "Shared Responsibility: Sweden's Policy for Global Development." Government Bill No. 2002/03:122, Stockholm.

GTZ (German Organization for Technical Cooperation). 2009b. "Compilation— Promising Practices on the Human Rights–Based Approach in German Development Cooperation." GTZ, Eschborn.

Heinz, Wolfgang S. 2006. "Menschenrechtsrelevanz in der Arbeit der KfW. Eine Portfolioanalyse ausgewählter Projekte." Berlin: Deutsches Institut für Menschenrechte.

International Civil Service Commission. 2002. "Standards of Conduct for the International Civil Service." New York

MCC (U.S. Millennium Challenge Corporation). 2011. *Guide to the MCC Indicators and the Selection Process, Fiscal Year 2011.* Washington, DC: MCC.

McInerney-Lankford, Siobhán. 2009. "Human Rights and Development: a Comment on Challenges and Opportunities from a Legal Perspective." *Journal of Human Rights Practice* 1 (1): 51–82.

Ministry of Foreign Affairs of Denmark. 2010a. "Peace and Stabilisation: Denmark's Policy Towards Fragile States." September, Copenhagen.

Netherlands Ministry of Foreign Affairs. 2005. "Track Record User Guide: What Level of Alignment Is Possible and What Are the Corresponding Aid Modalities?" Effectiveness and Quality Department, Netherlands Ministry of Foreign Affairs, The Hague.

New Zealand Ministry of Foreign Affairs and Trade. 2011. "International Development Policy Statement: Supporting Sustainable Development." March, Wellington.

Norad. 2001. *Handbook in Human Rights Assessment: State Obligations, Awareness and Empowerment.* Oslo: Norad.

NTF (Nordic Trust Fund. 2010. *Knowledge and Learning for Human Rights and Development: Nordic Trust Fund Progress Report Sept. 2009–Oct. 2010.* Washington, DC: World Bank.

———. 2011b. "Nordic Trust Fund Learning Brief: International Human Rights and Development, An Introduction." World Bank, Washington, DC.

NZAID. 2002. "Human Rights Policy Statement." New Zealand Agency for International Development Cooperation, Wellington.

———. 2004. "NZAID Human Rights Policy: Implementation Plan of Action 2004-09." New Zealand Agency for International Development Cooperation, Wellington.

OECD (Organisation for Economic Cooperation and Development). 2005a. "Paris Declaration on Aid Effectiveness. Ownership, Alignment, Harmonisation, Results and Mutual Accountability." Statement endorsed at the High-Level Forum on Aid Effectiveness, March 2, Paris.

———. 2005b. "Piloting the Principles for Good International Engagement in Fragile States." Concept Note, OECD, Paris.

———. 2007a. "DAC Action-Oriented Policy Paper on Human Rights and Development." February, OECD, Paris.

———. 2007b. "Human Rights and Aid Effectiveness." DAC Update, April, OECD, Paris.

———. 2007c. "DAC Principles for Good International Engagement in Fragile States and Situations." April, OECD, Paris.

———. 2011b. "Aid Effectiveness 2005–10: Progress in Implementing the Paris Declaration." Paris.

———. 2011c. "The Busan Partnership for Effective Development Cooperation." December 1, Paris.

OHCHR (UN High Commissioner for Human Rights). 2003. "Draft Guidelines: Human Rights Approach to Poverty Reduction Strategies." Prepared by Paul

Hunt, Manfred Nowak, and Siddiq Osmani, Office of the United Nations High Commissioner for Human Rights, Geneva.

———. 2008a. *Claiming the Millennium Development Goals: A Human Rights Approach.* New York and Geneva: UN.

———. 2008b. *Report on Indicators for Promoting and Monitoring the Implementation of Human Rights.* Geneva: OHCHR.

OHCHR and CESR. 2011. "The Millennium Development Goals: Who's Accountable?" Concept Note, November, Geneva.

Piron, Laure-Hélène, and Julius Court. 2004. "SDC's Human Rights and Rule of Law Guidance Documents: Influence, Effectiveness and Relevance within SDC." Independent evaluation commissioned by the Swiss Agency for Development and Cooperation, Bern.

Salomon, Margot E. 2007. "International Economic Governance and Human Rights Accountability." LSE Law, Society and Economy Working Papers 9/2007, London School of Economics and Political Science Law Department, London.

SDC (Swiss Agency for Development and Cooperation). 2008b. "Implementation of Governance as a Transversal Theme with a Human Rights–Based Approach." SDC Governance Division, May, Bern.

Sida (Swedish International Development Cooperation Agency). 2011a. "Integrating and Strengthening a Human Rights–Based Approach to Development in Programme Based Approaches: A How-to Note." Draft, Sida, Stockholm.

Stewart, Frances, and Michael Wang. 2005. "Poverty Reduction Strategy Papers within the Human Rights Perspective." In *Human Rights and Development: Towards Mutual Reinforcement.* Ed. Philip Alston and Mary Robinson. 469. Oxford: Oxford University Press.

Tran, Mark. 2011. "EU Aims to Make a Bigger Impact with Its Aid." Poverty Matters Blog, *The Guardian,* London, October 20.

UN (United Nations). 2000. "United Nations Millennium Declaration." September 8, A/RES/55/2, New York.

———. 2003b. "Monterrey Consensus of the International Conference on Financing for Development." March 18–22, 2002, New York.

———. 2005a. "2005 World Summit Outcome." Resolution adopted by the General Assembly, A/RES/60/1, New York.

———. 2007. "Common Country Assessment and United Nations Development Assistance Framework: Guidelines for UN Country Teams on Preparing a CCA and UNDAF." February 15, New York.

———. 2008b. "Optional Protocol to the International Covenant on Economic, Social, and Cultural Rights." December 10, A/RES/63/117, New York.

———. 2009. "Guidelines for UN Country Teams on Preparing a CCA and UNDAF." February, New York.

————. 2010d. "Keeping the Promise: United to Achieve the Millennium Development Goals." A/RES/65/L.1, October 19, New York.

————. 2010e. "Right to Development; Report of the High-Level Task Force on the Implementation of the Right to Development on Its Sixth Session." A/HRC/15/WG.2/TF/2/Add.2, March 8, New York.

————. 2010f. "The Human Right to Water and Sanitation." A/RES/64/292, July 28, New York.

————. 2011b. "Joint Statement on the Occasion of the 25th Anniversary of the United Nations Declaration on the Right to Development." September 14, New York.

UNDG-HRM (United Nations Development Group Human Rights Mainstreaming Mechanism). 2011. "Mapping of UN Agency Human Rights Mainstreaming Policies and Tools." April 18, UNDG-HRM, New York.

UNDG-UNDAF Programming Network (UPN). 2011. "Synthesis of an Interagency Peer Desk Review of 2010 Signed UNDAFs." August 25, New York.

UN-DOCO. 2011a. "Overview of Methodology and Selection Process for Identifying Good Examples of Rights-Based UNDAFs." January, New York.

UNDP (United Nations Development Programme). 2006b. "Indicators for Human Rights–Based Approaches to Development in UNDP Programming: A User's Guide." March, UNDP, New York.

————. 2007. "Human Rights and the Millennium Development Goals: Making the Link." January 1, UNDP, New York.

————. 2010b. "The Path to Achieving the Millennium Development Goals: A Synthesis of Evidence from Around the World." July, UNDP, New York.

UNDP and OHCHR. 2010. "UNDP-OHCHR Toolkit for Collaboration with National Human Rights Institutions." December.

UNESCO (UN Educational, Scientific, and Cultural Organization). 2006. "Economic, Social and Cultural Rights: Report of the Special Rapporteur on the Right of Everyone to the Enjoyment of the Highest Attainable Standard of Physical and Mental Health, Paul Hunt." E/CN.4/2006/48, March, New York.

UNFPA (UN Population Fund). 2004a. "Policy Note on Implementing a Human Rights–Based Approach to Programming in UNFPA." UNFPA, New York.

UNFPA and the Harvard School of Public Health. 2010. *UNFPA: A Human Rights–Based Approach to Development Programming; Practical Implementation Manual and Training Materials.* New York: UNFPA.

UNICEF (UN Children's Fund). 1998. "A Human Rights Approach to UNICEF Programming for Children and Women: What It Is, and Some Changes It Will Bring." Executive Directive, CF/EXD/1998-04 of 21, April, UNICEF, New York.

————. 2011a. *UNICEF Annual Report 2010.* New York: UNICEF.

UNIFEM (UN Development Fund for Women). 2001. *Turning the Tide: CEDAW and the Gender Dimensions of the HIV/AIDS Pandemic.* New York: UNIFEM.

———— 2004b. *Pathway to Gender Equality. CEDAW, Beijing and the MDGs.* New York: UNIFEM.

————. 2008. *Progress of the World's Women, 2008–2009, Who Answers to Whom? Gender and Accountability.* New York: UNIFEM.

UNIFEM et al. 2000. *Gender, HIV, and Human Rights: A Training Manual.* Prepared by Madu Bala Nath. New York: UNAID/UNIFEM.

UN Women (UN Entity for Gender Equality and the Empowerment of Women). 2011a. *Progress of the World's Women, 2011–2012: In Pursuit of Justice.* 102–17. New York: UN Women.

USAID (U.S. Agency for International Development). 2011a. *Evaluation of the Implementation of the Paris Declaration: United States Government, Millennium Challenge Corporation. MCC Case Study.* Prepared by James W. Fox, Social Impact Inc., January. Washington, DC: USAID.

WHO (World Health Organization). 2011a. *Human Rights and Gender Equality in Health Sector Strategies: How to Assess Policy Coherence.* Prepared by staff at WHO, OHCHR, and Sida. Geneva: WHO.

World Bank. 2011b. *World Development Report 2011: Conflict, Security, and Development.* Washington, DC: World Bank.

Part II
Case Studies

5

The Realization of Human Rights Policies

UNICEF

UNICEF—the United Nations Children's Fund—is the UN agency with the longest experience of working with a human rights–based approach. With external funding, it has invested substantially in documenting its experiences, providing a solid basis for analysis.

Context

UNICEF's human rights–based approach to programming is shaped by its role in contributing to the drafting and adoption of the Convention on the Rights of the Child (CRC) in 1989, as well as its special relationship to the Committee on the Rights of the Child and its interpretations of the CRC. During the 1990s, UNICEF moved away from advocating for CRC ratification and started using it as a framework for program design and implementation. That has made UNICEF particularly receptive to the concept of a human rights–based approach (HRBA). The Convention on the Elimination of All Forms of Discrimination against Women (CEDAW) has also played a role, though to a lesser degree. In addition, the UN human rights mainstreaming process, started in 1997

with the support of the UN Secretary-General, created an overall supportive environment (box 5.1).

Key Steps

In 1998, a human rights–based approach to programming was declared
to be an institutional priority of UNICEF, and guidelines were provided
by the executive director (UNICEF 1998). Since then, the organization has invested considerable effort in defining what such an approach
means in practice, so that the policy can be implemented, in particular through country programs. Specific instructions accompanied the
Executive Directive, giving responsibilities for dissemination and implementation to heads of offices, regional directors, and division directors. UNICEF's Medium-Term Strategic Plan 2002–2005 combined a
reinforced result-based management approach and a human rights–
based approach to programming. It was developed through widespread
consultations involving staff from headquarters, regional and country offices. In fact, ultimately every staff member and country office is
responsible for implementation.

A book suggesting steps for the implementation of an HRBA to
programming was published in 2003 (Jonsson 2003). In addition,

Box 5.1 UNICEF's Human Rights–Based Approach

UNICEF's human rights–based approach to programming is clearly based on international human rights instruments, combining a focus on standards and principles
(such as the four CRC principles). Programming was based on the "Triple-A" model
of assessment, analysis, and action, requiring participants to analyze immediate and
structural problems, roles and obligations, and resources. It also encourages drawing
on the CRC monitoring and reporting procedures.

For UNICEF, an HRBA has ushered in an institutional transformation, away from direct
delivery of services built on a needs-based approach, toward developing the capacity
of local actors and collaborating with a range of partners (UNICEF 2010b). The agency's
Medium-Term Strategic Plan 2006–2013 requires all offices to provide "continued support for building national capacities to fulfill children's rights, with increased emphasis on
strengthening policy frameworks, service delivery and protection systems and institutions." At the end of 2010, UNICEF integrated a refocus on equity, citing the widening gap
between rich and poor children, even in countries that show overall progress towards
meeting the MDGs (UNICEF 2010a). The new Medium-Term Strategic Plan for 2014–2017
will continue to employ a human rights–based approach while reflecting UNICEF's refocus on equitable outcomes and the most disadvantaged children (UNICEF 2011c).

UNICEF's Program Policy and Procedures Manual was updated several times over the past decade (UNICEF 2007). The first manual was issued in January 2000, reflecting UNICEF's organizational transition to an approach to programming for children and women based explicitly on human rights principles. It provides up-to-date guidance on UNICEF program operations for use by country and regional offices. In 2004, the updated manual sharpened guidance on a human rights–based approach to programming to reflect the consensus (including a consensus among UN agencies) and provided new expertise on topics such as gender mainstreaming. The 2007 version reflected updated guidance on harmonization and simplification in the common programming process and offered new guidance for operating in crisis, post-crisis, and unstable environments. Training materials were developed by UNICEF headquarters and by some regional offices. There are two levels of training, introductory and advanced, as well as a programming course that includes a module on the human rights–based approach.

A human rights–based approach to programming was first adopted in Africa and Latin America, and that experience has inspired the rest of the organization. The five-year programming cycle means that not all country programs moved to an HRBA immediately in 1998. The approach was progressively applied within UNICEF to its different sectors, beginning with protection, and moving to education, health, and, more recently, water and sanitation programs.

A significant effort was also made in documentation. The 35 case studies commissioned by UNICEF country offices and undertaken by UNICEF are a rich source of experiences in promoting an HRBA, both programmatically and organizationally (Theis 2004). The case studies contain a strong emphasis on excluded and marginalized groups. Most addressed the use of the principles of indivisibility and interdependence, which helped planning officers to strengthen child protection projects and to integrate child protection issues with health or education projects.

Two global consultations (Tanzania 2002 and Ecuador 2003) brought HRBA experts together to identify issues requiring further study and to assess how to refine the approach. In addition, UNICEF's more advanced stage of implementation helped it play an influential role in the 2003 Stamford UN interagency meeting and the resulting UN Interagency Common Understanding of an HRBA (appendix 1).

Internal Institutional Change

Responsibility for developing and implementing a human rights–based approach to programming was shared between headquarters and country offices. An evaluation of UNICEF's capacity-building project points out that headquarters' role was "to provide support, coordination, guidance, and often to push a HRBA agenda" (Robert and Engelhardt 2005).

UNICEF has invested significantly in staff training. Senior staff appear to have played a particularly important role. In addition to individuals in formal management positions (such as heads of country offices), there have been signs that influence has come from beyond formal management structures, such as semiretired senior staff who "command respect and exercise leadership"

UNICEF reviews implementation of its human rights–based approach to programming annually. In 2004, a study assessed progress over a five-year period (Raphael 2005). Staff responses indicated that a human rights–based approach to programming had taken root. Over half (56 percent) of reporting countries had used it to design their country program or undertake a country analysis, and more than one-third (36 percent) reported taking a more multisector approach. The approach was seen to improve UNICEF effectiveness, primarily through improved cooperation with partners, but also within UN country teams, in projects, and in planning. There were fewer examples of improved cooperation with CRC/CEDAW committees, PRSPs, or resource mobilization. Understanding of principles and theory seemed to be good. However, country offices were considered to need documentation of existing UNICEF good practices for operational use, in particular for the regions that had had less exposure to the approach.

Further changes were made to UNICEF's institutional approach in 2010, following completion of the study "Narrowing the Gaps to Meet the Goals" (UNICEF 2010a). The study examined whether targeting services and support to the most marginalized groups could be a cost-effective and practical way to make greater strides in reaching the MDGs—equitably. UNICEF had been concerned that gains made toward realizing the MDGs were based on improvements in national averages, despite widening disparities in poverty and children's development within countries. The 2010 study concluded that an equity-focused approach could significantly improve returns on investment and accelerate progress toward the MDGs. As a result, equity-focused strategies are being developed to reduce barriers resulting from geographic location, income poverty, and lack of awareness of services. For example, UNICEF partnered with CIDA on a new international assistance strategy to target district health plans in 12 countries with high numbers of unimmunized children, with priority given to areas that are farthest behind.

Adapting to Context

UNICEF's Quito Global Consultation in 2003 showed that the organization used different approaches successfully, according to country settings. In Latin America, for example, an initial focus on reforming national laws to conform to the CRC led many country offices to promote policy and institutional reform, with an eye toward establishing an environment in which children's rights would be guaranteed and standards to which duty-bearers would be held accountable would be clearly spelled out. In countries where laws, policies, and institutions are often not well developed, country offices have developed community capacity to demand and fulfill children's rights—while at the same time exposing state-level duty-bearers to human rights principles and the policies required to guarantee them. This is the approach adopted in eastern and southern Africa. UNICEF's work in Vietnam shows how progress can be slowly achieved, even in difficult environments where notions of human rights appear not to coincide with the political system and culture (chapter 6).

UNICEF has adapted capacity development strategies for its work at various levels within countries to focus on promoting the rights of women and children. The approach in each country is determined by a consensus of stakeholders. At the community level, UNICEF has supported capacity development initiatives by training key individuals within the Community-Based Disaster Preparedness program in West

Bengal, India, since 2001. At the institutional level, UNICEF works with UN partners, the ministry of justice, and NGOs to provide capacity development support to networks of civil society organizations in Mozambique. The program has promoted the involvement of young people, and its networks have influenced policy makers to pass influential legislation, such as the 2008 Children's Act and the 2009 Law on Domestic Violence against Women. At the policy level, UNICEF has fostered capacity development in Ecuador by engaging in the national budgeting process to increase the awareness of the need to invest in children and social expenditures. Finally, UNICEF cooperatively supports national capacity development strategies in myriad ways, such as providing critical resources to national institutions, conducting trainings, and supporting legal reforms related to children and women (UNICEF 2010b).

Challenges

The 1998–2003 progress review (Raphael 2005) recognized a major challenge in the operations of government structures in partner countries, in particular when they operate in a highly centralized manner, with limited accountability. Some country contexts present even greater challenges, such as war-torn societies, widespread poverty, or extremely weak capacity, where basic survival or institution building is seen as a priority. There can also be open political resistance to human rights, for example, in the context of sharp ethnic divisions, where collecting disaggregated data or providing education in native languages is not politically acceptable. Yet resistance to human rights goes beyond governments and can include social norms and values, such as opposition to child and adolescent participation and a preference for seeing aid as charity. (Responses included communications strategies and paying more attention to the cultural context.) The review also pointed out that a community-focused HRBA could be demanding for communities and slow in delivering results (see also box 5.2).

Lessons

Some bilateral agencies may feel that UNICEF should be considered an exception, given the special role played by the CRC and the focus on less-controversial and more clearly defined children's rights. However,

Box 5.2 UNICEF's Operational Constraints

- Like other donor agencies, UNICEF is hampered by internal capacity gaps, such as limited understanding, high staff turnover, overstretched staff, or resistance to an approach that may be perceived to be more difficult (such as focusing on process and not just outcomes), and it may have inadequate resources to handle confrontation with governments.
- Bringing other partners on board can be difficult: it requires time, training, and dialogue. Other donors may not always be favorable to a human rights–based approach and may put cost recovery or private sector legal security first.
- A few country offices reported the need for more practical guidance focusing on results.
- A weak global economy and reduced public budgets have left UNICEF short of resources in critical areas, such as polio and measles immunization efforts.

a number of lessons, particularly with regard to institutional change and approach to country programming, are relevant for other agencies. UNICEF has invested considerably in documenting its change process. Clear instructions from the very top of the organization, as well as revisions to the "Program Policy and Procedures Manual" (UNICEF 2010a), have given prominence to the approach at an institutional level. The agency sees a difference between country offices that have been working on a human rights–based approach for some years and those where the approach is still relatively new.

International Financial Institutions

For some international financial institutions (IFIs) human rights present potential legal challenges because of political prohibitions in their mandates. A 2011 survey conducted by the EIB found that the World Bank, the African Development Bank (AfDB), Inter-American Development Bank (IADB), the Islamic Development Bank (IsDB), and the International Finance Corporation (IFC) have a range of political restrictions in their foundational documents, prohibiting interference in the political affairs of a member country or taking member governments' political character into account. Other related provisions proscribe decision making based on political considerations (EIB 2011). Despite these limitations, the World Bank, the IADB, and the IFC have developed a range of policies that are supportive of human rights while staying within the limits of their mandates. In many instances, the practices and policies developed by such institutions have in fact supported the realization of human rights in development.

With the exceptions of the EIB, the CEB, and the EBRD, the international financial institutions tend not to have an explicit legal basis for considering human rights in their activities, nor do they typically have a distinct human rights policy framework articulating a separate set of the fundamental principles and implementing measures related to human rights. The Asian Development Bank (ADB) and the Nordic Investment Bank (NIB), for example, have adopted policies that address protection of human rights in their lending operations, as has the European Investment Bank (EIB 2011). The World Bank, ADB, and IADB also have policies and procedures pertaining to indigenous peoples (World Bank 2005d; Asian Development Bank 1998; IADB 2006), gender equality (World Bank 2003; Asian Development Bank 2003; IADB 2010), and involuntary resettlement (World Bank 2011l; Asian Development Bank 1995; IADB 1998) that are supportive of human rights and in some instances mention human rights.

European Instrument for Democracy and Human Rights (EIDHR)

Originally created in 1994, the European Initiative for Democracy and Human Rights was the EU's main financial instrument to implement its human rights and democracy policy, complementing geographic cooperation programs and foreign policy tools. It funded predominantly civil society and nongovernmental organizations and did not require the consent or involvement of state authorities. That allowed it to operate in sensitive political contexts. The initiative ended in 2006 upon expiration of its legal authorization (Regulation [EC] Nos. 975/1999 and 976/1999) by the European Parliament and Council of the European Union.

In its place, the European Instrument for Democracy and Human Rights (EIDHR) (Regulation [EC] No. 1889/2006) was launched by the EU to enhance respect for human rights and fundamental freedoms, strengthening the international and regional framework for the protection of human rights, justice, and the rule of law, the promotion of democracy, and election monitoring (EU 2006b). It is a self-standing funding instrument administered by the European Commission's Development and Cooperation Directorate General—EuropeAid— alongside nine other thematic funds. A first strategy paper was adopted for 2007–10 by the European Parliament and the Council, with a second, largely consistent strategy following for 2011–13 (European Commission 2010b). Like its predecessor, the EIDHR can grant aid where no established cooperation exists and can intervene without the agreement of the governments. The new Finance Regulation also allows the EIDHR to finance not only registered organizations but also more informal partners, such as groups of natural persons "who do not have legal personality under the applicable national law" (EU 2006b). Civil society organizations can also "re-grant" small grants to other local groups or individual human rights defenders. For the period 2007–13, the EIDHR has a budget of €1.104 billion, including €40 million in support of human rights defenders; its current budget proposal for 2014–20 is €1.4 billion (European Commission 2011f). In 2010, activities in nearly 20 countries, predominantly in Africa, operated at a cost of €100 million; a total of 66 local calls for proposals were launched, and 434 grants contracts were signed with a total value of €69 million. More than 1,600 EIDHR projects were ongoing (including those from both the initiative and the instrument), not including more than 50 election-related missions that took place (European Commission 2010b).

One example of an EIDHR-supported project involved supporting the rights of ethnic minorities in Cao Bang Province, North Vietnam, through improved access to information and communications and increased participation in decision making. From 2007 to 2010, the EIDHR also financed more than 60 projects to fight torture, focusing on rehabilitation of torture victims, as well as human rights training for the judiciary and for prison officers, the setting up of national prevention frameworks, and legal aid to defend victims from injustices. Other examples include EIDHR's support to human rights defenders, such as emergency protection, reimbursement of medical or legal fees, the purchase of secure information technology equipment or cell phones, and temporary support for a grassroots human rights organization during a difficult situation. A recent evaluation by EIDHR of this support concluded that to improve the effectiveness of its funding, attention should be paid to avoiding duplication of effort, reinforcing the quality of local partnerships, increasing direct support to human rights defenders, and ensuring a cohesive and strategic approach in the overall selection of projects (European Commission 2011b).

The EIDHR is just one of the external aid instruments providing EU financial support to development cooperation. Another such instrument is the Development Cooperation Instrument (DCI) that, with a €16.9 billion budget for 2007–13, supports a wide range of programs in developing countries. Launched in 2007, the DCI has many geographic programs focused on achieving the Millennium Development Goals and providing support to democracy, human rights, and institutional reforms. The DCI covers thematic areas as well; together with the European Development Fund (EDF) and European Neighbourhood and Partnership Instrument (ENPI), these programs address five different fields. One program, Investing in People, supports actions on health, education and skills training, gender equality, and other aspects of human and social development (European Commission 2007). The initiative's mandate incorporates a specific focus on human rights, such as the rights to good reproductive and sexual health, the promotion of gender equality and women's rights, cultural rights of indigenous peoples and persons belonging to minorities, and protecting the rights of youth and children (EU 2006a).

The EDF is an older fund (launched in 1959), serving as the main instrument for providing community development aid in the African, Caribbean, and Pacific countries and the overseas countries and territories. It supports actions in economic, social, and human development as well as regional cooperation and integration. The 10th EDF Governance Initiative, currently under way, emphasizes dialogue between the EU and partner countries and includes innovative financial incentives for countries to improve their democratic governance. Additional financial support is provided to certain North African countries through the European Neighbourhood Policy (ENP) Governance Facility, following an assessment of progress made on "core governance issues," including "democratic practice, respect for human rights and fundamental freedoms and the rule of law" (European Commission 2009a).

CIDA: Implementation of the Official Development Assistance Accountability Act

For the past few years, the Canadian International Development Agency (CIDA) has operated under a clear mandate to target development assistance specifically toward long-term poverty reduction in developing countries. The Official Development Assistance Accountability Act of 2008 (ODAAA), Bill C-293, established three conditions that international aid must satisfy to qualify as official development assistance: (1) it must contribute to poverty reduction; (2) it must take into account the development priorities and perspectives of aid beneficiaries; and (3) it must be consistent with international human rights standards (Canada 2008). Internal accountability and transparency are supported by ODAAA requirements to consult with three groups (governments, international agencies, and Canadian civil society organizations) at least once every two years and to submit an annual report on official development assistance to Parliament.

The ODAAA was quickly followed by an Aid Effectiveness Agenda, released in 2009 and 2010. The agenda enumerates five thematic priorities, including food security; children and youth; sustainable economic growth; security and stability; and democracy, although the first three themes direct CIDA's programming decisions. Three additional themes are integrated across the priority areas: environmental sustainability, equal opportunity for men and women, and effective, accountable governance. One example of the overlap of these priorities and themes is a project in Tarritos, Honduras, funded by CIDA and the World Bank, which trains women to be plumbers in water sanitation projects, to assist with the provision of safe drinking water and effective sanitation. As of 2011, 28 women graduates of the program maintained 13 water systems in 20 different communities (CIDA 2011a).

To facilitate implementation of this aid agenda, CIDA produced an Aid Effectiveness Action Plan for 2009–12 (CIDA 2009b) organized around seven goals related to focus, efficiency, accountability, predictability, alignment, inclusive partnerships, and fragile states. In an effort to focus its work, CIDA limited 80 percent of its bilateral country aid to 20 countries (down from approximately 34). In doing so, the agency cited its interest in meeting its commitments to the Paris Declaration and the Accra Agenda for Action.

Sida—Swedish International Development Cooperation Agency

Over the 1980s and 1990s, Sweden gradually developed a special form of cooperation involving direct work promoting democracy and human rights (box 5.3). The foundation for Sida's development cooperation in the field of human rights is formed by the international conventions and declarations. Sida's human rights work can be divided into two areas: work in countries in cooperation with their own governments or in cooperation with civil society, and work at an international level to promote democracy and human rights within the UN or other international bodies.

Box 5.3 Rationales for Sida's Democracy and Human Rights–Based Approach

Sida closely links human rights and a democratic culture and institutions. It considers that democracy is essential in upholding human rights and on that basis promotes free and fair elections, party systems, free media, rule of law, participation, tolerance, and dialogue.

For Sida, a democracy and human rights approach contributes to development cooperation by building a shared pool of values based on the international conventions on human rights and fostering a process in which participation is a fundamental principle. This approach draws a clear division of responsibility based on the state's obligations and the individual's human rights. It takes a holistic view of the individual person's problem and potential, as well as a society's power relationships and power structures, which form the framework within which individuals act, alone or in a group. The democracy and human rights approach provides an analytical tool that makes it possible to identify target groups, problem areas, power relations, and structures, and thereby leads to a more efficient collaboration with cooperation partners and countries. It also provides measuring instruments and indicators that facilitate a clearer scrutiny of gains.

Policy Development

Sweden has invested considerably, over a number of years, in human rights policy development. In 1997, Sida issued an action program called "Justice and Peace: Sida's Program for Peace, Democracy and Human Rights" (Sida 1997). Three key government communications provided Sida's initial policy framework:

- "Human Rights in Swedish Foreign Policy" (Government of Sweden 1997; 2003b)
- *Democracy and Human Rights in Sweden's Development Cooperation* (Government of Sweden 1997)
- "The Rights of the Child as a Perspective in Development Cooperation" (Government of Sweden 2002).

In 2002, Sweden adopted a National Human Rights Action Plan, demonstrating its domestic commitment to human rights. In 2003, a new Swedish Policy for Global Development was adopted (Government of Sweden 2003a), encompassing all Swedish overseas policy; it required coherence across trade, development, migration, and so forth. The policy called for annual reporting back to Parliament. It required that a rights-based approach, defined as including not only human rights and the rights of the child but also democracy and gender equality, be adopted across Swedish activities. It took a number of years to develop this official policy, and Sida was very active in the process. Human rights NGOs also pushed for human rights to be part of the policy.

The 2003 global policy was seen as creating a higher degree of awareness on human rights and democracy within Sida. It was complemented by shorter policy documents that incorporate a rights-based approach, such as the position paper *Poverty Reduction Strategies* (Sida 2005e) or the method document *Country Level Analysis for Poverty Reduction* (Sida 2005f). At the same time, a range of existing policy documents on children's rights (2005a) and human rights in the health (2002b) and education (2005b) sectors were updated. These policies were followed in 2010 by the Swedish Policy for Democracy and Human Rights (Ministry for Foreign Affairs of Sweden 2010a; box 5.4).

Box 5.4 Sweden's Development Cooperation Policy

Sweden's Policy for Global Development (Government of Sweden 2003a) is at the top of Sweden's policy hierarchy, as it was adopted by Parliament and would require parliamentary action to be amended. Guided by this policy and others that have succeeded it, Swedish development cooperation aims to help build an environment supportive of poor people's own efforts to improve their quality of life. It must be based on two perspectives: the perspectives of the poor and the rights perspective. The rights perspective (HRBA) is based on the global values expressed in the Universal Declaration of Human Rights and subsequent conventions. Key principles are equality in dignity and rights, participation, openness and transparency, and accountability. Democracy, human rights, gender equality, children's rights, and respect for international humanitarian law are part of the rights perspective. The policy identified eight global components: democracy and good governance, respect for human rights, equality between women and men, environment, economic growth, social development, conflict management, and global public goods.

In 2010, Sweden published an ambitious new policy on democratic development and human rights in development cooperation (Ministry for Foreign Affairs of Sweden 2010a). Entitled "Change for Freedom," the policy explains how a rights-based approach should be mainstreamed into the Swedish development cooperation program (both bilateral and multilateral), particularly activities that focus on democratic development and human rights. It explicitly states, "People's enjoyment of their human rights is both a foreign policy goal and a means of achieving development and a sustainable peace. Sweden's basic position is that all development cooperation must be human rights-based, i.e., that a rights-based approach must be applied in all areas." The policy covers 2010–14 and has three focus areas: (1) civil and political rights; (2) the institutions and procedures of democracy and the rule of law; and (3) actors of democratization.

Sida's other recent policy and methods documents include Sweden's "Strategy for Multilateral Development Cooperation" (Sida 2007a), which reiterates that a rights-based approach helps direct Swedish development goals and that aid resources should be allocated to organizations that effectively pursue matching goals. The 2010 "Guidelines for Cooperation Strategies" discuss the importance of engaging in dialogue on key thematic issues, including democracy, human rights, and gender quality, and include among their assessments the partner country's commitments and measures taken to promote democracy and human rights (Ministry for Foreign Affairs of Sweden 2010b). These documents have been supplemented by sector-specific policies, action plans, and papers that incorporate a rights-based approach. For example, in addition to a multiyear action plan (2009–12) on incorporating the rights of persons with disabilities into Sida's development work (Sida 2009a), Sida produced both a baseline study on its interventions and capacity to effectively work with disability issues (Sida 2010c) and a background paper on dialogues on the rights of persons with disabilities (Sida 2010a). Other action plans on specific groups and issues were compiled in recent years, including one on gender-based violence and another on the rights of LGBT persons.

Relationship to the Ministry for Foreign Affairs

The close relationship between Sida and the Swedish Ministry for Foreign Affairs has been vital in developing and implementing Sida's human rights and democracy approach. Sida is an independent government agency but it works closely with the ministry on human rights issues. The ministry's Division for International Law and Human Rights is responsible for the international human rights framework and the ministry has a duty to mainstream human rights within all its divisions.

Institutional Capacity

In 2011, Sida lost close to a quarter of its total staff capacity through administrative budget cuts. That loss has affected all areas of working including the agency's HRBA work. In addition to the downsizing, Sida has undergone two reorganizations in recent years. At present, out of 725 staff at Sida, 150 are members of Sida's democracy and human rights network, which means that they have operational responsibility for human rights and democracy, including implementation of a human rights–based approach. In addition, three human rights and democracy policy specialists within the Department for International Organizations and Policy Support advise the rest of the agency (including country programs) on implementing a human rights–based approach by providing methods, tools, and lessons learned. Responsibility for implementing the rights-based approach, however, rests with the whole agency.

Tools

For historical reasons, only environmental and conflict issues are mandatory aspects of Sida's operating rules. To assist in a more systematic approach, Sida developed its "Guide for Country Analysis from a Democratic Governance and Human Rights Perspective" (Sida 2001a;

see box 5.5). This questionnaire helped staff conduct a country analysis, with questions covering human rights democratization, participation, and good governance. Overall, it is not clear what impact this tool has had on Sida country strategies, and its use is not mandatory.

Other, more recent tools are posted on an interim HRBA Helpdesk website, for example, a "guiding checklist" that helps those involved in a development intervention apply a human rights–based approach (Sida 2009b). The HRBA Helpdesk also has links to a number of briefs with information on how to apply HRBA to specific sectors (e.g., democratic governance; education; health, HIV, and AIDS; infrastructure, energy, and water; and research) and thematic areas (disability rights and LGBT rights).

In addition, Sida has invested in "power analyses," which it also considers to be a way of putting its democracy and human rights approach into practice (Dahl-Østergaard et al. 2005). Such analysis looks at the "issues of power asymmetries, access to resources and influence over politics" to better understand how development cooperation and donor activities are affected by the "informal political landscape" (ODI 2009). It was used by Sida to understand the local political, social, and economic power structures in rural Bangladesh (Lewis and Hossain 2008). The 2010 policy on democratic development and human rights refers to this tool as "power and actor analyses" and notes its importance for "identifying drivers of democratic change and processes that Sweden can support" (Ministry for Foreign Affairs of Sweden 2010a).

Box 5.5 Country Analysis from a Human Rights Perspective

The "Guide for Country Analysis from a Democratic Governance and Human Rights Perspective" (Sida 2001a) was piloted in Zimbabwe starting in 1998. The process involved the Swedish foreign ministry and Sida staff, mostly at headquarters level, though there was a mission to the country.

The process was felt to lead to a richer and longer country analysis, with a better understanding of actors and processes. However, the initial effort was found not to have influenced the country strategy to a significant degree, despite touching on political dialogue issues for the first time. Political events (land crisis and irregular elections) led to the expiration of the cooperation agreement between Sweden and Zimbabwe without renewal. In that context, the country analysis was considered useful: it had identified issues for political dialogue and meant that Sida was better informed.

Mainstreaming

The 2002 government communication "The Rights of the Child as a Perspective in Development Cooperation" (Government of Sweden 2002) comprised a 10-point program: put children first, listen to children, invest in the future, exclude no one, education for all, equal opportunities for girls and boys, health for all, protect children in war, combat HIV/AIDS, and stop exploiting children. The document highlighted four strategic areas: right to health and medical care, social reforms, education for all, and contributions for disadvantaged children.

In 2003, Sida reported back to the government on how it had implemented the 10-point program of children's rights (Sida 2005a). The report showed that Sida was able to mainstream a child rights perspective. Sida's policies and programs contribute to the four strategic areas. They integrate well the principles of the best interest of the child, gender equality, and nondiscrimination, but participation was more difficult to achieve. Sida's policy documents have increasingly emphasized children's rights. In 1999, the position paper "The Rights of the Child in Swedish Development Cooperation" was issued as a guide (Sida 2000a). The document "Perspectives on Poverty" gives attention to children and adolescents in vulnerable positions (Sida 2002a). A child rights perspective also became more visible in country strategies, such as in the regional South America strategy and Zambia country strategy. The Guide for Country Analysis (Sida 2001a), which required paying attention to children's rights, was seen as a contributor to this process.

The report found that Sida exerts international influence on children's rights by working with the UN, EU, and other bilaterals. Sida's cooperation with the UN system highlights children's rights. Support to WHO is based on a human rights–based approach. Its support to the International Labor Organization includes the project "Understanding Children's Work and Its Impact." UNICEF is Sida's largest channel, with responsibility for 40 programs in partner countries. Swedish NGOs also receive Sida funding and work with local organizations, in particular, Swedish Save the Children. However, quantifying the resources allocated to mainstreaming children's rights beyond support to UNICEF and Save the Children is difficult.

Sida currently has a "30 percent position" at the policy level for children's rights mainstreaming. To date, Sida continues to mainstream child rights in all aid interventions (see box 2.3, chapter 2).

In 2011, Sida circulated a draft how-to note to assist Sida and the Ministry for Foreign Affairs in integrating a human rights–based approach into the six phases of a program-based approach by identifying potential entry points (Sida 2011a). Sida has also invested in developing policies and tools to mainstream human rights, democracy, and child rights in other sectors, such as health or education.

Sweden's 2010 policy, "On Equal Footing: Policy for Gender Equality and the Rights and Role of Women in Sweden's International Development Cooperation 2010–2015" (Ministry for Foreign Affairs of Sweden 2010c), replaces its 2005 policy "Promoting Gender Equality in Development Cooperation" (Sida 2005g). The new policy relies on gender mainstreaming as a strategic approach in all Swedish development cooperation, through targeted measures, integrated measures, and policy dialogue. Activities addressing poverty reduction must be based on a gender equality analysis or a gender impact assessment. The 2010 policy also fills some of the void left by the now-expired 2008–10 action plan on gender-based violence (Sida 2007b). The Swedish Secretariat for Evaluation conducted an evaluation of support for gender equality in 2010, as well, and found that although Sida successfully integrates gender during the program planning process, it continues to omit gender during the program monitoring and evaluation phases (Sida 2010b).

Dialogue

Sida makes it clear that its partnership with the countries, organizations, and people it supports is "based on the human rights conventions that both parties have ratified, which further strengthens the rationale for promoting democratic governance" (Sida 2001a). Sida has experienced a range of political dialogues on human rights, as well as the application of human rights conditionality in some countries. In 2010, Sida emphasized the central role that dialogue plays in its development cooperation by producing a human rights dialogue kit, with concise briefs on freedom of expression (Sida 2010g), the rights of children and young people (2010h), young people's political participation (2010i), child protection

(2010j), disability as a human rights issue (2010e), and the human rights of gay, bisexual, and transgender persons (LGBT) (2010k).

Global Initiatives

Sweden hosted an important international conference on human rights and development in 2000 (Frankovits and Earle 2001). Sida has been a strong supporter of mainstreaming human rights across the UN system (e.g., OHCHR, HRM, HURIST and its successor initiative GHRSP [see box 2.12, chapter 2], Action 2, WHO, UNDP, UNFPA, UNICEF). It also provides funding to international NGOs and is a funding donor of the World Bank Nordic Trust Fund.

Evaluation

Democracy and human rights projects and programs are difficult to evaluate because of the challenges of measurement (e.g., What are the right indicators?) and attribution (What caused the change? Can it be attributed to a donor project?). Moreover, there are challenges with reporting when human rights are being put into operation by many components in the field. The 2010 Guidelines for Cooperation Strategies instruct Sida to submit an assessment memorandum at the end of a strategy period that "tak[es] into account the various dimensions of poverty." In so doing, a rights perspective and the perspectives of people living in poverty are to be applied. The assessment memorandum would include a summary of the partner country's commitments and measures taken to support gender equality, respect for the rule of law, democracy, and human rights. The guidelines further specify that the assessment should "examine the extent to which international human rights conventions that the country has ratified have actually been implemented, and assess the willingness of the government to implement them" (Ministry for Foreign Affairs of Sweden 2010b; also see the discussion of the evaluation of Sida's program in Kenya, in chapter 7).

Challenges

Sida has a very strong set of policy commitments. The challenge, as with all other donor agencies, has been to translate policy into practice. Agencies are only now entering a period of more systematic implementation. However, the process of decentralization means that the center has less influence; staff in field offices are overcommitted and may not know the policy. Although training on human rights, democracy, and the rights of the child is not compulsory, significant opportunities for training have been provided over the years. Furthermore, donors experience pressure to harmonize their aid at a country level. Human rights may lose out as a result of that process if donors' country-level offices are not aware of their agencies' policies.

In 2010, Sida's HRBA Helpdesk compiled a paper on 12 lessons learned applying a human rights–based approach in Sub-Saharan Africa (Sida 2010f), based on challenges that staff faced in the field and at headquarters. Among the recommendations shared are (1) to communicate a human rights–based approach in consistent, simple terms, to minimize confusion and maximize understanding of the approach; (2) to provide relevant, tailor-made support to staff; (3) to develop and maintain contacts with local stakeholders; and (4) to begin by identifying sectors or issues where the agency already has an advantage in terms of influence and knowledge, when the timing is right and the partner government is interested in the issue. It also identifies the challenge of working with all four human rights principles. Although "participation" is easiest to address, "nondiscrimination," "accountability," and "transparency" all require specific attention.

Achievements

Because Sida's democracy and human rights–based approach dates from 1997, it is possible to identify a number of enabling factors over the past 17 years. For example, a favorable domestic political environment contributed to human rights overseas. An implementation approach based on human rights and democracy principles, rather than international human rights instruments, has worked better because the principles provide an entry point for discussion. That was the lesson of Sida's synthesis work on democratic governance (Sida 2003), which is being integrated into Sida's human rights work. Sida's four principles are equality in dignity and rights; participation; openness and transparency; and accountability. These principles are rooted in the international human rights framework, which remains at the core of Sida's work.

Sida's how-to note on integrating an HRBA, "lessons learnt" document, and numerous dialogue briefs have proved to be useful methodological tools, particularly as they are made easily accessible on the agency's website and online HRBA Helpdesk (Sida 2011b). Sida's mapping of experiences with equal access to justice interventions (Sida 2011c) and subsequent guide to equal access to justice programs (Sida 2011d) provide a conceptual understanding, as well as practical instructions on employing an HRBA into such justice initiatives. A steadily increasing share of Sida's total development support goes toward democracy, human rights, and gender equality (28 percent in 2011), with its largest financial contributions in Afghanistan, West Bank and Gaza, Mozambique, Cambodia, Tanzania, Zimbabwe, Guatemala, Liberia, Uganda, and Colombia. An openness to both internal and external evaluations of Sida's work has enabled the agency to learn from its experiences integrating a human rights–based approach.

DFID—U.K. Department for International Development

The ways in which human rights can make a wide range of contributions to poverty reduction was shown by the "DFID Human Rights Review" (Piron and Watkins 2004), which described how DFID integrated human rights into development policy and programs on three levels: central, country, and sector. An important constituency of staff, across departments and professional backgrounds, also have had an interest in human rights and are developing innovative approaches and activities.

Prompted in part by a 2006 white paper, "Eliminating Poverty: Making Governance Work for Poor People," a subsequent "scoping study" was published in 2007, which concluded that the policy framework for DFID's work on human rights had successfully created an "enabling environment for the more systematic integration of human rights into DFID's policy and practice" (O'Neil et al. 2007). It highlighted the requirement that DFID country offices include human rights considerations in their planning processes but found that despite an increasing number of explicit references to human rights in its sectoral policy documents, such references were not necessarily well integrated into the document, making them harder to implement in practice.

Further review of DFID's human rights policy in practice was completed in 2008 and concluded, based on examination of a limited number of country cases, that DFID country offices do not "regularly explicitly integrate the international human rights framework" (Braunholtz-Speight et al. 2008). More often, an implicit human rights approach, rather than an explicit one, is being implemented in practice, as exemplified by the economic and legal empowerment themes contained in DFID's 2011 strategic vision for girls and women (DFID 2011b). More recent changes of government in the UK have not changed DFID's human rights policy, which still stands. Its approach has shifted, however, as have those of several other donors, to focusing on the value of money, tangible results, and deliverables in the MDG framework (DFID 2011e). DFID's recent policy statement "Empowering Poor People and Strengthening Accountability" reflects the shift, as it examines ways to "make every penny count and increase the reach of development initiatives" (DFID 2011c).

Central Level

DFID has channeled support to a number of international organizations in support of human rights. That includes building capacity for developing and monitoring international human rights standards (Office of the UN High Commissioner for Human Rights), developing a UN interagency common understanding of the meaning of a human rights–based approach to development (2003 meeting), and fostering the adoption of human rights–based approaches in the UN (e.g., UNICEF) and among international NGOs (e.g., ActionAid).

DFID has favored innovative research activities, drawing on field experiences in country programs to feed directly into new strategies. It promotes voice, participation, and accountability and supports processes to make budgets more transparent and participatory. It has piloted new participatory tools, such as the Participatory Rights Assessment Methodologies (Brocklesby and Crawford 2004). In its research activities, DFID has explored issues such as linkages between livelihoods and rights and analyzed the relationship among rights, poverty, growth, and inequality.

DFID has developed rights-based policies that guide its interventions. It has encouraged and supported the move within civil society away from solely a service delivery role, toward developing local capacity for policy engagement, monitoring, and advocacy. In addition, it has a pro-poor approach to safety, security, and access to justice and has worked hard to develop new policy on core labor standards and poverty reduction.

Country Level

In some countries, DFID has used a human rights analysis to inform strategy and set overall objectives. Its three human rights operational principles of participation, inclusion, and fulfilling obligations have been used to highlight social exclusion and inequality in Latin America (Bolivia, Brazil, and Peru). DFID has identified improving the economic and social status of women as one of three key themes running through its country program in Bangladesh (DFID 2011f) and has used an analysis of international human rights standards and reporting obligations in its work in the Overseas Territories. It has incorporated shared human rights commitments into its 10-year Development Partnership Arrangements, such as the 2006 arrangements with Afghanistan and Pakistan, allowing for longer periods of time over which to establish human rights as a legitimate aspect of the relationship (Braunholtz-Speight et al. 2008).

An analysis of integration of human rights into country programs has been a key feature in DFID's work in Malawi, where it has focused on pro-poor governance and the development of rights-based sectoral interventions in health, education, and livelihoods. It has also commissioned research on human rights and citizenship to inform the direction of the country strategy and program in Rwanda.

The agency has integrated human rights into strategic aspects of its program delivery, such as human rights dialogue in bilateral talks (China), a Memorandum of Understanding detailing a shared commitment to the promotion and protection of human rights (Rwanda), the use of aid instruments in direct budget support (Uganda), and its work with the European Commission in the Middle East and North Africa.

Sector Level

At the sector level, DFID has worked to help particular groups claim and enforce their rights, for example,

- Women, by supporting the implementation of the Convention on the Elimination of All Forms of Discrimination against Women (China) and collaborating with UNIFEM on gender and racism (Brazil)
- Children, by developing a child protection strategy (Overseas Territories)
- Minorities, by promoting social inclusion of the Roma minority (Eastern Europe)
- Indigenous peoples (Latin America)
- Workers, by improving core labor standards, including support to the International Labor Organization and work on child labor and child trafficking (India and South-East Asia).

DFID works on the "demand side" of justice reform by enabling poor people to know, claim, and defend their rights through public information campaigns on land inheritance rights for women (Zimbabwe) or public interest litigation (Bangladesh).

Over the years, DFID has launched a number of initiatives designed to make governments more respectful of the rights of citizens. It has collaborated with civil society to promote human rights principles (Bangladesh), civic education, and women's political empowerment (Kenya). DFID has strengthened accountability of parliament by its work with civil society (Malawi). And it has promoted free and fair elections in many parts of Africa. DFID has helped communities to ensure proper management of public expenditures by supporting their right to participate in resource allocation decisions through district-level monitoring committees (Uganda).

DFID has promoted the radio as a source of information for peacebuilding efforts (Democratic Republic of Congo) and encourages media self-regulation to balance freedom of speech with legitimate restrictions (Russia).

Other initiatives have focused on poor people's access to justice by undertaking sectorwide reforms in the security and justice sector (Malawi), developing culturally relevant policies and systems to provide protection from domestic violence and child abuse (Jordan), and bringing a rights-based approach to health service delivery (Peru and Nepal). DFID funding has helped those trying to protect communities during and after conflict (UN human rights presence in Iraq, UN Special Representative of the Secretary-General on Children in Armed Conflict, and UNIFEM in protection of women in conflict situations).

BMZ—German Ministry for Economic Cooperation and Development

Policy Development

Human rights considerations have been a part of German development policy since the early 1990s, and the BMZ has funded a number of human rights projects in developing countries over the years. More systematic policy development started in the early 2000s with issuance of a first human rights action plan in 2004 and a second one in 2008. The plans included a number of measures and identified Guatemala and Kenya as pilot countries. The plans were not binding on German implementing agencies, however, and lacked a monitoring framework, though they were later to become part of the German National Human Rights Action Plan. In 2011, after extensive consultation among all departments in the ministry itself and with German civil society, the BMZ adopted a binding human rights policy with far-reaching commitments. The policy is framed as part of Germany's human rights obligations, flowing most explicitly from Article 32 of the Convention on the Rights of Persons with Disabilities (CPRD). Building on experience with support for gender equality (an important policy goal since the 1990s), the policy envisions a twin-track strategy based on the promotion of specific human rights programs (e.g., support for national human rights institutions, regional human rights protection systems, human rights defenders, and civil society groups), as well as the mainstreaming of a human rights–based approach in all sectors and priority areas of cooperation. Guidelines on how to implement the policy for specific vulnerable groups will follow the policy and guidelines have already been formulated for children's and youth rights (BMZ 2011c). Policy implementation will be reviewed regularly, with the first review planned for October 2012. Monitoring will include policy coherence and be conducted with cooperation countries, if possible.

Institutional Capacity

With human rights traditionally being in the remit of the foreign ministry, BMZ staff for human rights was, and continues to be, limited. However, policy champions beyond the human rights desk, particularly at the health, water, and governance desks, adopted a human rights–based approach in their respective strategies. Because Kenya and Guatemala were determined pilot countries in the first action plan, the respective desk officers were also key champions for a human rights–based approach. In 2005, the BMZ commissioned the project "Realizing Human Rights in Development Cooperation." It comprises a small team of human rights experts at the GTZ (German Organization for Technical Cooperation; later GIZ) head office to assist the ministry and its agencies in promoting and implementing a human rights–based approach. GTZ partnered with the German Institute for Human Rights to foster synergies with the human rights community. In addition to the human rights team at GIZ, the ministry had already commissioned teams on gender equality, children's rights, and disability, with similar tasks. All teams thus support the ministry and country programs run by the implementing agencies, for example, by being part of appraisal or project progress missions, or as trainers on the issues. This institutional set-up provides important learning and feedback opportunities.

Due to work overload, general training for BMZ staff was not feasible. All incoming BMZ staff, however, receive a brief overview on cross-cutting issues, including human rights, gender equality, and poverty reduction. The same holds true for incoming staff at the implementing agencies. However, human rights and cross-cutting issues are an elective. In addition, the GIZ-based human rights team offers training and on-the-job coaching for staff at all agencies, at headquarters or in-country. It has developed a number of formats for staff with different levels of responsibilities.

Tools

BMZ uses political dialogue as a key tool, and references to human rights concerns and possibilities for mainstreaming have increased markedly in government negotiations since 2006. Another key tool is the governance assessment developed by the ministry in 2007. The assessment includes three human rights questions, based on the indicator matrix developed by the OHCHR (OHCHR 2008b). Results of the assessment determine aid modalities along the lines of the Netherlands' Track Record framework (see box 4.14, chapter 4). Other BMZ tools include a checklist for program formulation in each sector, focusing on do no harm and possibilities for mainstreaming.

Another important tool, used in particular by the officer responsible for children's rights, is the creation of a task team on children's rights, composed of members from the ministry, desk officers from the implementing agencies, and civil society representatives. The task team serves as a sounding board for policy development with respect to children's rights (BMZ 2011c) and for piloting tools to implement children's rights.

Tools at the implementing agencies include, among others, a reformulation of the target group analysis at the KfW (KfW 2012); a set of Promising Practices, detailing program approaches and the value added of a human rights–based approach; a set of information materials (e.g., GIZ 2011); FAQs; and a training package, which focuses on demonstrating the value added and the "how-to." A key success factor in tool development was linking an HRBA to other cross-cutting issues, for example, to conflict transformation (Parlevliet 2011), instead of developing stand-alone tools and materials. Engaging sector and country experts in common work and products, as was done, for example, in Promising Practices, increased staff capacity to apply a human rights–based approach and in general provided a good learning tool.

Results

Applying a human rights–based approach has influenced a number of country programs in various ways: programs became more participatory and inclusive of vulnerable groups and increased work on accountability structures. For example, the health program in Tanzania addressed the expulsion of pregnant teenagers from schools and the discrimination of persons living with albinism. The health program in Kenya supported the Gay and Lesbian Coalition of Kenya to build its capacity as a network. The education program in Guatemala revised its program goals and objectives and adopted a set of human rights–sensitive indicators to steer and monitor progress.

Increasing accountability and transparency is a traditional focus of German support to promote good governance; an HRBA perspective led some programs to expand their choice of partners (e.g., national human rights institutions) and their methods (e.g., social audits, rights charters, or grant facilities for common projects undertaken by governmental and nongovernmental agencies and organizations). For example, the "Support to the Health Sector Reform Program" in Cambodia identified a lack of awareness on the part of both health care users and providers concerning their rights and responsibilities as a cause of inadequate standards in health care and, indirectly, a contributor to unnecessarily high morbidity and mortality. Therefore, the notion of clients' and providers' rights was incorporated in the implementation plan of the strategy for the health sector. A "Charter on Clients' Rights and Providers' Rights-Duties" was drafted in a participatory process and widely disseminated. It helped to improve service quality and utilization, with tangible benefits for clients and providers. In Bangladesh, a combination of capacity-building measures and the establishment of grievance mechanisms for the ready-made-garment sector led to much improved social compliance by a large number of factories (GTZ 2009b).

Challenges

To date, results have been achieved primarily because of enabling factors such as policy champions (at headquarters or in the field) or windows of opportunity in partner countries. HRBAs are therefore not routine operating procedure and not yet integrated into all phases of the program cycle. Staff capacity at all levels needs to be improved significantly (particularly given the high staff turnover rate), the human rights policy will need to be integrated into all relevant instruments for managing and implementing cooperation programs, and there is much room for improvement with respect to German policy coherence.

Private Sector Initiatives

Between 2005 and 2011 Professor John Ruggie was the special representative of the UN Secretary-General on the issue of human rights
and transnational corporations and other business enterprises. Professor Ruggie's mandate has led to the development of a framework
on business and human rights, which was unanimously approved by
the UN Human Rights Council in 2008 (UN 2008a). The subsequent
Guiding Principles on Business and Human Rights, endorsed by the
UN Human Rights Council in June 2011, contain three pillars: (1) the
state duty to protect against human rights abuses by third parties,
including business; (2) the corporate responsibility to respect human
rights; and (3) greater access by victims to effective judicial and nonju-
dicial remedies (UN 2011c).

The Ruggie framework and guiding principles influenced the policies
and guidelines of several institutions and multilateral organizations.
For example, when the OECD updated its Guidelines for Multinational
Enterprises, followed by 42 countries (including nonmembers such as
Brazil), it added a chapter on human rights that drew from the second
pillar of the framework regarding corporate responsibility to respect
human rights. The OECD guidelines now state that companies should
carry out risk-based due diligence to address any adverse impacts on
areas covered by the guidelines, as a result of a company's own activities, as well as its working relationships with others. In addition, the IFC
updated its Sustainability Policy and Performance Standards to include
the business responsibility to respect human rights. The IFC standards
are in turn followed by the 70 Equator Principal Financial Institutions, banks that commit not to provide loans to borrowers who cannot adhere to the IFC Performance Standards. Finally, the ISO26000
social responsibility standard adopted in 2010 by almost all members of
the International Organization for Standardization has a human rights
chapter that draws on the Ruggie framework (Ruggie 2011).

In support of Professor Ruggie's framework, the Institute for Human
Rights and Business (IHRB) focuses on the relationship between business and international human rights standards. It provides a forum for
understanding the human rights challenges that businesses face and
appropriate ways of addressing them. IHRB helps ensure that companies

"do no harm" but also seeks to raise corporate standards and thereby generate positive outcomes. Its work focuses on several key areas, including migrant workers, accountability, conflict, due diligence, and natural resources. To promote the protection of vulnerable workers, IHRB is helping develop the Dhaka Principles for Migration with Dignity, which address human rights concerns that migrant workers face during recruitment, employment, and return to home countries. IHRB also supports the use of UN human rights mechanisms and processes for addressing corporate accountability, such as contributions to the Universal Periodic Review process, assistance to UN thematic experts and rapporteurs, and collaboration with national human rights institutions.

Because businesses run the risk of complicity in human rights violations when operating in fragile situations, the IHRB and Professor Ruggie have also been studying the experiences of companies in delivering services or maintaining civilian infrastructure while operating in conflict zones. Both offices have supported the Red Flags Initiative, which seeks to communicate the legal liabilities that corporations face when operating in high-risk zones. The initiative highlights the following activities that may raise a "red flag," warning companies of legal liability:

1. Expelling people from their communities
2. Forcing people to work
3. Handling questionable assets
4. Making illicit payments
5. Engaging abusive security forces
6. Trading goods in violation of international sanctions
7. Providing the means to kill
8. Allowing use of company assets for abuses
9. Financing international crimes.

Finally, the IHRB has been studying human rights due diligence, a central theme of the corporate responsibility to respect human rights, as articulated in the Ruggie framework (IHRB 2011). The Voluntary Principles on Security and Human Rights (box 5.6) provide additional guidance on respecting human rights in the extractive and energy sectors.

Box 5.6 Voluntary Principles on Security and Human Rights

The Voluntary Principles on Security and Human Rights were developed in 2000 by governments, companies, and NGOs to help companies working in extractive and energy sectors maintain the safety and security of their operations while ensuring respect for human rights and humanitarian law. The focus of the voluntary principles is threefold:

- Risk Assessment. Effective risk assessment of a company's operating environment should consider, among other things, comprehensive identification of the source and target of security risks, the potential for violence, and available human rights records of public security forces, paramilitaries, law enforcement and private security, and the rule of law.
- Interactions between Companies and Public Security. Companies should consult regularly with host governments and local communities about the impact of their security arrangements on those communities, encourage public security providers to adhere to the company's policies on ethical conduct and human rights, observe international law enforcement principles, and maintain the rule of law, and should report and investigate allegations of human rights abuses by public security in their areas of operation.
- Interactions between Companies and Private Security. Where a company engages private security providers to protect its personnel or assets, private security should observe the policies of the contracting company regarding ethical conduct and human rights, act in a lawful manner, and have policies regarding appropriate conduct and local use of force, among other responsibilities. Companies are encouraged to include these principles in contractual provisions with and training for private security providers.

By the end of 2011, participation in the initiative included seven member governments, 19 companies, and 10 NGOs. A practical guide to implementing the voluntary principles—"Implementation Guidance Tools"—was recently launched by the International Finance Corporation, the International Council on Mining and Metals (ICMM), and the global oil and gas industry association for environmental and social issues (IPIECA), in collaboration with the International Committee of the Red Cross (ICMM et al. 2011).

References

Asian Development Bank. 1995. *Involuntary Resettlement.* August, Manila.

———. 1998. *The Bank's Policy on Indigenous Peoples.* April 1998.

———. 2003. *Policy on Gender and Development.* Policy approved by the ADB Board of Directors in May 1998, published June 2003.

BMZ (German Federal Ministry for Economic Cooperation and Development). 2011c. *Young People in German Development Policy.* Bonn: BMZ.

Braunholtz-Speight, Tim, Marta Foresti, Karen Proudlock, and Bhavna Sharma. 2008. "DFID Human Rights Practice Review." July 4, Overseas Development Institute, London.

Brocklesby, Mary Ann, and Sheena Crawford. 2004. "Operationalising the Rights Agenda: DFID's Participatory Rights Assessment Methodologies Project." DFID report, Swansea and Edinburgh.

Canada. 2008. *Official Development Assistance Accountability Act,* June 28, S.C. 2008, c. 17, Minister of Justice, Québec.

CIDA (Canadian International Development Agency). 2009b. "CIDA's Aid Effectiveness Action Plan. 2009–2012." CIDA, Québec.

———. 2011a. *Development for Results, 2009–2010.* CIDA, Québec.

Dahl-Østergaard, Tom, Sue Unsworth, Mark Robinson, and Rikke Ingrid Jensen. 2005. "Lessons Learned on the Use of Power and Drivers of Change Analyses in Development Co-operation." Review commissioned by the OECD-DAC Network on Governance (GOVNET). September, OECD-DAC GOVNET, Paris.

DFID (U.K. Department for International Development). 2011b. "A New Strategic Vision for Girls and Women: Stopping Poverty before It Starts." DFID, London.

———. 2011c. "Empowering Poor People and Strengthening Accountability." DFID, London.

———. 2011e. "Multilateral Aid Review: Ensuring Maximum Value for Money for UK Aid through Multilateral Organisations." March, DFID, London.

———. 2001f. "Operational Plan 2011–2015, DFID Bangladesh." April, London.

European Commission. 2007. "Investing in People: Strategy Paper for the Thematic Program 2007–2013." Brussels.

———. 2009a. "Supporting Democratic Governance through the Governance Initiative: A Review and the Way Forward." January 19, Brussels.

———. 2010b. "European Instrument for Democracy and Human Rights (EIDHR)." Strategy paper 2011–2013, April 21, Brussels.

———. 2011b. *2011 Annual Report of the European Union's Development and External Assistance Policies and Their Implementation in 2010.* Brussels.

———. 2011f. "Joint Communication to the European Parliament and the Council: Human Rights and Democracy at the Heart of EU External Action—Towards a More Effective Approach." COM (2011) 886 final, December 12, Brussels.

EIB (European Investment Bank). 2011. "Survey on Human Rights and the Activities of the International Financial Institutions." Presentation by Alfonso Querejeta, General Counsel, European Investment Bank, at the 2011 Annual Meeting of Chief Legal Officers of International Financial Institutions, June, Moscow.

EU (European Union). 2006a. "Regulation EC No 1905/2006 of the European Parliament and of the Council of 18 December 2006 Establishing a Financing Instrument for Development Cooperation." *Official Journal of the European Union,* L 378/41, Article 12.

———. 2006b. "Regulation EC No 1889/2006 of the European Parliament and of the Council of 20 December 2006 on Establishing a Financing Instrument for the Promotion of Democracy and Human Rights Worldwide." *Official Journal of the European Union,* L 386/1.

European Commission. 2010b. "European Instrument for Democracy and Human Rights (EIDHR), Strategy Paper 2011–2013." April 21, Brussels.

Frankovits, Andrew, and Patrick Earle. 2001. "Working Together." Report of the Workshop on the Human Rights–Based Approach to Development Cooperation, October 16–19, 2000. Part 1: Report of the NGO Workshop, October 16–17, 2000; Part 2: Report of the Donor Workshop, October 17–19, 2000, Swedish International Development Cooperation Agency (Sida), Stockholm.

GIZ (Deutsche Gesellschaft für Internationale Zusammenarbeit). 2011. *The ABC of Human Rights for Development Cooperation.* Update August 2011, GIZ, Eschborn.

Government of Sweden. 1997. *Democracy and Human Rights in Sweden's Development Cooperation.* Government Report No. 1997/98:76, Stockholm.

———. 2002. "The Rights of the Child as a Perspective in Development Cooperation." Government Communication No. 2001/02: 186, Stockholm.

———. 2003a. "Shared Responsibility: Sweden's Policy for Global Development." Government Bill No. 2002/03:122, Stockholm.

———. 2003b. "Human Rights in Swedish Foreign Policy." Government Communication No. 2003/04:20, Stockholm.

GTZ (German Organization for Technical Cooperation). 2009b. "Compilation—Promising Practices on the Human Rights–Based Approach in German Development Cooperation." GTZ, Eschborn.

IADB (Inter-American Development Bank). 1998. *Involuntary Resettlement in IDB Projects.* OP-710, July, Washington, DC.

———. 2006. "Operational Policy on Indigenous Peoples and Strategy for Indigenous Development." February 22, Washington, DC.

———. 2010. "Operational Policy on Gender Equality in Development." November 3, Washington, DC.

ICMM (International Council on Mining and Metals), et al. 2011. "Voluntary Principles on Security and Human Rights: Implementation Guidance Tools." Prepared by ICMM, ICRC, IFC, and IPIECA, London, Geneva, and Washington, DC.

IHRB (Institute for Human Rights and Business). 2011. "The 'State of Play' of Human Rights Due Diligence: Anticipating the Next Five Years." London: IHRB.

Jonsson, Urban. 2003. *Human Rights Approach to Development Programming.* Nairobi: UNICEF.

KfW Entwicklungsbank (German Development Bank). 2012. "Integrierter Analyserahmen zur Untersuchung von Zielgruppen und Betroffenen in Vorhaben der Finanziellen Zusammenarbeit. Eine Arbeitshilfe für die Bearbeitung von Modul B des Gemeinsamen PV." April, Frankfurt/Main.

Lewis, David, and Abul Hossain. 2008. "Understanding the Local Power Structure in Rural Bangladesh." Sida studies no. 22, November, Sida, Stockholm.

Ministry for Foreign Affairs of Sweden. 2010a. *Change for Freedom: Policy for Democratic Development and Human Rights in Swedish Development Cooperation, 2010-2014.* Stockholm.

————. 2010b. "Guidelines for Cooperation Strategies." Stockholm.

————. 2010c. "On Equal Footing: Policy for Gender Equality and the Rights and Role of Women in Sweden's International Development Cooperation 2010–2015." Stockholm.

ODI (Overseas Development Institute). 2009. "Mapping Political Context: Power Analysis." Excerpted from *Mapping Political Context, A Toolkit for Civil Society Organisations.* January, ODI, London.

OHCHR (Office of the UN High Commissioner for Human Rights). 2008b. *Report on Indicators for Promoting and Monitoring the Implementation of Human Rights.* Geneva: OHCHR.

O'Neil, Tam, Marta Foresti, Tim Braunholtz, and Bhavna Sharma. 2007. *DFID Human Rights Policy: A Scoping Study.* London: Overseas Development Institute.

Parlevliet, Michelle. 2011. "Human Rights and Conflict Transformation. Guidance for Development Practitioners." GIZ, Eschborn.

Piron, Laure-Hélène, and Francis Watkins. 2004. *DFID Human Rights Review. A Review of How DFID Has Integrated Human Rights into Its Work.* London: Overseas Development Institute.

Raphael, Alison. 2005. "HRBAP Programme Review 2003: Implementation of Human Rights Approach to Programming in UNICEF Country Offices. 1998–2003." UNICEF, New York.

Robert, Pierre, and Achim Engelhardt. 2005. "External Evaluation of DFID-Funded Project Strengthening UNICEF Human Rights-Based Programming, Phase 2." Inception Report, UNICEF, New York.

Ruggie, John G. 2011. "Keynote Remarks." Extraordinary Plenary Meeting of the Voluntary Principles on Security and Human Rights Initiative, Department of Foreign Affairs and International Trade, September 15, Ottawa, Canada.

Sida (Swedish International Development Cooperation Agency). 1997. "Justice and Peace: Sida's Program for Peace, Democracy and Human Rights." Stockholm.

————. 2000a. "The Rights of the Child in Swedish Development Cooperation." Stockholm.

————. 2001a. "Country Strategy Development: Guide for Country Analysis from a Democratic Governance and Human Rights Perspective." Stockholm.

————. 2002a. "Perspectives on Poverty." Stockholm.

————. 2002b. *Health and Human Rights.* Issue Paper prepared by Birgitta Rubenson, Sida, Stockholm.

————. 2003. "Digging Deeper: Four Reports on Democratic Governance in International Development Cooperation—Summary." Stockholm.

————. 2005a. "The Child Rights Perspective in Practice." Sida's report in response to the Government's Annual Directives, 2003. September 2005, Stockholm.

————. 2005b. "Education, Democracy and Human Rights." Position paper, Stockholm.

———. 2005e. "Poverty Reduction Strategies." Position paper, November, Stockholm.

———. 2005f. "Country Level Analysis for Poverty Reduction." Methods document, November, Stockholm.

———. 2005g. "Promoting Gender Equality in Development Cooperation." Policy document, October, Stockholm.

———. 2007a. "Strategy for Multilateral Development Cooperation." March 30, Stockholm.

———. 2007b. "Action Plan for Sida's Work against Gender-Based Violence 2008–2010." October, Stockholm.

———. 2009a. "Human Rights for Persons with Disabilities: Sida's Plan for Work." October, Stockholm.

———. 2009b. "The Human Rights–Based Approach to Achieve Results: A Guiding Checklist." Stockholm.

———. 2010a. "Disability as a Human Rights Issue, Background Paper to Conducting a Dialogue." Stockholm.

———. 2010b. "Gender Equality in Swedish Development Cooperation: Final Report." Sida Evaluation 2010:1, prepared by Gabriela Byron and Charlotte Örnemark, February, Stockholm.

———. 2010c. "Base Line Study of Sida-Funded Interventions on Disability and Sida's Capacity to Work Effectively with Disability Issues: Final Report." Stockholm.

———. 2010e. "Disability as a Human Rights Issue: Conducting a Dialogue." Stockholm.

———. 2010f. "Lessons Learnt on HRBA in Sub-Saharan Africa." Prepared by Annika Nilsson and Anna Schnell, HRBA Helpdesk, April, Stockholm.

———. 2010g. "Freedom of Expression: Dialogue." Stockholm.

———. 2010h. "The Rights of Children and Young People: Conducting a Dialogue," part 1. Stockholm.

———. 2010i. "Young People's Political Participation: Conducting a Dialogue," part 2. Stockholm.

———. 2010j. "Child Protection: Conducting a Dialogue," part 3. Stockholm.

———. 2010k. "Human Rights of Lesbian, Gay, Bisexual and Transgender Persons: Conducting a Dialogue." Stockholm.

———. 2011a. "Integrating and Strengthening a Human Rights–Based Approach to Development in Program Based Approaches: A How-to Note." Draft, Stockholm.

———. 2011b. "Sida's Portfolio within Democracy and Human Rights 2008–2010." Stockholm.

———. 2011c. "Equal Access to Justice: A Mapping of Experiences." Prepared by Henrik Alffram, April, Stockholm.

———. 2011d. "A Guide to Equal Access to Justice Programs." April, Stockholm.

Theis, Joachim. 2004. "Consolidation and Review of the Main Findings and Lessons Learned of the Case Studies on Operationalizing HRBAP in UNICEF." UNICEF, New York.

UN (United Nations). 2008a. "Protect, Respect, and Remedy: a Framework for Business and Human Rights; Report of the Special Representative of the Secretary-General on the Issue of Human Rights and Transnational Corporations and Other Business Enterprises," by John Ruggie. A/HRC/8/5, April 7, New York.

———. 2011c. "Report of the Special Representative of the Secretary-General on the Issue of Human Rights and Transnational Corporations and Other Business Enterprises, John Ruggie. Guiding Principles on Business and Human Rights: Implementing the United Nations 'Protect, Respect, and Remedy' Framework." A/HRC/RES/17/31, March 21, New York.

UNICEF (United Nations Children's Fund). 1998. "A Human Rights Approach to UNICEF Programming for Children and Women: What It Is, and Some Changes It Will Bring." Executive Directive, CF/EXD/1998-04, April 21, UNICEF, New York.

———. 2007. "Program Policy and Procedures Manual." Revised February 2007, UNICEF, New York.

———. 2010a. "Narrowing the Gaps to Meet the Goals." September 7, UNICEF, New York.

———. 2010b. "Oral Report Background Note, The Approach of UNICEF to Capacity Development." E/ICEF/2010/CRP.20, August 3, UNICEF, New York.

———. 2011c. "Road Map towards the Medium Term Strategic Plan for 2014–2017." E/ICEF/2012/5, November 30, UNICEF, New York.

World Bank. 2003. "Gender and Development." Operational Policy 4.20, March, World Bank, Washington, DC.

———. 2004b. "Involuntary Resettlement." Operational Policy 4.12, revised April 2004, World Bank, Washington, DC.

———. 2005d. "Indigenous Peoples." Operational Policy 4.10, July, World Bank, Washington, DC.

———. 2011l. "Involuntary Resettlement." Operational Policy 4.12, issued December 2001 and updated August 2004, March 2007, and February 2011, World Bank, Washington, DC.

6

Experiences Applying Tools

UN Common Country Assessments and Development Assistance Frameworks

The UN Common Country Assessment (CCA) is the common instrument of the United Nations system to analyze a national development situation and identify key development issues. The CCA takes into account national priorities, with a focus on the Millennium Development Goals (MDGs) and the other commitments, goals, and targets of the Millennium Declaration, and international conferences, summits, and convention. CCAs are conducted less often than in the past, as other documents or earlier CCAs are considered to identify sufficiently a country's priorities, commitments, and goals.

As a complement and follow-up to the CCA, the UN Development Assistance Framework (UNDAF) provides a common strategic framework for the operational activities of the UN system at the country level. In the case of Thailand, such framework (2007–11 and 2012–16) has instead been referred to as the UN Partnership Framework (UNPAF), to better reflect the two-way exchange of knowledge and expertise between the donor and partner country.

In 2004, the OHCHR conducted a review of the CCAs and UNDAFs (O'Neill 2004) and found increasing evidence of commitment to a human rights–based approach and a willingness to put it into practice. In fact, most CCA/UNDAFs explicitly stated that human rights formed the basis of their analysis and programs. The UNDAF for Guyana (2006–10) is one such example (UNDG 2008b). Most identified the international human rights treaties ratified by the country; some also noted that national legislation conflicted with certain international obligations and must be changed, and only a few referred to regional human rights treaties and mechanisms.

The review included a thorough analysis of the root causes of poverty, highlighting the pernicious effects that poverty has on the ability to claim and enjoy rights. Several CCA/UNDAFs identify lack of political will, rather than lack of resources, expertise, or knowledge, as the main impediment to greater enjoyment of human rights. This can lead to more frank exchanges with governments. There is a much more nuanced treatment of participation as a key element for enhancing the capacities of both rights-holders and duty-bearers (related to the right to information and the obligation of the state to make core information available to its citizens).

The most important and widespread improvement in the CCA/UNDAFs has been the thoroughness and clarity of the capacity analyses of both the duty-bearers and the rights-holders. Good discussions of weak state capacity to plan, budget, deliver, and assess programs involving basic public services such as education, shelter, and health care appear in the majority of CCA/UNDAFs reviewed. Likewise, many UN country teams dissect the inability of beneficiaries to claim, advocate for, and defend their rights, and base programming on addressing this weakness. Strengthening capacities at all levels—national, regional, local, state, and civil society—for effective action to realize rights is a hallmark of the UN's human rights–based approach.

A more ambitious approach to advocacy is evident, including statements of the need to provide civil society with the information and skills to make demands on the state and to build alliances with embassies, international financial institutions, and regional organizations (e.g., for sensitive issues such as racial discrimination and torture).

Several CCAs identify the important role that local culture and traditions play in the enjoyment of rights. They note that much discrimination, especially toward women, begins at home and must be addressed there. The report considered that a continued weakness in the CCA/UNDAFs was the

> failure to exploit the rich vein of jurisprudence and commentary provided by the ever-growing UN human rights treaty-monitoring/reporting system and the exciting work being done by a bevy of Special Rapporteurs and Working Groups on issues central to development like education, healthcare, shelter, poverty and violence against women. (O'Neill 2004)

The report made suggestions that would strengthen human rights and development programming. These included having a more fluid understanding of duty-bearer and rights-holder, focusing more on the interaction between them, rather than the labels.

The report suggested specifying more clearly the exact nature of the capacity gap of duty-bearers and rights-holders (e.g., shortfall in human, financial, and logistical resources, lack of knowledge or expertise, failure of political will, or interference from the outside). It should be made clear that responsibility entails accountability: documents should show that governments, civil society, and other duty-bearers are the true owners and as such are accountable, whereas the UN "assists and supports them in meeting their responsibilities." Programs should be designed to fill the various capacity gaps and highlight how they will identify those accountable for meeting obligations. The report called for a sharper understanding of how UN programs address power relations in the host country: politically, in the society, and even in the family. There should be a greater focus on the primary actors essential to better enjoyment of human rights, and that includes non-state actors such as parents, religious leaders, health professionals, and teachers. The report suggested reviewing existing accountability mechanisms and indicating how the UN can help states use them, by offering assistance to strengthen the state's regulatory and oversight capacity, including judicial reform and access to justice.

The report called for using the treaty bodies' recommendations and observations, along with those of special rapporteurs and the general comments, in designing new programs (box 6.1). For example, the UN

Box 6.1 Treaty Body Recommendations in UN Common Country Assessments and Development Assistance Frameworks (CCAs and UNDAFs)

The Serbia/Montenegro CCA (2003) noted the readiness and commitment of the government to assume its reporting responsibilities under the six core UN human rights treaties. While highlighting the actions taken to establish inter-ministerial committees to prepare overdue reports, it empha- sized the importance of "the extent to which the Government uses this as an opportunity to systematically review its legislation and practice against international standards" and "the readiness of the Government to implement the recommendations of the treaty bodies when the reports are reviewed."

The Guatemala CCA (2003) identified discrimination as the fundamental problem to tackle, based on the findings of the Special Rapporteur on Indigenous Peoples. It also linked its analysis to the findings of other Special Rapporteurs who visited the country, including the Special Rap- porteur on Violence against Women, who raised the alarm that there is a systematic tolerance of massive violence against women, regardless of the numerous treaties ratified by the govern- ment. The CCA also refers to the findings of the Special Rapporteur on Human Rights Defenders, who reported that defenders are specifically targeted in Guatemala, and emphasized that without real freedom of expression and association and genuine participation, no progress will be possible. Guatemala UNDAF identified the need to inject the issues of sustainable and equitable develop- ment and adherence to human rights into national policy debates as a top priority for UN action in the coming five years.

The Philippines CCA (2003) highlighted a key comment made by the Committee on the Rights of the Child concerning the Philippines' failure to comply with international standards relating to juvenile justice, especially the use of incarceration to punish rather than rehabilitate. It also identi- fied certain traditional beliefs and practices that tolerate abuse and exploitation of children and cited the ILO Convention 182 concerning the Prohibition and Immediate Action for the Elimination of the Worst Forms of Child Labour as an important tool for government and the private sector to end this scourge. Use of ILO Conventions in the analysis led to the identification of a variety of duty-bearers.

The CCA for the Kyrgyz Republic (2003) identified that "the rights guaranteed by international instruments are still to move off the page of official documents into people's lives" and stated that "human rights must actually be enforced and not just talked about." The CCA gives an example of a follow-up undertaken by the government in response to the Concluding Observations of the Committee on the Rights of the Child: it established the "New Generation" initiative, a coordina- tion committee with representation from relevant ministries, NGOs, and young people, to imple- ment policy changes and to coordinate fresh approaches for the realization of child rights.

country team in Uzbekistan, along with key embassies, used the find- ings of the Special Rapporteur on Torture to design programs to achieve practical, measurable results. OHCHR country profiles contain summa- ries of relevant recommendations from treaty bodies and special rap- porteurs/independent experts. The 2009–13 Kenya UNDAF also makes explicit reference to recommendations of UN human rights monitoring mechanisms and human rights conventions (UNDG 2008b). Among the 2004 report's specific recommendations are:

To provide training on CCA/UNDAFs before the process begins. Such training needs to emphasize the practical application of human rights jurisprudence in UN development programming. It should respond to the finding that the content of the first generation of training was too theoretical, legalistic, and academic, and did not concentrate sufficiently on how to apply international human rights law to real people with real development problems.

To pay greater attention to all aspects of public finance, to inform greater public spending on children, women, rural populations, the disabled, and other marginalized or excluded groups. That includes not only reviewing the proportions of national budgets spent on basic services (e.g., to assess whether it is reaching the 20/20 target), but also analyzing whether existing budget allocations actually support the requisite "duty-bearing," so that the state can meet its key national priorities.

To highlight the need for accurate and reliable data in many spheres (e.g., demographics, population, literacy, health indicators, government spending, budgets, trade figures, and labor statistics). All this data must be properly disaggregated to show any patterns of inequality or discrimination.

To dedicate a professional human rights officer responsible for ensuring that all relevant findings, comments, recommendations, and orders generated by the UN and regional human rights mechanisms are considered and included in the United Nations country teams' work.

The UN issued new CCA/UNDAF guidelines in 2007 that adopted a human rights–based approach as one of five mandatory principles in UN programming. The guidelines also placed greater emphasis on national ownership, provided increased flexibility to tailor analysis to country needs, and called for the mainstreaming of gender equality, environmental sustainability, and results-based management (UN 2007). Those guidelines referred to and built upon the "UN Common Learning Package on Human Rights–Based Approach (HRBA)," developed in 2006 by the Working Group on Training of the Action 2 Interagency Task Force (OHCHR, UNDP, UNFPA, UNICEF, UNIFEM), in collaboration with the UN System Staff College (UNSSC). The package contained a wealth of materials that enhance the capacity of UN country team staff to understand the concept of an HRBA as applied to UN common country programming. The learning package was most recently updated by the UNDG-HRM (United Nations Development Group Human Rights Mainstreaming Mechanism), in collaboration with the UNSSC, in 2011, by including a new HRBA results-based management element and strengthening the use of case studies.

An earlier guidance note provided technical direction on developing and applying indicators for HRBA programming that incorporate human rights principles and results-based management processes (UNDG 2008b). Additional direction was given to country teams in May 2008 with decision No. 2008/18 of the UN Secretary-General's Policy Committee on Human Rights and Development, which articulated the roles and responsibilities of resident coordinators (RC) in promoting human rights (UNDG 2008a). As the leader of the UN country team, which includes all UN System organizations that are implementing assistance for a country, the resident coordinator is responsible for supporting national priorities and capacity building, within the context of international treaty obligations and development goals, and coordinating efforts by the country team to mainstream human rights principles into their work. The RC Guidelines make clear that despite this role in promoting human rights, the resident coordinator has no role in human rights monitoring or investigation. With greater capacity building through increased access to knowledge products, trainings, and tools that explain how and why an HRBA is effective, RCs and country teams can play a more critical role in the mainstreaming of a human rights–based approach. The deployment of human rights advisers from OHCHR, to advise RCs and UN country teams, has assisted in this process. At the end of 2010, OHCHR had human rights advisers in 16 regional areas, with three more added in 2011.

The UNDG-HRM was established in 2009 to help accomplish the objectives of the Secretary-General's 2008 Policy Committee decision and to build on the successes achieved in promoting human rights at the country level by the "Action 2 Initiative" of 2003–08 (UNDG 2009; see box 2.13 in chapter 2).

The guidelines for UN country teams preparing an UNDAF were updated in 2009 (UN 2009) and 2010 (UNDG 2010) to take into account new agreements such as the Accra Agenda for Action, which gave greater attention to capacity development and aid effectiveness. In addition, links were added to new international treaties, such as those pertaining to persons with disabilities and enforced disappearances. Today the guidelines continue to emphasize integration of the five programming principles, including a human rights–based approach, gender equality, environmental sustainability, results-based management, and capacity development, all tailored to the country context.

More recently, two additional assessments of UNDAFs were conducted. For the purpose of identifying case studies to include in the UNDG-HRM update of the HRBA Common Learning Package, the UN Development Operations Coordination Office (DOCO) developed an internal matrix of 16 variables to select good examples of UNDAFs from 2010 and 2011 that used a human rights–based approach (UN-DOCO 2011a). The methodology remains a work in progress but provides a useful HRBA evaluation framework. Six countries (four of which conducted CCAs) were found to be particularly useful examples of applying a human rights–based approach to the UNDAF:

Azerbaijan 2011–15. The CCA identifies key duty-bearers and rights-holders, as well as the underlying causes of development challenges that they need to address. It includes a summary of recent Treaty Body and Universal Periodic Review recommendations, analyses of gaps in the legal framework, and an overview of implementation of that framework.

Botswana 2010–16. The CCA and UNDAF reference reports concerning land rights from the Special Rapporteurs on Human Rights (on indigenous peoples and the right to food). In addition, the CCA examines where gaps exist in bringing legislation into conformity with international law, as well as the accountability structures that would address this. The UNDAF employs a human rights–based approach and includes the promotion of human rights as a specific UNDAF outcome.

Chile 2011–14. The CCA identifies groups that are most marginalized in terms of access to political participation, services, and protection mechanisms, and incorporates the recommendations of Special Rapporteurs and Treaty Bodies. Analyses have also been conducted of how the national legal framework conforms with international human rights standards and of the capacity of rights-holders and duty-bearers. The UNDAF further follows up on the issues identified in the CCA, particularly those related to inequalities.

Ecuador 2010–14. Following HRBA training workshops for UN staff and alignment of the UNDAF with Ecuador's National Development Plan to encourage participation and ownership by the government, Ecuador's UNDAF planning process was undertaken from a human rights perspective, with the promotion of human rights as an explicit objective. The UNDAF phrases many development issues in the human rights framework and uses human rights standards, such as the right to education and the right to health, to help set UNDAF objectives. Likewise, a human rights–based approach is promoted in the legislative framework and in the national development policy and budget framework. Moreover, the UNDAF focuses on the importance of supporting the capacity of rights-holders to claim their rights and duty-bearers to fulfill their responsibilities.

Lebanon 2010–14. Similar to the other examples cited, the CCA identifies gaps in the human rights legal framework, legislation, and implementation. It also looks at the rights situation of a number of vulnerable and marginalized groups. The UNDAF addresses the issues raised in the CCA, with a particular focus on implementation of human rights standards.

Uganda 2010–14. As in Botswana, a human rights–based approach is a cross-cutting issue in Uganda's UNDAF, and human rights are a specific outcome focus. This was the result of an HRBA audit of the UNDAF conducted by the UN country team. It focuses on the incorporation of international human rights standards in domestic law, as well as the need for implementation. The UNDAF highlights the need to strengthen the capacity of duty-bearers and increase awareness of rights among rights-holders. Indicators also draw on reports from UN Treaty Bodies. (UN-DOCO 2011b)

The second assessment, conducted by the UNDG-UNDAF Programming Network (UPN), examined, among other things, how the five key programming principles (including HRBAs) have been applied to UNDAFs. The study concluded that HRBAs were among the best and most uniformly integrated principles across all the UNDAFs, including in their assessment, text, results matrix, and indicators. Indeed, many of the UNDAF texts refer to the adoption of legal instruments regarding good governance, gender equality, and mainstreaming of human rights into public policies (UNDG-UPN 2011).

Universal Periodic Review

The Universal Periodic Review, or UPR, was established in 2006 by UN General Assembly Resolution 60/251, the same resolution that established the Human Rights Council. The Council was mandated to "undertake a universal periodic review, based on objective and reliable information, of the fulfillment by each State of its human rights obligations and commitments in a manner which ensures universality of coverage and equal treatment with respect to all States." The process entails an examination of the human rights records of all 192 UN member states once every four years. The UPR Working Group, comprising the 47 members of the Human Rights Council, reviews information submitted by the state, compiled by OHCHR, and produced by other stakeholders, such as nongovernmental organizations, to assess the extent to which states fulfill their human rights obligations. The UPR aims to improve human rights at country level through the following:

- An assessment of positive developments and challenges faced by the state
- Enhancement of the state's capacity and of technical assistance needed, in consultation with, and with the consent of, the state
- Sharing of best practices among states and other stakeholders
- Support for cooperation among national stakeholders in the promotion and protection of human rights
- Encouragement of cooperation with the Human Rights Council, human rights bodies, and OHCHR. (UNDP Oslo Governance Centre 2008)

The UPR can have relevance for UN country teams endeavoring to promote human rights in development work at country level, and UN development activities may support a country's engagement in the UPR process. For example, Bahrain was randomly chosen in 2007 to be the first country to undergo the UPR process. As the ministry of foreign affairs began to prepare its report in early 2008, the government requested assistance from UNDP—an initial step that evolved into a long-term collaboration, resulting in governance reforms and the creation of a national human rights action plan that incorporates a human rights–based approach. It led to the creation of Bahrain's National Human Rights Institution in 2010 (UNDP Oslo Governance Centre 2008).

The UN also supported Ecuador from the earliest stages of the UPR process by engaging the ministry of foreign affairs, tasked with drafting the report, as well as other government offices, to explain the mechanics and significance of the review. UNDP and OHCHR provided funding for three national consultations in major cities, in addition to two consultants to organize the national consultation process and help Ecuador draft its report. UN staff explained the UPR process to civil society groups, human rights organizations, and the National Human Rights Institution to support their engagement. The resident coordinator was instrumental in following up on the recommendations made by the Human Rights Council by helping secure support from the international community. As a result, the UN has trained members of Ecuador's police force in human rights and has assisted the government in improving the prison system. Moreover, the resident coordinator subsequently led the Ecuador country team in applying a human rights–based approach to the UNDAF process beginning in 2008 (UNDP Oslo Governance Centre 2008).

MDG Acceleration Framework (MAF)

Initially developed by UNDP in 2010, the MDG Acceleration Framework (MAF) helps countries address slow progress on Millennium Development Goal targets. Following testing in 10 pilot countries (Belize, Colombia, Ghana, Jordan, Lao PDR, Papua New Guinea, Tajikistan, Tanzania, Togo, and Uganda), the UN Development Group's (UNDG) MDG Task Force concluded that it was a useful cross-agency approach to speeding up MDG progress at the country level. The MAF provides a way for stakeholders to identify goals that are off-track and helps governments focus on disparities and inequalities that are causing uneven progress. The output of the MAF process is a comprehensive action plan that is aligned to and complements the UNDAF by helping establish priorities (UNDG 2011a).

The MAF has incorporated a human rights perspective, as several of the questions used to identify categories of bottlenecks include human rights principles, such as accountability and rule of law, equality and nondiscrimination, participation, and inclusion. Questions also examine the availability, accessibility, and quality of economic, social, and cultural rights. This kind of inquiry has proved useful in Belize, where the government could more easily identify that the lack of representation and participation of rural Mayan communities on local water boards was preventing those areas from receiving adequate water and sanitation services. Similarly, human rights principles in the MAF helped the government of Uganda in establishing that women were avoiding the use of government-run health centers because some clinical practices were inconsistent with women's cultural beliefs (Mukherjee 2011).

A Human Rights–Based Approach to Achieve the Maternal Health Millennium Development Goal

In recognition of the centrality of women's rights to making progress toward MDG 5, on maternal health, DFID commissioned a desk review assessing the relevance of a human rights–based approach to maternal mortality (Hawkins et al. 2005). DFID's Ghana and Bangladesh country programs were involved in piloting the work. As a result, a how-to note (DFID 2005d) was prepared to guide DFID advisers and program managers in applying a human rights–based approach to maternal mortality, to strengthen their analysis, policy, and programming. The note recognized that an HRBA adds value to technical or public health responses to maternal mortality by directing attention to the underlying social and political factors that influence maternal health. Furthermore, it stressed that the practical application of a human rights–based approach needs to be grounded in the local context, including the type of language that is used. Country-specific tools need to be developed to accompany this generic guidance.

Reflecting DFID's *Realising Human Rights for Poor People* (2000a), the note explored how a commitment to the principles of participation, inclusion, and fulfilling obligation can strengthen analysis, planning, and implementation. It identified particular areas of work resulting from the application of a human rights–based approach to maternal health (box 6.2). The OECD reported on the use of the Human Rights of Women Assessment Instrument (HeRWAI) by Naripokkho, a women's rights organization in Bangladesh, to assess maternal health services. The 2006 assessment reviewed the Bangladesh National Strategy for Maternal Health against the government's national and international human rights commitments. The analysis revealed that the measures set out in the strategy were mainly benefiting middle- and upper-middle-class women. Rural and poor women had too little information about where they could get treatment and often failed to reach services in time. The assessment included recommendations for measure that would fulfill the government's human rights obligation to ensure equal access to maternal health services (OECD 2008b).

Strengthening Policy and Political Support

Political support for, and ownership of, making maternal health a priority are essential; human rights can provide an entry point (box 6.3). They can be used in dialogue and advocacy to strengthen the commitment to maternal health in national development policies, as a starting point for the implementation of international human rights obligations. Both government and civil society will need to be engaged to ensure the mix of aid instruments required to integrate a human rights–based approach into reducing maternal mortality, including dialogue, budget support, and NGO and multilateral funding.

Box 6.2 Services for the Poorest and the Socially Excluded

Funded by DFID, the Nepal Safer Motherhood Project adopted an "all-inclusive" approach to saving the maximum number of women's lives. In 2004, a study measuring use of emergency obstetric care found that the principal users of services were high-caste Brahmin/Chettri women. In one district, the rate of use per 1,000 population was more than four times greater for higher-caste women than for all other women. This has drawn attention to the need to target resources so that lower-caste and excluded ethnic groups can use emergency obstetric services at the same rate as the Brahmin/Chettri women, both to save lives and to be truly inclusive. The cost of providing services for the poorest and socially excluded will be higher than for the more accessible, high-caste women. This calls for difficult political choices. It also highlights the need to monitor who benefits.

Box 6.3 Community Support Groups in Bangladesh

Bangladesh is considered one of the few countries on target to achieve MDG 5, having achieved a 40 percent reduction of maternal mortality between 2001 and 2010. Despite this success, progress in ensuring skilled attendance at delivery has been very limited; only 29 percent of the women who experienced complications during or after childbirth attended medical facilities in 2010.

To address this problem, the Bureau of Health Education, Directorate General of Health Services, UNICEF, and the international NGO CARE collaborated to create Community Support Groups for villages covering 300 to 500 households in six *upazilas* (local subdistricts) that had comprehensive but underutilized emergency care services at local health centers. CSG members and community facilitators sensitize the community in identifying pregnant women, providing them information on maternal health issues, informing them of their right to access community support services, and encouraging them to seek care. Each Community Support System (ComSS) increased its local acceptance by generating its own resources through subscriptions and donations by members and communities.

By the end of the pilot phase (2006–09), the ComSS initiative had established 60 Community Support Groups in six *upazilas*, and use of emergency services had increased significantly. UNICEF identified community mobilization and engagement with local service providers as one of the key strategies in designing and implementing the initiative. The model and strategies used in the ComSS initiative were adapted to two other community-based maternal and neonatal initiatives. Although financial and technical support from CARE ended in October 2010, an exit plan workshop with all stakeholders resulted in an action plan for local and national execution, coordination, and follow-up.

Source: UNICEF 2011b.

Applying a Human Rights–based Approach

A human rights–based approach focuses attention on inequality in the health sector and can provide a powerful advocacy tool for the reallocation of resources to fight discrimination. It can also improve the quality of, and access to, health services by strengthening accountability and standards.

The law can be used to improve maternal health policy and practice at both the international and national levels (box 6.4). Actors can engage with the international treaty-monitoring bodies to encourage government compliance with their human rights obligations and, at national level, can work with governments to ensure that constitutional commitments are implemented and that legislation and policies are congruent with human rights standards and principles.

It is important to increase women's knowledge about their rights, but that should be done in a context-specific manner and be accompanied

Box 6.4 Impact of Abortion Law on Maternal Mortality in Romania

Legislation can save women from unsafe abortions. Restrictive abortion laws were passed in Romania in 1966. Maternal mortality ratios rose dramatically, from around 80 deaths per 100,000 live births in 1964, to 180 in 1988. After the repeal of those laws in 1989, the maternal mortality ratio fell to around 40 deaths per 100,000 live births in 1992. The decrease owed almost entirely to fewer deaths from abortion.

by support for social mobilization and community-managed support systems, if it is to have a positive impact on behavior.

The UN Population Fund's (UNFPA) Culturally Sensitive Health Programming

As a result of a review in 2002 of how its country offices were using the human rights–based approach, UNFPA realized that the scope of its activities varied among regions. Staff identified the perceived conflict with local culture or religion in some countries as a major obstacle to engaging with human rights. As a result, UNFPA created a Gender, Culture and Human Rights Branch that reviewed culturally sensitive programming approaches and partnerships with religious and faith-based organizations.

The review resulted in the publication *Culture Matters* (UNFPA 2004b). It explores the contribution of culturally sensitive approaches and partnerships with local power structures to the effective implementation of rights-based population and development programs. It is important to make clear the distinction between "cultures as broad ethnical and value systems" and certain "traditional practices" that are harmful in the individual and the community.

The report found that both constraints and entry points to rights-based programming resulting from sociocultural structures cannot be underestimated. Serious engagements with cultural factors lead to more effective outcomes. Building bridges between universal rights and local cultural and ethical values helps individuals and communities to understand and advocate universal rights standards. Culturally sensitive language is an invaluable negotiating and programming tool.

Research highlighted the fact that collaboration with local power structures and institutions, including faith-based and religious organizations, is instrumental in neutralizing resistance and creating local ownership of reproductive health and rights. Owing to the growing number of members of such organizations throughout the public services—including political leaders, policy makers, health professionals, and teachers—engaging with them meant that UNFPA was able to mainstream reproductive health concerns and services into many of those networks. However, participatory approaches must be adapted to the local context (box 6.5). It may be necessary to engage with leaders of local power structures before involving grassroots communities in project design and implementation.

Projects that are likely to lead to cultural or religious controversy must be preceded by strong advocacy campaigns. Religious organizations were willing to partner with UNFPA in a number of areas, and those partnerships were strengthened when it became clear that both sides working together addressed the needs and the rights of communities they both serve. In Muslim contexts, using Islamic sources in advocacy campaigns has facilitated project ownership.

Country offices developed strong in-house capacity to manage diversity and bring together various interests. They have been effective facilitators of change where there were challenges on sensitive issues. The identification of, and support to, local advocates for change has been central to this. The lessons learned by UNFPA in the areas of reproductive rights and health could serve as a starting point for culturally sensitive programming in other areas of human rights.

Box 6.5 The Literacy Movement Organization Project in the Islamic Republic of Iran

The Reproductive Health/Family Life Education Advocacy project (known as the "Literacy Movement Organization" project) integrates population and reproductive health messages into literacy classes at all levels in four provinces in Iran. The Literacy Movement Organization is affiliated with the ministry of education and has around 50,000 instructors working throughout the country to teach basic literacy.

UNFPA has provided support for the integration of population education into the government of Iran's literacy program since 1992. The project provides advocacy on issues such as health, family life, gender equality, women's empowerment, and male participation.

UNIFEM's Guide to Results-Based Management

Most practitioners are able to identify the ways in which human rights are relevant to particular areas of their work. It is far more challenging, however, to understand the implications of adopting a human rights–based approach for the entire programming cycle. UNIFEM's guide to results-based management from a human rights perspective (UNIFEM 2005a) can help in that process.

As a result of the explicit adoption of an HRBA in its main planning tool (the Multi-Year Funding Framework 2004–07), UNIFEM was one of the first agencies to produce a guide to results-based management from a human rights perspective, that is, developing and measuring results based on the difference they make to the ability of all women to realize their human rights (UNIFEM 2004a). This new entry-level guide, which is supported by three online training modules, helps UNIFEM staff to plan, implement, assess, and report on their programs, using results-based management premised on a human rights perspective. (CEDAW is the source of indicators.)

UNIFEM's Multi-Year Funding Framework establishes the broad framework of what the agency expects to achieve within the time frame, by providing a direct link between international human rights commitments and UNIFEM's daily work. The central focus of the results-based management system is to support the capacity of rights-holders and duty-bearers. Crucially, UNIFEM recognizes that adopting a human rights–based approach has implications for the way it works, as well as what it actually does, Thus it advocates that, rather than being a technical exercise, results-based management should be empowering and embody the kinds of participatory planning and change that UNIFEM wants to see in society in general.

Within this framework, the guide outlines how capacity development, human rights standards, and participatory processes can be applied to the various stages of the programming cycle:

- Context or situation analysis. What is the specific right to be furthered? Which capacity gaps on the part of both duty-bearers and rights-holders need to be filled? What baseline data are necessary?
- Conceptualizing expected results. What capacities are expected to change and in what time frame? What processes are necessary to

achieve the results? Who is accountable for the results? How is this represented in the program Logframe?

- Developing rights-based indicators. How do we measure transformative change? How can we determine indicators that measure improvement in the capacity of duty-bearers and rights-holders to realize rights that accurately reflect an expected result?
- Planning for monitoring. What is the role of the Performance Monitoring Framework? How does this relate to the baseline information identified in the context or situation analysis? How is progress toward capacity development monitored?
- Reporting results. How does reporting contribute to ensuring accountability for meeting objectives and to lesson learning?

New Zealand Aid Programme's Human Rights Policy Implementation Plan

The New Zealand Aid Programme's (formerly NZAID) Human Rights Policy Implementation Plan of Action 2004–09 (NZAID 2004) set out a process and time frame to integrate human rights into all aspects of its operations: its practices and organizational culture as well as policies, strategies, and programming. It focused on steps to be taken within the agency that would enable NZAID's policy to be reflected in its external activities. The plan described activities and assigned responsibility to individuals and teams and included performance indicators.

The plan recognized that integration is time and resource intensive and that it would take several years to achieve. It proposed to review the human rights plan of action after five years. NZAID was required to report to ministers on the implications and longer-term options of moving toward a human rights–based approach to development.

Organizational Capacity

In terms of organizational capacity, the aim was to ensure that NZAID had the capacity to identify whether, when, and how human rights are being integrated across the agency. Areas for action included the following:

- Adequate resourcing to support integration of human rights, providing access to country-specific information to staff on country status related to human rights instruments

- Data capture and accessibility, by identifying and incorporating appropriate markers for a new agency database to allow monitoring and reporting of issue-specific activity and issue-integrated activity (and monitoring the database to see if markers and procedures are being used effectively)
- Cross-agency learning, for example, by developing effective mechanisms to ensure regular exchange of experience on implementation of human rights policy (e.g., program information, experience, and lessons) across NZAID
- Training for NZAID staff in Wellington and at post (covering human rights issues and principles; planning for implementation at agency, group, and individual levels; and identifying expectations on all staff to implement policy).

Organizational Culture

NZAID aimed to transform its organizational culture so that its language, attitudes, and behaviors are consistent with human rights principles. This was also advanced by applying human rights obligations and principles as part of NZAID's Walking the Talk/Wananga process, as well as by creating a process for responding to staff concerns about human rights abuses within the agency or in partner countries. NZAID developed appropriate human rights–specific questions for inclusion in all staff recruitment processes; required an appropriate level of awareness of human rights issues and principles in all consultancy selection processes; included human rights markers in financial and management procedures; revised contracting procedures for coherence with human rights policy; and referred to human rights issues in relevant communications.

NZAID has restructured and has renamed itself the "New Zealand Aid Programme." Many of its policies and action plans are currently being revised. It continues, however, to recognize human rights as a cross-cutting issue that has a significant impact on development outcomes and the management of negative unintended impacts. Human rights issues in development programs are regularly tracked and reported to management (New Zealand Ministry of Foreign Affairs and Trade 2011).

References

DFID (U.K. Department for International Development). 2000a. "Realising Human Rights for Poor People." Policy paper, DFID, London.

―――. 2005d. "How to Reduce Maternal Deaths: Rights and Responsibilities." How-to Note, DFID, London.

Hawkins, Kirstan, Karen Newman, Deborah Thomas, and Cindy Carlson. 2005 "Developing a Human Rights–Based Approach to Addressing Maternal Mortality." Desk Review for the DFID Health Resource Centre, London.

Mukherjee, Shantanu. 2011. "The MAF—Focusing Efforts on Speedier Acheivement of the Millennium Development Goals." *Human Rights for Development UNDP News Brief,* vol. 4, p. 11, New York.

O'Neill, William G. 2004. "Human Rights–Based Approach to Development: Good Practices and Lessons Learned from the 2003 CCAs and UNDAfs." Review prepared for the Office of the UN High Commissioner for Human Rights, December, Geneva.

UN (United Nations). 2007. "Common Country Assessment and United Nations Development Assistance Framework: Guidelines for UN Country Teams on Preparing a CCA and UNDAF." February 15, New York.

―――. 2009. "Guidelines for UN Country Teams on Preparing a CCA and UNDAF." February, New York.

UNDG (United Nations Development Group). 2008a. "Human Rights Mainstreaming within the United Nations." Background paper, Third Interagency Workshop on Implementing a Human Rights–Based Approach, October 1–3, Tarrytown, New York.

―――. 2008b. "Overview of a Human Rights–Based Approach in Selected 2007/2008 Common Country Assessment/UN Development Assistance Frameworks." Third Interagency Meeting on Implementing a Human Rights–Based Approach, October 1–3, Tarrytown, New York.

―――. 2009. "Delivering as One on Human Rights: A Proposal to Institutionalize Human Rights Mainstreaming in the UNDG." November 12. New York.

―――. 2010. "How to Prepare an UNDAF. Guidelines for UN Country Teams," Parts 1 and 2. January, UNDG, New York.

―――. 2011a. "MDG Acceleration Framework: Operational Note." October, New York.

UNDG-UPN (UNDG UNDAF Programming Network). 2011. "Synthesis of an Interagency Peer Desk Review of 2010 Signed UNDAFs." August 25, New York.

UN-DOCO (United Nations Development Operations Coordination Office). 2011a. "Overview of Methodology and Selection Process for Identifying Good Examples of Rights-Based UNDAFs." January, New York.

―――. 2011b. "Examples of Rights-Based UNDAFs 2010/2011: DOCO Input for Updating and Enhancing the HRBA Common Learning Package." January, New York.

UNDP (UN Development Program) Oslo Governance Centre. 2008. "The Universal Periodic Review of the UN Human Rights Council: What Is It and How Can UNCTs Engage in the Process?" *Huritalk Insight Series*, Issue 3, October.

UNFPA (United Nations Population Fund). 2004b. *Culture Matters: Working with Communities and Faith-based Organizations: Case Studies from Country Programmes.* New York: UNFPA.

UNIFEM (United Nations Development Fund for Women). 2004a. "Multi-Year Funding Framework, 2004–2007." UNIFEM, New York.

———. 2005a. "Results Based Management in UNIFEM: Essential Guide." UNIFEM, New York.

New Zealand Ministry of Foreign Affairs and Trade. 2011. "International Development Policy Statement: Supporting Sustainable Development." March, Wellington.

NZAID. 2004. "NZAID Human Rights Policy: Implementation Plan of Action 2004–09." NZAID, Wellington.

7

Experiences from Country Programs

UNICEF's Country Program in Vietnam

This UNICEF's country program in Vietnam demonstrates the results of long-term engagement built on high-level political dialogue in centralized, socialist political systems, using nonconfrontational language. When UNICEF first introduced child rights principles in its analysis and planning, explicit rights language would have been too sensitive. By broadening the range of its state and party counterparts, UNICEF was able to raise awareness of children's rights in a number of areas. As a result, UNICEF has made progress in legal reform, juvenile justice, and child protection. Patience, persistence, and appropriate strategies for the use of language were instrumental in the process.

UNICEF Achievements

To make children the subjects of rights in the legal system, UNICEF began working with a variety of partners in 1996. Training on children's rights with the Ho Chi Minh Political Academy led to a network on children's rights, which meets twice a year to explore how to promote child rights in academic training. In partnership with the ministries of justice and public security, the sessions have trained judges, lawyers, prosecutors, police, prison staff, and border guards. Work on juvenile justice started in 1996, with a focus on disseminating international standards and integrating them into the reform of the Criminal Court and Criminal Procedure Code. UNICEF trains a wide range of staff and is the only agency allowed to work in prisons. By 2002 the Communist Party called on the government to create a special court for families and juveniles. UNICEF has supported discussion of the proposal and an intersectoral Plan of Action for Juvenile Justice. Constraints to further progress have included the scale of UNICEF support, based in a small rights promotion project; the sensitive nature of reforms aimed at strengthening the status of citizens vis-à-vis the state; and the priority given by the government to legal reform in relation to the economic sector (e.g., for accession to the World Trade Organization).

Work in the area of child protection has also been challenging. The Convention on the Rights of the Child (CRC) recommends national systems of social work and counseling and noninstitutional forms of child care. However, the country has few trained professionals, including social workers, and few independent NGOs, which would typically have a central part in such systems. In the 1990s, however, UNICEF and others were able to advocate for alternative care. Following a conference in Stockholm in 2002, the government reviewed its policy of institutional care and replaced it with models of community-based care. This called for a wide range of consultations with officials, though less participation by nonstate actors such as parents or children themselves. (The policy change was also prompted by rising numbers of children in need of care and a state budget insufficient to meet the need.)

Other areas of progress have included a more integrated approach to the development of child policy, with UNICEF supporting the development of Vietnam's first national family strategy (which does not mention the need for establishing a national profession of social workers) and efforts to encourage more participation within UNICEF programs. In 2001, UNICEF supported the review of the National Action Plan for Children and the preparation of the next one. That marked the first time that children from all parts of the country discussed child policies and programs with the political leadership.

Main Experiences

In documenting its experiences with a human rights–based approach to programming, UNICEF commissioned a Vietnam case study (Salazar-Volkmann 2004). The study produced a number of findings.

First, HRBAs can be applied in challenging and complex environments. It requires a careful analysis of the functioning of political, economic, and social systems to identify national windows of opportunity. UNICEF requires government approval for all its activities. Although tight control characterized UNICEF's work until the *doi moi* reform process, staff then became able to travel and interact with subnational counterparts and engage in policy advice. As Vietnam opened to the international economy, it also worked on nationalizing international concepts, and that created a favorable context for introducing child rights. "Human rights-based programming can become acceptable within a political environment such as Vietnam only when it has evolved from a successful political dialogue at the very highest levels." UNICEF made inroads in the more traditional social and economic rights areas, while using appropriate political momentum to include more sensitive civil, political, and cultural rights.

Second, UNICEF adopted a progressive approach that yielded results over time. Without using the sensitive language of rights, situation analyses and master plans of operations promoted the principles and underlying ideas behind a rights perspective. Government partners became progressively more comfortable with the approach. Trust was built thanks to UNICEF's continuous presence since the war in 1975, even during the Western-led embargo. Senior UNICEF management staff were among the most important agents of change in a process that included a broadening of counterparts, including the Committee for the Protection and Care of Children and the Women's Union. The committee increased understanding of child rights across the state and society, so that eventually child rights language could even be found in official documents. Thus "patience, persistence and appropriate strategies for the use of language were instrumental in the process."

Third, child rights, based on the Convention on the Rights of the Child, provided an entry point for a human rights-based approach. As the convention was developed with the support of socialist countries during the 1980s, the Vietnamese Communist Party found it politically acceptable. The government ratified the convention early, starting a process of implementation measures, such as legal reforms and action plans to harmonize laws, policies, and practices.

The rights of indigenous people, by contrast, can be more difficult to address. In Vietnam, and East Asia generally, the rights of indigenous peoples have been seen as a matter of national security and in some cases taboo. There has also been less progress on women's rights. Though CEDAW was ratified before the CRC, it took longer to disseminate it across government and society. Its integration into the national legal system was weaker than that of the CRC, reflecting stronger cultural and political resistance.

Finally, economic liberalization can constrain the realization of economic and social rights. Vietnam's process of privatization and economic reform is seen as having contributed to poverty reduction but has also been associated with processes of marginalization, as subsidies were cut back and service delivery reformed. Vietnam has continued to struggle with issues of inequity and disparity, particularly regarding children of ethnic minorities and in rural areas. UNICEF has encouraged use of a human rights–based approach, to recognize the distinct cultures of ethnic minorities and prevent them from being subjected to discrimination or marginalization (UNCT Vietnam 2009).

In 2006, Vietnam became the first pilot country for the "One UN" program, in which multiple UN agencies function as a single team within a country to maximize efficiencies and promote interagency coordination. In the Final Common Country Program Document for Vietnam 2012–2016, UNICEF, UNDP, and UNFPA collectively highlighted the need to strengthen the rule of law in Vietnam. The organizations identified how greater institutional accountability, equal enforcement of the law, improved access to justice, and increased government engagement in implementing human rights treaties will facilitate the strengthening of the rule of law. Over the next few years, the UN will be implementing a human rights–based approach to development and plans to help coordinate stakeholders in Vietnam as they engage on cross-cutting issues, including a human rights–based approach (UNICEF, UNDP, UNFPA 2011).

Sida's Kenya Program

The work of Sida, the Swedish International Development Cooperation Agency, in Kenya, provides a good illustration of how to integrate a focus on democracy and a human rights–based approach at different country programming levels.

Country Strategy

The Swedish Ministry for Foreign Affairs and Sida worked together closely to adopt a strategic approach. They began by designing a more coherent strategy for dialogue with the government toward the end of the Kenya African National Union era, in 2002, in view of the large number of donor dialogue mechanisms at the time. The resulting strategy focused on equality, participation, and good governance and allocated responsibilities to all staff to engage in dialogue.

At the same time, they drew up a new country strategy. The country analysis revealed that a lack of good governance and government commitment to fulfilling human rights obligations was a fundamental obstacle to development. The process required internal negotiation within the embassy (e.g., between the economist and the human rights adviser). As a result, the overall objective of Swedish development cooperation for Kenya during 2004–08 was to contribute to Kenyan efforts to reduce poverty by improving democratic governance. Improving service delivery—central to the effort—called for integration of the principles of nondiscrimination and equality (regardless of regional differences, gender, and age), accountability, transparency, and participation.

Sida's strategy rested on three pillars:

- Democracy and human rights as a focus program area, directly supporting human rights organizations and also sustaining the Governance, Justice, Law and Order Reform Program through support to both government and civil society
- Dialogue on human rights and democracy, focusing on inequality and discrimination

- The integration of a democracy and human rights-based approach across the program, in particular in roads, urban development, health, agriculture, water, and justice.

Dialogue

To promote dialogue, the embassy launched a project to put "equality for growth" on the public agenda, working with civil society organizations, research bodies, media, other donors, and decision makers in the executive and Parliament. A Memorandum of Understanding was established between the Ministry for Planning and National Development, the Society for International Development (an implementing NGO), and Sida, in which they agreed to focus on gender, regional, and income inequalities. Project activities included collecting data on inequality in Kenya and helping the ministry to disseminate its poverty map to line ministries. The ambassador wrote in the press about inequalities. As a result, inequality became a national issue, and the project grew to include other partners such as UNDP and ActionAid.

Mainstreaming

Since 2003, the Mainstreaming in Action Project (MAINIAC) has worked to better integrate human rights and democracy principles (nondiscrimination, participation, accountability, and transparency) into the sector programs funded by Sida. It has aimed to develop the capacity of the government of Kenya and other key actors to identify and use mainstreaming indicators, undertake implementation in a manner that promotes mainstreaming, participate in dialogue, and develop an adequate monitoring and evaluation system. Target sectors were roads; water; health; integrated land and urban sector; governance, justice, law and order; and agriculture.

An extensive evaluation of how a human rights–based approach was integrated into Swedish-Kenyan development cooperation was conducted by the Swedish Agency for Development Evaluation (SADEV) in 2008 (SADEV 2008). The evaluation found that there "has been a strong and committed leadership emphasizing the embassy's priority of working with the principles of the rights perspective which has created conditions and practices conducive to capacity development on the rights perspective and its principles, through initiatives such as training, structures for follow-up and internal feedback." It concluded that embassy knowledge and awareness of a human rights–based approach in programming had increased and that the project developed the capacity of Sida program staff to work out indicators and participate in dialogue with government on mainstreaming issues in the assessment and implementation of programs. Some ambiguity about the relationship between an HRBA and cross-cutting issues promoted under the MAINIAC Project remained, however, generating confusion among staff, additional and follow-up training was recommended.

The program also succeeded in developing a network of local resource persons working on the human rights–based approach, which meets quarterly at the Kenya National Commission on Human Rights. This network supports the design and implementation process by commenting on program documents, participating in seminars, and developing the capacity of staff in ministries. The resource people are drawn from local organizations, such as the International Federation of Women's Lawyers, the Institute for Law and Environmental Governance, or the Child Rights Advisory Documentation and Legal Centre, as well as UN agencies such as UNIFEM and UNICEF. The evaluation found that the network would benefit from ongoing and long-term maintenance of these working relationships.

In the agriculture sector, the SADEV evaluation found that "the integration of HRBA has been intensified in all programming phases." Decision making has become more participatory and accountable following policy changes, the development of mechanisms to engage groups at the local level, and increased information sharing among stakeholders. The roads project was generally a success due to a high degree of local participation (with attention paid to how women and children can benefit), local accountability structures, and public information about the initiatives at local markets. The decentralization of responsibilities to district committees and engineers improved accountability and participation, but there was a lack of documentation about how the human rights–based approach was decentralized. In the water sector, transparency and participation by marginalized groups were increased through the establishment of planning tools and the use of complaint mechanisms.

Moreover, government has taken ownership of the process. The president of Kenya announced that he wanted Kenya to be "a rights-based state," and a new constitution was promulgated in 2010. The Kenya National Commission on Human Rights has played "an instrumental role in providing training on HRBA." Overall, government prioritization of human rights created an enabling environment for dialogue and for integrating a human rights–based approach into sectors and programs (SADEV 2008).

DFID's Rights-Based Programming in Peru

Between 2000 and 2005, the U.K. Department for International Development—DFID Peru—applied an innovative, rights-based approach to its programming. The following description of key lessons is based on a study that DFID commissioned to document its experiences in Peru, prior to its departure in March 2005 (DFID 2005b). Additional practical guidance on assessing and monitoring human rights in country programs more generally was published by DFID in 2009 (DFID 2009b).

Context

DFID's country program in Peru was particularly shaped by two factors: DFID's analysis of the causes of poverty in Peru and the conceptual framework shared by the DFID Peru advisory team. That framework was built on three themes—a human rights–based approach, citizenship, and accountability—that guided the team in addressing poverty in Peru. Although the rights-based approach that the Peru team adopted drew on the policy paper "Realising Human Rights for Poor People" (DFID 2000a), it is also clear that team members were able to take a human rights–based approach farther than has been the case in most other DFID programs. That they did so was partly due to the experience and relative autonomy of the advisory team in Peru (and the strong links that it had with the DFID Bolivian office). It was also due to the dominant views within DFID regarding the issues of inequality, governance, and rights in Latin America.

DFID's main analytical entry point in Peru was the country's extreme inequality. Despite its status as a middle-income country, Peru continues to have high levels of poverty. DFID Peru's analysis of the historical causes of poverty and exclusion in Peru made it clear: working toward

poverty reduction would require a strategy that addressed the exclusion-
ary power relations and ethnic discrimination that underlay the country's inequality. That led to a focus on inclusive citizenship and rights,
through the strengthening of relations between state and society.

Translating Concepts into Action

For the Peru team, the concept of active citizenship provided the bridge
between state and citizen. Political events in Peru provided the opportunity for the team to give greater weight to the roles of both government
and civil society in supporting poor people's actions. This concept was
translated into practice through activities aimed not only at developing
the capacity of duty-bearers and rights-holders, but also at strengthening the relationships between state and society. As a result, DFID Peru
strengthened accountability through support to the mechanisms of citizen
participation and oversight and to the formal institutions of representative
democracy. Furthermore, the team cultivated new alliances for change and
nurtured existing networks within and beyond Peru. In so doing, it tried
to bring together civil society actors working on civil and political rights
(human rights organizations) and those working on economic, social, and
cultural rights (organizations working on sustainable development and
poverty reduction).

Supporting Institutions for Political Inclusion

The change of government in Peru in 2000 opened the door for DFID
to encourage public participation at the local and national levels—in
an attempt to transform Peru's top-down system of governance. DFID
launched various programs to implement this part of the country strategy.

The Program in Support of Electoral Processes and Program in
Support of Regional/Municipal Elections (El Gol) worked with a
coalition of state and civil society organizations to facilitate electoral
education and oversight during national (presidential and congressional) and regional (regional and municipal) elections. By fostering the
active involvement of poor people in the electoral process, the programs set out to strengthen citizenship. It was hoped that this would
make the political elite more responsive to the voices of the poor and
their call for economic and social rights, through the exercise of their
political rights.

While the first program had limited impact in combating political exclusion, it did allow DFID to establish new working relationships and provided valuable lessons for the subsequent regional program. DFID saw a need to facilitate debate and the adoption of common positions between partner institutions. It also highlighted the difficulty of promoting citizenship among the most disadvantaged, as relationships with local communities tended to be mediated by the local political elite. As a result, the El Gol program, which provided training to mayors and helped citizens to undertake participatory budgeting, provided closer coordination among the institutions involved. It helped them to pool resources, establish common platforms, and focus efforts on reaching poor, voters in the most marginalized areas.

DFID also provided support to political parties and the system in which they operated. DFID was concerned that for poor people to capitalize on the opportunities presented by a more democratic environment, Peru's political parties needed to provide a more effective bridge between state and society. DFID's strategy had two main components:

- Support to the redesign of the institutional and legal framework in which the political parties operated. DFID brought together state and civil society actors to find consensus on a new law of political parties and a reformed electoral code. The new law would create a system of incentives to establish a responsive party system. It encouraged party consolidation by creating barriers to small, unrepresentative parties and created obligations with respect to internal democracy and financial transparency. After the law was adopted by parliament, DFID supported its implementation.
- Working with the parties themselves. Although this is a sensitive area for any donor, DFID helped the parties to interact and encouraged them to think more about poverty and how to tackle it. DFID contributed to (and benefited from) work undertaken at a regional level, particularly by the Inter-American Development Bank. DFID participated in the Agora project, a series of meetings that brought together militants from a wide range of parties to explore how to strengthen party governance. It emphasized inclusiveness by facilitating the participation of all parties and by encouraging the

involvement of local party activists (including the women and the young), and it held meetings outside Lima.

The Political and Financial Accountability Program encouraged political inclusion through the review of fiscal issues (notably tax reform and budget transparency) and by promoting accountability and responsiveness to poor people. This innovative program was inspired by collaborative work on tax reform with the Inter-American Development Bank, which had allowed DFID to broach a politically sensitive issue. The program focused on the equity potential and accountability functions of fiscal policy (rather than simply efficiency). It set out to ensure that resources reached excluded groups, on the expenditure side, and promoted the perspective that paying taxes is not only a duty but also creates rights, on the revenue-creation side.

Supporting Networks

DFID Peru took the strategic decision to broaden networking and alliance-building activities with government and civil society, as well as the international community, so as to influence different arenas of dialogue and negotiation. The Improving the Health of the Poor through a Rights-Based Approach program took a rights-based approach to health care: it was designed to improve access for Peru's poorest citizens by supporting existing networks of health professionals, including the Social and Economic Research Consortium.

The consortium had produced a study in the late 1990s that challenged the success of Peru's supply-side health sector reform. It found that a quarter of Peru's population lacked access to health care and that the most marginalized communities were excluded. In the face of government attempts to close down public debate on the issue, the consortium sought institutional support from DFID. The DFID program was designed to improve the public services run by the ministry of health and defend citizens' health rights by supporting the Ombudsman's Office and civil society organizations. For example, one project established a national umbrella network, ForoSalud, to spark debate about health policy and generate alternative proposals to those of the government.

Lessons

Innovative thinking about rights and pro-poor change in Peru was shaped both by institutional factors (such as the autonomy and experience of DFID advisers and the prevailing assessment within DFID of the key causes of poverty in Latin America) and by the wider environment in which the team was working (such as political changes within Peru).

The advisory team grounded the program in a deep understanding of Peru's history and the ways in which it had shaped the country's structures, institutions, and power relationships. Combined with a shared conceptual framework and the team's commitment to engaging with wider conceptual debates about political and social change, this provided a lens through which to analyze the causes of poverty in Peru, to understand recent national and local changes, and to translate them into a program for action. One of the key conclusions was that many of Peru's problems lay in the political, not technical, domain. Hence DFID adopted an approach to tackling inequality that fostered inclusive political institutions through support for alliances for change.

An innovative element of the rights-based approach adopted in Peru was the explicit recognition that—because it attempted to change power relations within society—it was an inherently political approach. That meant that DFID was itself a political actor. That raised difficult issues regarding the legitimacy of action, the practice of power, and lines of accountability and meant that the potential existed for conflict between DFID and the state. For instance, questions regarding the right of a donor agency to intervene in domestic political processes emerged from, among other things, DFID's work with political parties and its health sector program (which supported organizations overtly critical of the government's policy).

DFID's programs in Peru underline the importance of fostering a bridge between state and civil society (rather than working simply with one actor) and of seeking to build broad coalitions involving a variety of actors. However, many programs also highlighted the difficulties that that entailed in practice. For instance, the critical stance of the organization involved in the health network, ForoSalud, undermined its ability to achieve internal consensus and foster relations of trust with the ministry of health.

Although Peru's middle-income status meant that the country program budget was relatively small, the team made an impact because its assessment was that poverty and inequality in Peru prevailed, not from lack of knowledge about what to do to reduce poverty, but from uncertainty about how to do it. The Peru team therefore focused its efforts on supporting processes rather than providing technical assistance.

The departure of DFID from Peru underscored the need for long-term approaches to rights-based programming. For example, although some of the networks that DFID supported became institutionalized, others struggled to survive in the absence of support. Other, pre-existing, political groups that were collaborating with DFID risked losing momentum once DFID withdrew completely.

References

DFID (U.K. Department for International Development). 2000a. "Realising Human Rights for Poor People." Policy paper, DFID, London.

———. 2005b. *Alliances against Poverty: DFID's Experience in Peru 2000–2005.* London: DFID.

———. 2009b. "How-to Note: A Practical Guide to Assessing and Monitoring Human Rights in Country Programmes." September, DFID, London.

SADEV (Swedish Agency for Development Evaluation). 2008. "Integrating the Rights Perspective in Programming: Lessons Learnt from Swedish-Kenyan Development Cooperation," prepared by Sara Brun et al. SADEV Report 2008:2, Karlstad.

Salazar-Volkmann, Christian. 2004. "A Human Rights-Based Approach to Programming for Children and Women in Viet Nam: Key Entry Points and Challenges." UNICEF, New York and Vietnam.

UNCT Vietnam. 2009. "Toolkit: A Human Rights–Based Approach. A User-Friendly Guide from UN Staff in Viet Nam for UN staff in Viet Nam." UN, Vietnam.

UNICEF, UNDP, UNFPA. 2011. "Final Common Country Programme Document for Viet Nam 2012–2016." DP/FPA/OPS/ICEF/CCPD/2011/ALB/1, October 21, UN, New York.

8

Experiences from Specific Projects and Programs

SDC–UNICEF Girl Child Project in Pakistan

The Girl Child Project was a collaboration by UNICEF and the Swiss Agency for Development and Cooperation, or SDC. It was implemented by Family Planning Association of Pakistan (FPAP) as a component of both SDC Pakistan's Rights and Non-Formal Education Sector Program and UNICEF's Advocacy and Communication Program.

The project addressed the deep-seated structural discrimination faced by women and girls in Pakistan by developing the capacity of adolescent girls from marginalized rural and urban communities and raising awareness about rights. Initially piloted in 10 locations, the project reached 730 communities and 35,500 girls by the end of 2004.

The project was designed to mobilize girls to become role models and agents of change in their communities. Two groups of activities gave them visible and useful skills. First, home school training addressed the lack of equal access to education for girls and their lower levels of literacy by training girls to set up their own home schools. This provided them with a source of income and non-formal education for other girls in the community. In each community, about 12 girls received basic education—a total of 1,185 by the end of 2004. Second, a course in first aid techniques helped meet the need for trained medical professionals in marginalized areas by training girls to provide first aid in their communities and treat minor ailments.

These capacity development activities enhanced the perceived value of the girls and improved their status within their family and community. Moreover, by motivating the girls to initiate small-scale activities, such as the home schools, they also had a positive and cascading impact on other girls in the community.

Providing the girls with leadership and negotiation skills is also of tremendous importance. Those involved in the project reported that one of its biggest contributions was transforming the sense of self-worth and confidence of participants. The training inspired leadership and volunteer spirit in the girls, giving them an impetus to improve conditions in their homes and communities. Furthermore, by teaching the girls persuasion skills, the project helped them to win support for these activities from their family and community elders in a culturally sensitive and nonconfrontational manner (box 8.1). The result was increased community commitment to educating girls. With the realization that boys play a key role in creating an environment in which girls' rights can be exercised, communities began to include adolescent boys in the project.

The project enabled girls to obtain their rights without inducing a negative reaction from the family and community. A key constraint that the project initially faced was resistance within some communities—including resistance from religious leaders—to the involvement of their

Box 8.1 Using New Negotiation Skills

Jannat Bibi, who lives in a village near Badin, Sindh, in South Pakistan, was engaged to an older man at the age of 3. After participating in the Girl Child Project when she was 16, Jannat became aware that she had the right to make her own decisions about her life. The project trainers encouraged Jannat not to rebel against her family but to instead work to convince her elders to support her choices. The training that Jannat had received gave her knowledge about her rights and the confidence to begin the long process of persuading her family that she should be able to cancel the engagement. Despite initial strong resistance, Jannat was able to achieve her aim. She feels that, by giving her the skills to do this, the Girl Child Project has changed her life.

girl children in the project. By concentrating on one-to-one advocacy efforts, FPAP managed to convince key members of the community of the benefits of the project.

The project's unique approach clearly increased the sustainability of its achievements. To ensure sustainability further, FPAP developed an exit strategy by identifying potential links with existing community mechanisms. The organization also conducted a Training of Master Trainers course. Participants evaluated the project and helped to produce a film documenting its impact as they saw it. The film was used as an advocacy tool at local, national, and international levels. Thanks to its success, the project was selected for a number of awards, and girls from the project participated in a number of UN events.

UNIFEM's Women's Rights to Land in Central Asia Program

It can be difficult for field offices to identify entry points for strengthening the capacity of duty-bearers and rights-holders. UNIFEM's Women's Rights to Land in Central Asia Program is an innovative example of how agencies can support and engage with national processes to further the realization of human rights. UNIFEM seized the opportunity provided by a regional land reform process to design a program that would strengthen the capacity and accountability of key actors to ensure women's economic rights and security. The program reflects best practices in project design, approaches to implementation, and creative collaboration with partners from government and civil society.

Field staff sometimes fail to use a human rights framework because they lack the knowledge to do so. UNIFEM has produced "bridging analysis" that translates human rights conventions into practical programming guidance by providing tools for human rights based programming.

Linking Women's Rights to Country Processes

The program combats the growing marginalization of rural women and seeks government accountability in upholding women's rights in the land reform process in Kyrgyz Republic, Tajikistan, and Kazakhstan.

The program is currently at a different stage in each of the three countries, reflecting their different conditions: the status of the land reform process, the capacity of implementing partners, and the political commitment on the part of the respective governments.

Kyrgyz Republic

The program was launched in 2002, in partnership with the Women Entrepreneurs Support Association and local government. Staff have set up training programs in seven provinces (reaching 80 percent of local administration) and established commitments to take into account the needs of "the missing" to correct the shortcomings of previous work in the land reform process. They have collected and analyzed practical cases during the process of drafting amendments to the land law and produced practical manuals on land reform implementation.

Among its successes, the program has established an efficient monitoring and result tracking system based on a good baseline study. It has submitted draft amendments to the existing Land Code and related policies to the relevant government agencies and the Parliament of Kyrgyz Republic. It has strengthened the capacity of local government officials and staff to protect women's rights to land, developing partnerships with various stakeholders and increasing public understanding about the importance of women's land rights.

Tajikistan

Following a series of assessments based on fieldwork and legal and policy analysis, the participants (members of government, civil society, and donor agencies) at a 2002 workshop put forward a series of challenges specific to Tajikistan, in light of the government land reform efforts and the privatization of a large number of collective farms. That led to the launch of the Land Rights and Economic Security for Rural Women Project, designed to ensure gender equality in access to and use of land for economic initiatives.

This project has already made an impact on policy and legislation. Amendments to the Land Code, policies, and legislation and advocacy for state programs became law in February 2004. Amendments in relation to women's access to land were incorporated into the government's

2001–10 policy on the equal rights and opportunities of men and women and approved by the government. Finally, a new method for the disaggregation of land reform data by sex was developed and presented for government endorsement, for use in statistical reporting from 2005.

Along with working to influence policy and legislation, UNIFEM helps local partners provide legal advice to rural women on land reform issues by, among other things, conducting training workshops at district, village, and local government levels.

Bridging Analysis

To provide human rights based programming tools, UNIFEM produced a bridging analysis to demonstrate how human rights treaties could be used to respond to the violation of women's rights to land. The analysis identifies the government of Tajikistan's obligations with respect to women's right to land under the treaties to which it is a party, and then outlines the measures it should take to meet those obligations, to provide possible program entry points. It identifies four project areas: women's right to land in the land reform process, women's rights and the family, women's access to credit and the impact of stereotypes, and discriminatory customs and religious laws on women's access to land and property.

BMZ-Funded Kenyan-German Cooperation in the Water Sector

The German Federal Ministry for Economic Cooperation and Development, or BMZ, funds a human rights based water sector program that has been implemented by GIZ, KfW, and the former DED since 2003. Planned to continue through 2013, the Kenyan-German International Cooperation Program works at the national, regional, and local levels. Its focus is to increase the sustainable access of the urban poor to water and sanitation and to improve the management of water resources. As part of its advisory services to the Ministry of Water and Irrigation (MWI), the program introduced a human rights–based approach in 2006. The MWI, as partner institution, was supported to implement an intensive dialogue with key stakeholders to familiarize them with the right to water and sanitation and its contents, as outlined in Committee on Economic, Social, and Cultural Rights General Comment No. 15 (2002), namely, that water for domestic and personal use must be available, accessible, acceptable, and of appropriate quality. Such dialogue also clarified misconceptions about the nature and scope of the right to water and triggered a change of perspective toward human rights responsibility among those in charge of sector reforms (GTZ 2009a). During the process, new partners were identified, among them civil society organizations, and accountable service provision was greatly strengthened (GTZ 2009b).

The government of Kenya formally recognized the right to water and sanitation, reflecting it also in the Water Act of 2002 in its national strategies and policy documents. By 2006, a pro-poor, human rights–based approach had been adopted; an assessment of the water sector was conducted from a human rights based perspective in 2007. The National Water Services Strategy that followed refers to safe water and basic sanitation as a basic human right. The Kenyan-German Program supported the development of a Water Services Trust Fund for water service suppliers to acquire funding to extend services to informal settlements, as well as the creation of a Pro-Poor Implementation Plan for Water Supply and Sanitation. In combination with national regulation oriented toward the poor, these developments led to pro-poor water tariff structures, subsidies, and water kiosks among the water companies as duty-bearers, to make quality and price-controlled water more accessible and affordable. In 2010, the new Kenyan constitution included the human right to water and sanitation as part of its Bill of Rights. The new Water Policy of 2012 prescribes, among other provisions linked to human rights, that water institutions and water resource user associations must have at least 30 percent women members.

Human rights standards were developed into indicators and integrated in the National Water Resource Management and National Water Services Strategies. Water governance and accountability were also strengthened through clear lines of responsibility and reporting. The MWI established a regulator to monitor compliance with human rights principles in every aspect of service provision (GTZ 2009b).

Implementation of the DAC Action-Oriented Policy Paper on Human Rights and Development

Chapter 3 and box 1.1 (chapter 1) discuss the "DAC Action-Oriented Policy Paper on Human Rights and Development" (AOPP) (OECD 2007a) and enumerate its 10 principles for areas and activities in which harmonized donor action is of particular importance. The following are examples of the ways in which donors and partners are implementing the principles in practice. Many of the accounts below are derived from the draft results of a donor survey conducted by the DAC Human Rights Task Team, which examined implementation of the Paris Declaration and Accra Agenda for Action principles related to human rights (OECD-DAC 2011a).

1. **Build a shared understanding of the links between human rights obligations and development priorities through dialogue.**

In the context of the German-Kenyan water sector program, the representative of KfW, as spokesperson for the German Cooperation in the water sector, and the GIZ technical adviser in the sector reform program (based at Kenyan Ministry of Water and Irrigation) are permanent members of the donor and NGO Round Table in the water sector. This setting has provided an opportunity to support synergies between the efforts of governmental institutions, civil society, and donors with regard to human rights fulfillment in the water sector. GIZ is also supporting the Kenyan Ministry of Water and Irrigation to better communicate with donors and civil society concerning joint actions and alignment to make progress toward the human right to water and sanitation (OECD-DAC 2011a; GTZ 2007).

In Kenya and Tanzania, GIZ has been actively supporting a human rights–based approach in the health sector, including promoting an HRBA and dialogue among other donors active in this sector. GIZ also brought together partners and donors in the Kenyan health sector to address the serious problem of access of terminally ill children to palliative care. Another example is the close collaboration between GIZ, the African Development Bank, and the Danish International Development Agency (DANIDA) in Kenya on evaluating gender differentials in HIV/AIDS and other areas of health care (OECD-DAC 2011a).

At country level, Denmark often participates in dialogue forums and working groups where human rights priorities and challenges are discussed in relation to the development cooperation; for example, "justice sector" working groups in the PRSP/budget support set-up and EU human rights working groups (OECD-DAC 2011a).

2. Identify areas of support to partner governments on human rights.

Irish Aid is a lead donor in the justice sector in Uganda, where the justice delivery ministries and actors (police, prisons, etc.) work together to ensure the protection of human rights and access to justice for all. Irish Aid supports the Uganda Human Rights Commission within the Justice Law and Order Sector in Uganda, for its valuable work in monitoring, promoting, and adjudicating on human rights in Uganda (OECD-DAC 2011a).

CIDA also supports projects that are specifically aligned with government commitments on human rights. The UNIFEM CEDAW Southeast Asia Program (CEDAW SEAP) has been working since 2004 to support governments, civil society organizations, and partners within the UN system and international community to facilitate better implementation of the CEDAW to advance women's rights in Southeast Asia (OECD-DAC 2011a).

3. Safeguard human rights in processes of state building.

Danish support to human rights is centered around the strengthening of the capacity of relevant national institutions to promote the rule of law and human rights. Examples include support to ministries of human rights (e.g., in Burkina Faso), national human rights commissions (e.g., in Uganda and Bangladesh), and ministries of justice (e.g., in Mozambique) (OECD-DAC 2011a).

SDC supports the creation and strengthening of national human rights institutions in several countries. The agency works with the Civil Society and Human Rights Network in Afghanistan, which strengthens the rule of law and respect for human rights by promoting the understanding of human rights concepts among civil society organizations through human rights awareness trainings. SDC also supports the minister of justice in Bolivia in its implementation of the Human Rights Action Plan (OECD-DAC 2011a).

USAID works with government human rights institutions, such as the ombudsman, human rights commission, and temporary investigative commission, to build their capacities to execute their mandates beyond capital cities. It also supports government efforts to protect human rights defenders in places such as Colombia, where the ministry of justice is creating programs that protect individuals and communities at risk of harm from armed groups.

ADC supports state building in Uganda through a project aimed at strengthening the capacities of parliamentarians in Uganda and the participation of civil society via elected representatives. Austria also supports women's rights in Uganda through the civil society organization Federation of Women Lawyers (FIDA), thereby strengthening women's rights but also contributing to civil society as a vibrant force in society. Finally, the ADC supports human rights institutions in Uganda through initiatives such as the Legal Aid Basket Fund or the Justice, Law and Order Sector (OECD-DAC 2011a).

4. Support the demand side of human rights.

Through support to the Organization of American States, CIDA's Modernization of Haiti's Civil Registry project (2008–14) helps Haiti's national identification office (Office National d'Identification, or ONI) to consolidate and modernize its capacity to maintain a unified national civil registration and identification system that is permanent, universally accessible, secure, and nondiscriminatory. The lack of a civil identity in Haiti leaves millions of people unable to access basic services, apply for credit, obtain title to property, or find jobs in the formal sector. This project has become particularly important since the January 2010 earthquake in Haiti, during which many lost their identification documents. By the end of the project in 2014, the registration rate for children is expected to rise from 30 percent to 95 percent, and the overall registration rate to near 100 percent (CIDA 2011c; OECD-DAC 2011a).

Human rights awareness-raising campaigns conducted in a municipality in Benin have led to what one UNDP practitioner described as an awakening of conscience ("un éveil de conscience"), marked by dramatically increased participation of the population, especially women, in local development and policy processes. In its 2006 Participatory Poverty Reduction Strategy Paper (PRSP) project, UNDP partnered with the NGO Social Watch to reach out to the population and ask them their views on each Millennium Development Goal. On the basis of the information, Social Watch lobbied the government to incorporate these views into the national 2006 PRSP. To encourage stronger public engagement in the PRSP process, Social Watch and UNDP conducted a number of civic education campaigns to build awareness among the people of the municipality about their rights and how to claim them. Due to high levels of illiteracy, many people had no knowledge of these issues. As a result of the campaign, women started to engage more in the local development policy processes. On their own initiative they proceeded to train other women in human rights concepts. This development was also positive for the authorities, who reported that a more informed and responsive citizenry helped them with their work. They thus encouraged UNDP to employ further awareness-raising activities to strengthen community involvement (UNDP 2007).

USAID also helps strengthen governance and human rights institutions by fostering demand by NGOs and civil society organizations that assert their rights. Funding is provided to build the capacities of a wide range of groups that address civic participation and the rights of women, lesbian/gay/bisexual/transgender communities, persons with disabilities, and indigenous people.

5. **Promote nondiscrimination as a basis for more inclusive and stable societies.**

In an effort to assist with the integration of all groups into the democratic process, the ADC supports the rights of the indigenous Maya people in Guatemala. A bilingual education scheme has been developed in cooperation with the national ministry of education and established at the regional level. Mayan culture, language, and traditional law are promoted through organizational development measures, to enable Mayan institutions to cooperate with national institutions and thus exert political influence. As a third component, priority is attached to promoting women by developing their occupational skills through further training. Awareness activities ensure that indigenous women can claim their rights (ADC 2010).

In Georgia, Armenia, and Azerbaijan, the ADC supports a project that aims at socioeconomically reintegrating mine victims, as a vulnerable group, into the societies of South Caucasus countries. This is part of ADC's overall strategy for integrating the needs of persons with disabilities in all activities (OECD-DAC 2011a).

6. Consider human rights in decisions on alignment and aid instruments.

One example of how Ireland's engagement is aligned with partner governments' international human rights commitments is the Department of Foreign Affairs' support of the Universal Periodic Review, (UPR) process. Ireland is actively engaged with government, human rights commissions, and civil society organizations at the country level in the program countries that are undergoing Universal Periodic Reviews. Irish Embassies in program countries are uniquely placed to play active diplomatic, political, and development roles there—and to make use of the synergy between them. Support has been provided for the UPR process in Malawi, Ethiopia, Zambia, Egypt, Lesotho, Vietnam, and currently in Sierra Leone and Uganda (OECD-DAC 2011a).

In Ethiopia, the Irish Embassy plays an active role within the human rights coordination forum of embassies, bilateral donors, and the UN. During the period of Ethiopia's UPR (the latter half of 2009 and early 2010) Ireland was political co-chair of the group. The Irish Embassy had two levels of engagement with the UPR process—promoting the UPR process and raising issues of concern at country level (such as on NGO legislation), along with other embassies and agencies, and raising certain issues of concern at the examination process in Geneva (OECD-DAC 2011a).

The results frameworks used in Danish-supported human rights and development programs typically feature several indicators that are sensitive to human rights obligations and principles. In Niger, for instance, a support program aimed at promoting gender equality and equity includes result indicators related to Niger's removing its reservations to the CEDAW and ratifying its additional protocol. In Mozambique, one of several justice/law and order indicators was concerned with a gradual increase in the percentage of criminal cases processed within the limits established by law. When relevant, Denmark actively supports the inclusion of human rights–related indicators in PRSP performance assessment frameworks (OECD-DAC 2011a).

As human rights standards and principles have increasingly become an explicit reference in GTZ policy, they have also materialized in program planning and in the definition of program indicators. In some cases, program objectives and indicators explicitly refer to human rights, and in others the substance of human rights or their key elements are incorporated into program indicators. One example of an indicator used in the water sector reform program in Kenya is as follows:

- *Overall objective:* The *sustainable access* to safe drinking water for *urban poor* has increased and water resource management has improved.
- *Indicator for overall objective:* At least 1.6 million *poor* living in cities have additional *access* to *safe* and *affordable* drinking water.
- *Indicator at component level:* 80 percent of the *Water Action Groups* report to the regulatory authority three times a year on the *current state of the realization of the human right to water* in their region (so far no regular reporting). (OECD-DAC 2011a)

7. Consider mutual reinforcement between human rights and aid effectiveness principles.

Nepal's Safe Motherhood Program, supported by DFID, has used a human rights–based approach to inform women from marginalized groups about their entitlements to free basic health care services and to nondiscriminatory access to services under Nepal's 2007 interim constitution. These women's views are used to inform improvements in health care service delivery. This program is part of a larger effort by DFID, the World Bank, and other donors to make aid more effective by addressing the problems of social exclusion and discrimination in Nepal (Ferguson 2008).

The WHO and OHCHR have facilitated the engagement of civil society organizations, such as the Uganda National Health Consumers Organization, with the Uganda Ministry of Health to inform people at the local level about their entitlements to health. They also worked cooperatively to develop a charter of patients' rights used in the planning of national health strategies. This type of partnership between local, national, and international organizations has bolstered partner country ownership on the right to health (Ferguson 2008).

8. Do no harm.

The incorporation of human rights standards can help mitigate harm to human rights by providing a binding legal standard against which development policies, processes, and outcomes can be assessed, (1) to determine risks to human rights and whether development activities are likely to result in harm, or in fact do so; (2) to ensure that development activities in fact promote human rights or create the conditions for the realization of human rights; (3) to prevent and redress unintended negative impacts on human rights in development processes and outcomes; (4) to better understand the claim that development advances human rights; and (5) to foster a deeper understanding of the relationship between the two fields (McInerney-Lankford 2009).

An example of the application of the "do no harm" principle can be found in the WHO's creation in 2005 of the World Alliance for Patient Safety. Its aim was to bring attention to the need to avoid unintentional harm caused in the delivery of health care in developing countries and countries in economic transition (WHO 2004). The "do no harm" principle is further raised in the health care context where human rights impact assessments are needed for public health programs, such as immunization campaigns.

9. Take a harmonized and graduated approach to deteriorating human rights situations.

In cases where Irish Aid provides sector and budget support through joint donor processes (e.g., the joint budget support operations in Mozambique, Tanzania, and Uganda), human rights and the respect for the rule of law are specified as underlying principles that must be in place for that support to be provided. This provides the basis for dialogue with partner governments on human rights, especially when cases arise in which human rights are being threatened (OECD-DAC 2011a).

The ADC and ADA have elaborated a policy in the context of budget support that fosters a harmonized and graduated approach to deteriorating human rights situations, creating a harmonized assessment of when a human rights situation remains challenging, despite the fact that instruments were developed in the past (OECD-DAC 2011a).

10. Ensure that the scaling-up of aid is conducive to human rights.

Addressing the problems faced by those living with HIV is critical to achieving the MDGs, but most existing HIV-related legal services are provided on a small scale. To address this problem, UNDP collaborated with the International Development Law Organization (IDLO) and UNAIDS to develop a toolkit that advises people involved in expanding and improving HIV-related legal services on how to scale up their programs, while continuing to protect and promote the human rights of those living with HIV. The toolkit encourages the use of a participatory needs assessment prior to scaling up services nationally, to ensure that local perspectives inform the analysis and community trust and ownership in the programs are fostered. When HIV-related legal services are scaled up in ways that are client centered, nondiscriminatory, participatory, gender inclusive, confidential, and accountable to the communities they serve, demand for services increases and care becomes more universal (IDLO, UNAIDS, and UDP 2009).

Nordic Trust Fund Grants

To execute the Nordic Trust Fund's (NTF) grant program (box 2.14, chapter 2), the NTF Secretariat works with teams within the World Bank's Regions and Networks, in addition to the IFC and World Bank Institute, to identify interest for an NTF-funded program. The NTF advises teams on substantive human rights issues, facilitates links to human rights resources, and offers practical inputs. The grants are intended to support client countries' development strategies, rather than engage in monitoring, assessment, or compliance functions. Moreover, although the grants must have an explicit link to human rights, the Nordic Trust Fund does not promote a human rights–based approach or work on World Bank policies or procedures. Grants are typically $400,000 per project, and a total of 55 grants have been made thus far. The following are examples of NTF-funded projects.

Supporting Women's and Children's Rights in the Artisanal Mining Sector

An NTF grant is supporting work to address women's and children's rights in the artisanal mining sector in the Democratic Republic of

Congo. The grant is also supporting the creation of an action plan to eradicate child labor in coltan and copper mining at an artisanal mining site in Katanga province; the plan will look at stakeholder analysis as well as the Congolese legal framework. Additional research will be conducted to understand the relationship between violence, conflict, artisanal mines in the Kivus, and women's rights.

At the outset of the project, a human rights portfolio review of the country was conducted, and it was determined that the intersection of women's and children's rights and the artisanal mining sector was a promising entry point. Although a few publications appeared on the link between mining and sexual violence, there was little analysis of the gender dimensions of artisanal and small-scale mining more generally or of how the sector could bring economic returns to both men and women. The context of the Democratic Republic of Congo also provides an opportunity to examine how human rights considerations can improve Bank work in post-conflict settings. The draft analytical tool (World Bank 2011h) produced in early 2011 draws from the IFC HRIAM (chapter 3) and the Bank's draft gender assessment in the artisanal mining sector. Possible opportunities for integrating human rights analysis are identified, including project identification and concept documents, activities at project preparation and design stages, and project appraisal documents.

Implementing the Right to Health in Colombia

The 1991 Colombian constitution guarantees the right to health, including health insurance for all citizens, by subsidizing health services for the poor. To implement this constitutional requirement, the Colombian government passed the Law 10 in 1993, creating a national health insurance system with two regimes, one for workers in the formal labor market and those who have the ability to pay, and the other for workers in the informal sector and those unable to pay for insurance. Despite the law, nearly 12 percent of the population remains without health insurance, and persons receiving subsidized services encounter poorer quality and less access to care. As a result, Colombians have increasingly filed judicial complaints in recent years ("tutelas"), demanding payment for health procedures not covered by the regimes. Courts have been receptive to these complaints, ordering insurance providers to pay various medical bills, resulting in immense pressure on the public budget.

In July 2008, Colombia's supreme court issued "Sentencia T-760," a "Bill of Health Rights" that obliges the government to protect all citizens under a series of circumstances. The court also required the government to expeditiously establish a strategy for eliminating coverage disparities between the two regimes. Health regulations were promulgated in 2009. Later that year a Nordic Trust Fund grant provided for an economic analysis of the mid- and long-term financial sustainability of the state's plan to ensure the right to health. The grant will also support an analysis of the process of litigation of health rights and the implementation of the Sentencia. Finally, the grant will support analytical work on possible models for a new legal framework on health rights, as well as research on access to justice and alternatives to health litigation to enforce the right to health. Overall, the grant will foster dialogue among the various branches of government and stakeholders on health rights and will also shed light on the significance and value added of an approach predicated on the right to health and how it is distinct from approaches that do not employ the language or framework of rights.

Finnish Rights-Based Approach Applied to Rural Village Water Resources Management Project in Nepal

Although the new Finnish development policy of 2012 emphasizes a human rights–based approach to development, many of these principles are already reflected in the Rural Village Water Resources Management Project (RVWRMP) at work in 10 districts of the Far-Western Region and Mid-Western Region of Nepal (Ministry for Foreign Affairs of Finland 2012a). This is implicitly a human rights based project in which water resources are taken as the point of entry into addressing poverty. Water rights are discussed, as are other issues relating to empowerment and good governance, such as transparency and accountability. Working on water resources related physical infrastructure provides an opportunity for learning by doing (capacity development) and introduces further livelihoods and institutional development opportunities. The project mainstreams additional human rights based principles through its Gender Equality and Social Inclusion Strategy. Although this strategy could be revised to incorporate an HRBA more explicitly, its current action plan and inclusive planning tools help ensure participation, empowerment, and systematic capacity building.

One of the challenges faced in the RVWRMP has been confusion about identification of the duty-bearer. As the Village Development Committee (VDC)–level strategic planner and leading institution for water use master plans, the Water Resources Management Committee can be seen as the immediate duty-bearer in practical terms, along with the user committees as local water system managers. Because it is a highly decentralized environment, it is unreasonable to expect that the Nepalese government would be the immediate duty-bearer, in terms of fully providing the numerous rural water systems and their operation and maintenance. This issue is further complicated by the way in which water is viewed in the context of integrated water resources management, which includes a range of land- and water-based development activities and related "duties." Rights discussions are not new for these communities, but they tend to be raised at the community level with an exclusive focus on rights, with the roles and responsibilities of duty-bearers often ignored.

There is a cross-boundary impact as well. India has traditionally been closer to the people of Far-Western districts than the rest of Nepal. This proximity appears to influence the way people think about the government's role as duty-bearer. For instance in Darchula district, communities that are closer to India's border feel more strongly that citizens have greater rights to get free services from the government. They view it as the government's duty to provide services free of cost, whether it has the capacity to do so or not. The issue arises during discussions about subsidies, household contributions to sanitation (in the context of private household latrines), and the use of World Food Program food aid as part of the community contribution to large infrastructure development.

Many communities continue to think along lines of a charity approach or to mix different approaches depending on which one seems to offer the best or most immediate benefits. The focus is not on long-term sustainability. Numerous NGO projects continue to be driven by the charity approach as well, which can influence communities to think accordingly. For example, the right to sanitation put into effect under the National Sanitation Master Plan has materialized as a right to a free latrine, regardless of whether the property is private or a person has the resources to build one on his or her own. This was one of the lessons learned from the first phase of the RVWRMP and was subsequently added to feasibility study "reality checks."

In its effort to adhere to the underlying principle that the right to water, sanitation, and livelihood are universal and inalienable, the project targets the poorest and most disadvantaged (including those disadvantaged based on gender, caste, ethnicity, socioeconomic status, or geographic isolation). Consequently, 18 of the 28 monitoring indicators have a social inclusion dimension. Using a participatory and inclusive community funding and governance mechanism, project communities have managed to complete water and sanitation schemes for the benefit of 225,000 people.

DFID Right to Identity Project in Bolivia

DFID co-funded a project to foster the right to identity in Bolivia. It set out to promote more inclusive political participation by strengthening the capacities of the state and citizens to demand rights and fulfill obligations. Documentation and registration campaigns can reduce the number of undocumented persons in Bolivia. Laws, procedures, and processes, however, also need to change if results are to be sustainable. Therefore, DFID aid helped provide identification documents to undocumented Bolivians (especially the poor, women, and indigenous people). It helped inform civil society, civil registration officials, and members of the electoral court by raising awareness about citizens' rights and the processes, to promote greater participation in referenda and municipal elections. In addition, it increased the capacity of the National Electoral Court and Registration Service to efficiently and effectively undertake referenda and elections, and it helped create a plan to strengthen those institutions for the medium term.

Political tension and poor communication between the state and civil society made formal coordination at the national level difficult. It was easier at the departmental level, where departmental electoral courts, national police, and ombudsmen constituted registration brigades.

From the Rule of Law to Access to Justice

Rule of Law

Good practices in the area of rule of law can be used to develop state capacity to meet fundamental rights standards, for example, in criminal justice.

USAID has been one of the leading bilateral agencies in the field of the rule of law. It has worked in this area for over 20 years and has significant capacity at headquarters to undertake lesson-learning exercises and develop new tools. Contractors have delivered rule of law activities in more than 50 USAID country offices. Though USAID does not have a human rights policy, a number of its rule of law activities have contributed to improving respect for civil and political rights. In the 1980s, for example, justice programs were developed in Latin America aimed at reducing abuses. USAID started working in Bolivia in 1986. Beginning in 1992 it supported efforts to modernize the national rule of law. The reform of the criminal justice system was a significant achievement. In 2001, when an oral accusatory process (based on a UN model criminal code) was introduced, USAID helped tailor the process specifically for Bolivia. It funded training in the new code for criminal court judges and the establishment of an Office of Public Defense in the Ministry of Justice, so that the constitutional right to defense could be respected in practice. Public defenders provided representation to the majority of criminal justice defendants, and time spent in pre-trial detention was being reduced.

BMZ has undertaken rule of law projects in several contexts as well. At the national level, the ministry has been working since 2004 to strengthen respect for the rule of law in Colombia by improving the capacity, efficiency, and accountability of legal institutions and fostering the law's role in finding a peaceful resolution to conflict. The early stages of the program focused on enabling the judiciary, the ombudsman's office, and the inspector general to execute their respective mandates more efficiently and effectively.

Within the field of law enforcement, Inwent (now part of GIZ) conducted human rights trainings for officials working with the Iraqi police, penal system, and ministries, including the Iraqi Ministry of Human Rights. As part of that program, Inwent supported the development of the first human rights education manual in Arabic that was designed for practical training sessions and training of trainers. The manual is now in use in other Arabic-speaking countries and was adapted to country contexts in Egypt and Tunisia, supported by a project funded by BMZ. At the regional level, BMZ has directly supported capacity building for the African Court on Human and People's Rights by supporting the establishment of the court's secretariat at its headquarters in Arusha, Tanzania. From 2008 to 2010, experts provided specialist knowledge, including expertise in library systems and legal informatics. Overall, these improvements helped create the conditions essential for the court to perform its adjudicative functions and thereby contribute to the con-tinued evolution of human rights standards in Africa.

Access to Justice

Several donor policies and practices have moved toward adopting a human rights–based approach to rule of law and law enforcement work (either explicitly or implicitly). Agencies that have not embraced such an approach (such as the World Bank or USAID) have nevertheless adopted a focus on access to justice as an aspect of programming.

In Bolivia, for example, USAID is supporting the development of Integrated Justice Centers to improve access to justice for isolated and predominantly indigenous populations, in areas where the central gov-ernment has tenuous authority. Trained professionals provide advice on the formal judicial system, as well as conciliatory services to help resolve local conflicts.

Another example is German collaboration in Zambia in support of women's rights, to institutionalize gender equality in law and work with customary law and lay judges. Legal information and awareness train-ing has fostered greater confidence among women and greater respect and support among men. Austria is also working to support women's rights in Uganda. In addition to directly funding government institu-tions in the justice, law, and order sector, including the Human Rights Commission, the ADC provides financial support to the Rights, Justice and Peace program component of the Uganda Democratic Governance Facility (DGF). The DGF program promotes and protects women's rights in northern Uganda by improving their access to justice and to legal aid services.

DFID's involvement in security and justice sector reform uses a people-centered approach that combines work on security sector reform with safety, security, and access to justice (Ball et al. 2007). As a result, an integrated or sectorwide approach examines how a justice system operates as a whole and recognizes the need to work better across institutions, rather than with individual partners. DFID has not "branded" its new policy as a human rights–based approach, though it can be considered to be implicitly following it, with the exception of the lack of systematic attention to human rights standards. A 2005 strategy for security and development (DFID 2005d) committed DFID to integrating safety, security, and access to justice more systematically with security sector reform and human rights.

The South Africa juvenile justice project (implemented in collaboration with UNDP) helped develop a more appropriate youth justice system. Its goal was set in human rights language by referencing the Convention on the Rights of the Child (Article 37) and other international norms and standards. The project demonstrated that it was possible to work on policy reform even before the legal framework was finalized and to prepare partners for implementation. Significant efforts were made to cost the Child Justice Bill adequately, setting a standard for future policy development processes. A ministry team with a range of skills managed the project. The team adopted an intersectoral approach (bringing in treasury and provincial-level officials), but the set of potential institutional partners and beneficiaries was limited (an annual average of 100,000 to 200,000 candidates for diversion). The team developed a strong relationship with NGOs. In fact, NGOs established a coalition, the Child Justice Alliance, even though this was a governmental project.

ADC launched a similar project in the area of child justice. It helped the government of Namibia to amend its legislation and regulations so that they are consistent with its constitution and its international human rights commitments. The Child Justice in Namibia Project corrected structural and professional deficits in the legal system by building an autonomous, integrated child justice system. The project strengthened the ability of the government of Namibia to protect the rights of children who come into conflict with the law by establishing laws, procedures, and institutions specifically applicable to them.

UNDP developed an access to justice policy that emphasizes a human rights–based approach. It prioritized people's equal ability to use justice services—regardless of their gender, ethnicity, religion, political views, age, class, disability, or other sources of distinction. In the Asia-Pacific region, it documented lessons learned. As DFID did, UNDP focused on the various stages and capacities needed for citizens to move from grievance to remedy, ushering them through a process of recognition of a grievance, awareness of rights, claiming, adjudication, and enforcement. Using this approach, the justice system is analyzed from the perspective not just of institutions, but also of citizens and the barriers they face.

Intensive participatory research, with local researchers, found barriers to accessing justice. Small-scale pilot projects are shrinking some of those barriers by bringing together duty-holders and rights-bearers, and efforts are directed at the informal sector in this first phase. An earlier case study (UNDP 2004a) pointed out that this approach is resource intensive: it requires that the donor agency commit time, funds, and staff and management capacity; it also calls for local partners willing to work in this way.

CIDA's Approach to Child Protection

In 2010, at the Davos Economic Forum, Canadian Prime Minister Stephen Harper announced that maternal, newborn, and child health would be the chief goal for the Muskoka G-8 summit agenda. He acknowledged that action was needed, as global progress in meeting the MDGs in these areas was lagging (CIDA 2011a). Canada's international development policy includes governance as a priority, with human rights as a key focus area. Governance programming includes promotion of the rights of children, particularly those affected by conflict, gender-based violence, and natural disasters. CIDA's Children and Youth Strategy (CIDA 2009a) supports human rights in the context of its work to improve child and maternal health, improve access to quality education opportunities (especially for girls), and protect children from violence, exploitation, and abuse. Its strategy ensures that "equality between women and men, environmental sustainability, and governance and human rights are integrated across all CIDA programming."

This approach and its earlier *Action Plan on Child Protection* (CIDA 2001a) are consistent with the four fundamental principles that the CRC set to guide the interpretation of its articles: the best interests of the child as a primary consideration in all actions concerning children; the right to nondiscrimination; the right to life, survival, and development; and the right to participation. The strategy also points to the Official Development Assistance Accountability Act of 2008 (ODAA), which applies to all of Canada's federal departments (including CIDA) providing official development assistance, which states that the ODAA's purpose is

> to ensure that all Canadian official development assistance abroad is pro-
> vided with a central focus on poverty reduction and in a manner that is
> consistent with Canadian values, Canadian foreign policy, the principles
> of the Paris Declaration on Aid Effectiveness of March 2 2005, sustain-
> able development and democracy promotion and that promotes interna-
> tional human rights standards. (Canada 2008)

In 2003 CIDA undertook a mid-term review of its action plan (Roth-man 2003), which reported that capacity development measures had been undertaken in line with the commitments in the plan. Notably, CIDA established a Child Protection Unit within the Human Rights and Participation Division, in Policy Branch, reflecting the emphasis on participation and human rights based programming. This was supported by a Child Protection Advisors Group drawn from CIDA's programming branches, whose mandate was to support the effective implementation of the action plan. The plan also led to more frequent and comprehensive child rights training (including an increased focus on human rights–based approaches), the establishment of a knowledge network, and the publication of more than 30 tools and resources. CIDA also increased awareness within Canada of children's rights, mainly through the public engagement program of retired Lieutenant-General Roméo A. Dallaire, Special Advisor on War-Affected Children to CIDA and the Minister of International Cooperation.

The review found that the five child protection pilot projects were the "most tangible and visible manifestation of the effective implementation of the Action Plan." All five included strategies for the participation of children in decision making throughout the project cycle. Whereas some of these projects were rights-based from the outset, others were originally child protection or education projects and subsequent efforts were then made to make them consistent with a human rights–based approach, with a particular focus on child participation. Some of these kinds of participatory projects remain instructive more than a decade later (box 8.2). CIDA has also funded the participation of children in several major international conferences, in policy dialogue on issues such as national plans of action for children, and in research.

Another element of the action plan that was anchored in a human rights–based approach was the establishment in 2001 of a Child Protection Research Fund, designed to provide evidence to support more relevant, inclusive, and effective programming. Thirteen projects were funded at a cost of Can $2 million, and the findings from these have underlined the importance of contextual research and analysis to human

---

Box 8.2 Protecting the Interests of Working Children and Youth in Egypt

When CIDA reviewed two projects supporting small business development, it found that half of the businesses involved in the projects relied on the labor of children. However, it discovered that child labor often benefited the children and their families.

Launched in March 2002, "Promoting and Protecting the Interests of Children Who Work" (PPIC) empowered girl and boy participants to identify labor hazards in their workplace and to design and deliver interventions to improve their working and learning conditions. The creation of a network of child workers to facilitate access to services beyond the project increased discussion about child labor among government, civil society, and private sector stakeholders. A school loan fund was set up for families of working children. Despite initial reservations about a human rights–based approach, the Egyptian government asked to use the project as an example of the approach at a national conference. The National Council on Childhood and Motherhood asked the project to advise on the development of a participatory, rights-oriented national strategy for children. The project was extended by a further three years in recognition that participatory approaches require more time and resources than traditional projects.

In coordination with the ILO, CIDA has recently begun its five-year "Decent Employment for Youth" project, which aims to support the government of Egypt's efforts to stimulate sustainable economic growth and provide appropriate jobs for young people, especially among groups such as women-headed households, people with disabilities, poor people living in rural areas, and unemployed graduates. This project will provide assistance to key government ministries, private sector partners, and nonprofit organizations to implement youth employment policies and programs. The project is focusing on providing training and expertise aimed at helping young people secure jobs and start businesses. The project is implemented at both national and regional levels and through pilot projects; it is expected to strengthen local capacities for implementing policy frameworks and best practices that can be scaled up at the national level.

rights based programming. The first project produced a landmark study on girls' lives during and after war in northern Uganda, Sierra Leone, and Mozambique (McKay and Mazurana 2004). The study was used by various UN agencies to train staff and develop standard operating procedures for demobilization and reintegration programs. Another project, involving research conducted by young people on the impact of a recent drought in tribal communities of Rajasthan, led to changes in local government resource allocations for those communities.

More recently CIDA has taken a human rights–based approach to its work with children and youth in Colombia. CIDA supports UNI-CEF to help government and civil society develop public policies for the rights of children and adolescents, their social inclusion, and access to education. Working with Save the Children Canada and the Norwegian Refugee Council, CIDA is supporting the implementation of programs for access to high-quality education for vulnerable children, youth, and adults. Finally, CIDA supports local initiatives for the rights of children and youth, helping protect them from the consequences of violence and conflict (CIDA 2011b).

Minority Rights Policies and Programs

In a paper submitted in 2003 to the UN Working Group on Minorities, the Minority Rights Group International (MRG) reviewed donor agencies' support to minorities. It concluded that whereas some agencies had made progress toward considering indigenous peoples in policy and programming, much less work had been done on other ethnic, religious, and linguistic minorities. The group concluded that minorities do not have a strong voice to articulate their needs in development and that governments do not give enough attention to the situation of minorities, with the result that they are not adequately reflected in poverty reduction strategies. It also noted that agencies lack internal capacity to work on minority issues.

The MRG report nevertheless highlighted a number of good initiatives. In the wake of the UN World Conference on Racism, UNDP commissioned a discussion paper from MRG to inform a new policy note and identified the need for more programming. To develop staff capacity, SDC had agreed to a three-year backstopping mandate with MRG, to train staff and develop tools to assess the situation of minorities and promote their participation in SDC programming. In the meantime, SDC has continued to support the rights of indigenous people by providing core contributions to doCip (Indigenous People's Centre for Documentation, Research, and Information) and Incomindios (International Committee for the Indigenous of the Americas). In 2002, the Inter-American Development Bank adopted its Action Plan for Combating Social Exclusion Due to Race or Ethnic Background (IADB 2002), strengthening its capacity to work on exclusion and racism. The IADB is also reaching out to other agencies, such as the European Commission.

MRG notes that minority issues are usually considered by donors as part of poverty and social inclusion, human rights and governance, or conflict prevention. For example, AusAID's programs that affect minority groups in China's Yunnan province are seen as part of Australia's interest in addressing poverty issues more directly (AusAID 2006). MRG's recommendations for developing donor capacity include greater dialogue between donors and minority representatives and development of institutional policies to mainstream minority rights and move from policy to practice.

MRG calls upon agencies to review their internal ability to uphold nondiscrimination and to ensure that aid is delivered in nondiscriminatory ways, including the use of adequate monitoring mechanisms. To increase capacity and understanding, agencies can train and hire minorities. Programming options include mapping minorities and legal frameworks; including minorities in country strategies; targeting programs using disaggregated data; enhancing accessibility of donor programs by using minority languages and culture; adapting participatory processes to enable genuine participation by minorities; advocating in support of minorities when engaging with governments; and building and using minority capacity, such as that of local businesses or NGOs in minority regions.

Development for All: A Disability-Inclusive Australian Aid Program

Disability is a development issue because of its strong link to poverty: disability may increase the risk of poverty, and poverty may increase the risk of disability. New research released in the 2011 "World Report on Disability" (World Bank and WHO 2011) shows that more than one billion people, or 15 percent of the world's population, experience some form of disability, and one-fifth, or between 110 million and 190 million, encounter significant difficulties. It is apparent that the Millennium Development Goals cannot be achieved unless development efforts reach and benefit people with disabilities.

In November 2008 the Australian Government launched its strategy "Development for All: Towards a Disability-Inclusive Australian Aid Program" (AusAID 2008). The strategy marked a significant change in the way Australia's aid is designed and delivered. Development for All (DFA) aims to improve the reach and effectiveness of development assistance by ensuring that persons with disabilities are included, contribute to, and benefit equally from development efforts. DFA was made available in braille, large print, and audio formats to make it as accessible as possible.

The Development for All strategy is aligned with human rights principles and helps Australia meet its obligations under the UN Convention on the Rights of Persons with Disabilities (CRPD), which came into force in 2008. The convention was intended to build on existing human rights standards and apply them within a disabilities context to ensure that persons with disabilities can exercise and enjoy all fundamental human rights. Accordingly the strategy seeks to ensure that persons with disabilities are included in and benefit equally from Australia's aid program, in line with Article 32 of the CRPD. The strategy's primary outcome is to support persons with disabilities to improve the quality of their lives by promoting and improving access to the same opportunities for participation, contribution, decision making, and social and economic well-being as others.

The Development for All policy (1) supports the inclusion of the strategy across all areas of the aid program, with a particular focus on education and infrastructure; and (2) supports targeted initiatives to enable persons with disabilities to participate in development.

A Human Rights–Based Approach to Water Programming

By demanding rigorous political and social analysis, a human rights–based approach to water program design and implementation can help improve access to water (box 8.3) and prevent interventions that inadvertently reinforce existing conflicts and power imbalances.

In the Kileto District, Tanzania, the International NGO WaterAid implemented a project to improve water access for residents. By integrating human rights principles into the programming process (WaterAid, 1999)—in particular participation, non-discrimination, equality and

---

Box 8.3 Access to Water as a Human Right

The human right to water has been recognized by most states, as well as by international organizations, NGOs, and the business community. It is explicitly recognized in the Convention on the Elimination of Discrimination against Women (1979) and the Convention on the Rights of the Child (1989), as well as in a number of regional human rights and environmental treaties and political declarations. It is implicit in the rights to an adequate standard of living and to health that are guaranteed in the International Covenant on Economic, Social and Cultural Rights (1976).

In its General Comment No. 15 on the Right to Water (2002) the UN Committee on Economic, Social and Cultural Rights affirms this right and clarifies its scope. Although the general comment is not legally binding, it is an authoritative interpretation of the International Covenant on Economic, Social and Cultural Rights by the committee responsible for monitoring its implementation in the countries which have ratified the covenant.

In July 2010, the UN General Assembly formally recognized the right to water and sanitation and acknowledged that clean drinking water and sanitation are integral to the realization of all human rights. In September 2010, the UN Human Rights Council adopted a resolution further affirming that water and sanitation are human rights.

- The right to water is connected with several other human rights, and in some instances, is a precondition for their enjoyment: The right to food—unsafe water consumption and absence of basic sanitation and hygiene undermine the efforts to ensure basic nutrition and consequently the right to food.
- The right to life and the right to health—unsafe water, inadequate sanitation, and lack of basic hygiene are the main causes of infant mortality worldwide.
- The right to education for all—in many countries fetching water is the task of women and girls. Where there is no easy access to water, girls have to help their mothers with this heavy task, and they often refrain from going to school as a result. In other cases, the lack of adequate sanitation facilities in schools poses a particular risk to the dignity and safety of girls and encourages parents to prohibit the schooling of their daughters. Moreover, waterborne diseases often keep children from going to school.
- The right to adequate housing—sanitation is also an important aspect of the right to adequate housing, included in the right of everyone to an adequate standard of living.
- The right to security of person is an important issue in situations where it is unsafe to fetch water or use the existing sanitation facilities, particularly for women and girls.
- Civil and political rights are essential for effective participation in shaping decisions in the water sector, as well as for the accountability mechanism to function.

Source: SDC 2008c.

empowerment—and including these as explicit program goals, WaterAid was able to identify the underlying obstacles to equitable access to water. The participatory approach and analysis revealed that power imbalances, lack of land rights, and exclusion from national policy decisions had impeded access to water for two of the three main ethnic groups. The project was therefore able to work with the communities to overcome the intergroup conflict.

By involving each ethnic group in the analysis and assessment stage of the project, WaterAid was able to identify each group's water needs. A participatory assessment and planning methodology enabled WaterAid to develop an understanding of inter- and intragroup power relations and the wider social context. WaterAid improved understanding among the groups by bringing all project stakeholders into the discussion.

To influence national policy and practices, WaterAid developed a coherent advocacy strategy in Tanzania. The strategy included working with and training national government staff responsible for water services and policies. WaterAid analyzed the political and legal context to see how national policies and legal issues positively and negatively affected the access of the groups. The organization looked at inequitable distribution of land, and subsequent lack of access to water because of a lack of knowledge of land rights and processes for application on the part of the least powerful.

WaterAid found that considerable time and effort had to be invested in discussions among the Kileto partnership management team, field staff, and project communities. Yet it was able to achieve genuine community management of water services by building partnerships with civil society organizations and training them in the planning and implementation of the program.

References

ADC (Austrian Development Cooperation). 2010. *Human Rights Manual: Guidelines for Implementing a Human Rights–Based Approach in ADC*. Vienna: ADC.

AusAID (Australian Agency for International Development). 2006. "China Australia Development Cooperation Program: Review of Human Rights Technical Cooperation Program." Report, AusAID, Canberra.

———. 2008. "Development for All: Towards a Disability-Inclusive Australian Aid Program, 2009–2014." AusAID, Canberra.

Ball, Nicole, Piet Biesheuvel, Tom Hamilton-Baillie, and Funmi Olonisakin. 2007 "Security and Justice Sector Reform Programming in Africa." Evaluation Working Paper 23, April, DFID, London and Glasgow.

Canada. 2008. *Official Development Assistance Accountability Act*, 28 June 2008, S.C. 2008, c. 17, Minister of Justice, Québec.

CIDA (Canadian International Development Agency). 2001. *CIDA's Action Plan on Child Protection: Promoting the Rights of Children Who Need Special Protection Measures*. CIDA, Québec.

————. 2009a. "Securing the Future of Children and Youth: CIDA's Children and Youth Strategy." November, Québec.

————. 2011a. *Development for Results, 2009-2010*. Québec: CIDA.

————. 2011b. "Colombia: CIDA Report." CIDA, Québec.

————. 2011c. "In Haiti, Having an Identification Card Means 'Having a Say.'" August 3, Canadian International Development agency, http://bit.ly/vg4ue7.

DFID (U.K. Department for International Development). 2005d. "How to Reduce Maternal Deaths: Rights and Responsibilities." How-to note, DFID, London.

Ferguson, Clare. 2008. "Linking Human Rights and Aid Effectiveness for Better Development Results: Practical Experience from the Health Sector." Report for the Human Rights Task Team of the OECD-DAC Network on Governance. OECD-DAC GOVNET, May 14, Paris.

GTZ (German Organization for Technical Cooperation). 2007. "Kenyan-German Development Cooperation in the Water Sector, Assessment from a Human Rights Perspective," prepared by Munguti Katui Katua et al. June 5, GTZ, Eschborn.

————. 2009a. *The Human Right to Water and Sanitation: Translating Theory into Practice*. December, GTZ, Eschborn.

————. 2009b. *Compilation—Promising Practices on the Human Rights–Based Approach in German Development Cooperation*. GTZ, Eschborn.

IADB (Inter-American Development Bank). 2002. *Action Plan for Combating Social Exclusion Due to Race or Ethnic Background, June 2002–December 2003*. Inter-American Development Bank, Washington, DC.

IDLO (International Development Law Organization), UNAIDS, and UNDP. 2009. "Toolkit: Scaling up HIV-Related Legal Services." Rome. http://bit.lyWVGi62.

McInerney-Lankford, Siobhán. 2009. "Human Rights and Development: A Comment on Challenges and Opportunities from a Legal Perspective." *Journal of Human Rights Practice* 1 (1): 51–82.

McKay, Susan, and Dyan Mazurana. 2004. *Where Are the Girls? Girls in Fighting Forces in Northern Uganda, Sierra Leone and Mozambique: Their Lives During and After War*. International Center for Human Rights and Democratic Development, Montréal.

Ministry for Foreign Affairs of Finland. 2012a. *Rights Based Apprach to Development in Rural Village Water Resources Management Project (RVWRMP) in Nepal*. MFA – Finland, Helsinki.

————. 2012b. "How Do We Know that It Works? Inclusion Indicators in Rural Village Water Resources Management Project in Far and Mid West of Nepal." MFA, Helsinki.

OECD (Organisation for Economic Cooperation and Development). 2007a. "DAC Action-Oriented Policy Paper on Human Rights and Development." February, OECD, Paris.

OECD-DAC (OECD Development Assistance Committee). 2011a. "Draft Results of the Human Rights Donor Survey, May 2011." Final publication forthcoming, OECD, Paris.

Rothman, Margot. 2003. "Mid-Term Review of CIDA's Action Plan on Child Protection. Final Report." Unpublished mimeo, available from the Child Protection Unit, CIDA, Gatineau, Québec.

SDC (Swiss Agency for Development and Cooperation). 2008c. "A Human Rights–Based Approach to Water and Sanitation: Briefing Paper," prepared by Catherine Favre and François Münger. Sepember 2, Bern.

UNDP (United Nations Development Program). 2004a. "Access to Justice." Practice Note, New York.

————. 2007. "Human Rights and the Millennium Development Goals: Making the Link." January 1, Oslo.

WaterAid. 1999. "A WaterAid Briefing Paper: The Right to Water, Sanitation and Hygiene and the Human Rights–Based Approach to Development," prepared by Belinda U. Calaguas. July, London.

WHO (World Health Organization). 2004. *World Alliance for Patient Safety: Forward Programme 2005.* WHO, Geneva.

World Bank. 2011h. "Draft Guide to Artisanal Mining Sector Analysis," prepared by Robert Mugisha and Bernard Harborne. March, World Bank, Washington, DC.

World Bank and WHO. 2011. *World Report on Disability.* Washington, DC: World Bank and WHO.

Appendix 1
The Human Rights–Based Approach to Development Co-operation—Towards a Common Understanding among UN Agencies

Introduction

The United Nations is founded on the principles of peace, justice, freedom, and human rights. The Universal Declaration of Human Rights recognizes human rights as the foundation of freedom, justice, and peace. The unanimously adopted Vienna Declaration and Program of Action states that democracy, development, and respect for human rights and fundamental freedoms are interdependent and mutually reinforcing. In the UN Program for Reform that was launched in 1997, the Secretary-General called on all entities of the UN system to mainstream human rights into their various activities and programs within the framework of their respective mandates.

Since then a number of UN agencies have adopted a human rights–based approach to their development co-operation and have gained experiences in its operationalization. But each agency has tended to have its own interpretation of approach and how it should be operationalized.

However, UN interagency collaboration at global and regional levels, and especially at the country level in relation to the CCA and UNDAF processes, requires a common understanding of this approach and its implications for development programming. What follows is an attempt to arrive at such an understanding on the basis of those aspects of the human rights–based approach that are common to the policy and practice of the UN bodies that participated in the Interagency Workshop on Implementing a Human Rights–Based Approach in the context of UN reform, 3–5 May, 2003.

This Statement of Common Understanding specifically refers to a human rights–based approach to development co-operation and development programming by UN agencies.

Common Understanding

1. All programs of development co-operation, policies and technical assistance should further the realisation of human rights as laid down in the Universal Declaration of Human Rights and other international human rights instruments.

2. Human rights standards contained in, and principles derived from, the Universal Declaration of Human Rights and other international human rights instruments guide all development co-operation and programming in all sectors and in all phases of the programming process.

3. Development co-operation contributes to the development of the capacities of "duty-bearers" to meet their obligations and/or of "rights-holders" to claim their rights.

4. All programs of development co-operation, policies, and technical assistance should further the realisation of human rights as laid down in the universal declaration of human rights and other international human rights instruments.

A set of program activities that only incidentally contributes to the realisation of human rights does not necessarily constitute a human rights–based approach to programming. In a human rights–based approach to programming and development co-operation, the aim of all activities is to contribute directly to the realisation of one or several human rights.

5. Human rights standards contained in, and principles derived from, the universal declaration of human rights and other international human rights instruments guide all development co-operation and programming in all sectors and in all phases of the programming process.

Human Rights principles guide programming in all sectors, such as: health, education, governance, nutrition, water and sanitation, HIV/AIDS, employment and labor relations, and social and economic security. This includes all development co-operation directed towards the achievement of the Millennium Development Goals and the Millennium Declaration. Consequently, human rights standards and principles guide both the Common Country Assessment and the UN Development Assistance Framework.

Human rights principles guide all programming in all phases of the programming process, including assessment and analysis, program planning and design (including setting of goals, objectives and strategies); implementation, monitoring and evaluation. Among these human rights principles are: universality and inalienability; indivisibility; interdependence and inter-relatedness; non-discrimination and equality; participation and inclusion; accountability and the rule of law. These principles are explained below.

- Universality and inalienability: Human rights are universal and inalienable. All people everywhere in the world are entitled to them. The human person in whom they inhere cannot voluntarily give them up. Nor can others take them away from him or her. As stated in Article 1 of the UDHR, "All human beings are born free and equal in dignity and rights."
- Indivisibility: Human rights are indivisible. Whether of a civil, cultural, economic, political or social nature, they are all inherent to the dignity of every human person. Consequently, they all have equal status as rights, and cannot be ranked, a priori, in a hierarchical order.
- Interdependence and inter-relatedness: The realisation of one right often depends, wholly or in part, upon the realisation of others. For instance, realisation of the right to health may depend, in certain circumstances, on realisation of the right to education or of the right to information.

- Equality and non-discrimination: All individuals are equal as human beings and by virtue of the inherent dignity of each human person. All human beings are entitled to their human rights without discrimination of any kind, such as race, color, sex, ethnicity, age, language, religion, political or other opinion, national or social origin, disability, property, birth or other status as explained by the human rights treaty bodies.

- Participation and inclusion: Every person and all peoples are entitled to active, free and meaningful participation in, contribution to, and enjoyment of civil, economic, social, cultural and political development in which human rights and fundamental freedoms can be realized.

- Accountability and rule of law: States and other duty-bearers are answerable for the observance of human rights. In this regard, they have to comply with the legal norms and standards enshrined in human rights instruments. Where they fail to do so, aggrieved rights-holders are entitled to institute proceedings for appropriate redress before a competent court or other adjudicator in accordance with the rules and procedures provided by law.

6. Programs of development co-operation contribute to the development of the capacities of duty-bearers to meet their obligations and of "rights-holders" to claim their rights.

In a HRBA human rights determine the relationship between individuals and groups with valid claims (rights-holders) and state and non-state actors with correlative obligations (duty-bearers). It identifies rights-holders (and their entitlements) and corresponding duty-bearers (and their obligations) and works towards strengthening the capacities of rights-holders to make their claims, and of duty-bearers to meet their obligations.

Implications of a Human Rights–Based Approach to Development Programming of UN Agencies

Experience has shown that the use of a human rights–based approach requires the use of good programming practices. However, the application of "good programming practices" does not by itself constitute a human rights–based approach and requires additional elements.

The following elements are necessary, specific, and unique to a human rights–based approach:

- Assessment and analysis in order to identify the human rights claims of rights-holders and the corresponding human rights obligations of duty-bearers as well as the immediate, underlying, and structural causes of the non-realisation of rights.
- Programs assess the capacity of rights-holders to claim their rights and of duty-bearers to fulfill their obligations. They then develop strategies to build these capacities.
- Programs monitor and evaluate both outcomes and processes guided by human rights standards and principles.
- Programming is informed by the recommendations of international human rights bodies and mechanisms.

Other elements of good programming practices that are also essential under a HRBA include:

- People are recognized as key actors in their own development, rather than passive recipients of commodities and services.
- Participation is both a means and a goal.
- Strategies are empowering, not disempowering.
- Both outcomes and processes are monitored and evaluated.
- Analysis includes all stakeholders.
- Programs focus on marginalized, disadvantaged, and excluded groups.
- The development process is locally owned.
- Programs aim to reduce disparity.
- Both top-down and bottom-up approaches are used in synergy.
- Situation analysis is used to identify immediate, underlying, and basic causes of development problems.
- Measurable goals and targets are important in programming.
- Strategic partnerships are developed and sustained.
- Programs support accountability to all stakeholders.

Index

bridging analysis, 104
budgetary challenges, 129–30
Burkina Faso
    democratic support, 76, 109
    disabilities-inclusive aid programs, 44
    right-to-education initiatives, 38b
Burundi, right-to-education initiatives
    in, 38b
Busan Outcome Document. *See* Fourth
    High-Level Forum on Aid
    Effectiveness (2011)
Busan Partnership for Effective
    Development Cooperation, 122

C

Cambodia
    right-to-education initiatives, 38b
    women's rights, 98
Canada. *See also* Canadian International
    Development Agency (CIDA)
    aid budget, review of
        effectiveness, 130
    Official Development Assistance
        Accountability Act (ODAAA,
        2008), 71, 153–54, 237
    social development funding from, 49b
Canadian International Development
    Agency (CIDA)
    Aid Effectiveness Plan, 87, 129, 153
    child rights programming, 28–29,
        73b, 236–39, 238b
    community-level governance
        programs, 54
    identifying root causes of poverty, 79
    treatment of human rights in
        development assistance, 10
    UNIFEM CEDAW Southeast Asia
        Program, 98
capacity development, 85–86, 101b, 105,
    107–10, 146, 222–23
Carothers, Thomas, 54
CEB. *See* Council of Europe Bank

CEDAW. *See* Convention on the
    Elimination of All Forms of
    Discrimination against Women
Center for Economic and Social Rights
    (CESR), 117
Central American Institute of Fiscal
    Studies, 37
Central Asia
    livelihood programs, 40
    UNIFEM's bridging analysis, 70b
challenges and opportunities,
    xxxiv–xxxvi, 59–61, 95–139
Charter of Fundamental Rights
    (EU), 13b
Child Friendly Schools programs,
    38b, 39
Child Justice Alliance, 235
child rights, 28–31, 59–60, 73b, 159–61,
    167, 204, 236–39, 238b. *See also*
    Convention on the Rights of the
    Child (CRC)
Chile
    CCA, 187–88
    disability aid programs, 44
    right-to-education initiatives, 38b
China
    domestic violence laws, 98
    human rights dialogues with,
        46, 46b
    minorities' rights, 240
    citizenship rights, 75b
    civil and political rights, 54, 59
    civilian protection, 133
    civil society organizations
        accountability, 76
        support to, 48
    climate change, 52
    coherence challenge, 125–27, 126b
Colombia
    child rights, 239
    health rights, 229–30
    human rights dialogues with, 47
    rule of law projects, 233

human rights policy framework, 4,
9–10. *See* DAC Action-Oriented
Policy Paper on Human Rights
(AOPP 2007)
Principles for Good International
Engagement in Fragile States
and Situations, 108, 109*b*
statement on respect for human
rights (1997), 8
Development Cooperation Instrument
(DCI), 152
Development for All strategy (AusAID),
15, 241
development partnerships. *See*
partnerships and alliances
Development Policy Action Plan on
Human Rights for 2004–07
(Germany), 26*b*
DFID. *See* UK Department for
International Development
dialogue, 44–48, 46*b*, 60, 61, 111, 161,
221–22
DIHR (Danish Institute for Human
Rights), 101*b*
disabled persons. *See* persons with
disabilities, rights of
disaggregated data, review of,
80, 80*b*, 83
"do no harm" principle, 10, 24*t*, 41,
76–78, 104, 132, 173, 227
donor approaches to programming
experiences, xxxi–xxxiii, 23–67
global initiatives on human
rights, 49–50
human rights-based approaches
(HRBAs), 5–6*t*, 23–24,
24*t*, 25–26
See also human rights-based
approaches
human rights projects, 48–49
human rights research, 51–53
mainstreaming human rights. *See*
mainstreaming human rights

political conditionality and dialogue,
44–48, 46*b*, 60, 61
donor policies and rationales, xxx–xxxi,
3–22, 125–27
agency/institutional mandate
including human rights, 6*t*
entry points in absence of policy
statements, 14*b*
legal and policy considerations,
11–17, 16*b*, 69–71
multilateral agreements on human
rights, 6*t*
policies, 3–4, 5–6*t*
from policy to practice, 17
rationales, 4–11
instrumental rationale,
10–11, 74–85
intrinsic rationale, 8–10
second-generation policies, 6*t*

E

EBRD. *See* European Bank for
Reconstruction and
Development
economic, social, and cultural rights
(ESCR), 99*b*
Ecuador
UNDAF, 188
UN programming, 17
education rights, 37–39, 38*b*
Egypt, protection of children and youth
in, 238*b*
EIB (European Investment Bank), 13*b*
EIDHR. *See* European Instrument for
Democracy and Human Rights
energy sector. *See also* extractive sector
Voluntary Principles on Security and
Human Rights, 174*b*
ENPI (European Neighbourhood and
Partnership Instrument), 152
entry points in absence of policy
statements, 14*b*